Turkey Tails and Tales From Across the USA

Volume 2

By Tom "Doc" Weddle

ISBN: 978 - 1 - 7354419 - 3 - 1
Printed in the United States of America

This one's for my friend David Caudill

Being right there beside you on the final successful turkey hunt of your long and colorful life was an unbelievable honor for me; one that I shall never forget. Your stories and spirit are sadly missed by all of us who loved you.

Contents

Signed copies of this book or other Volumes in the series can be purchased directly from me. Hardcovers are $35 and Paperbacks are $25. I'll take care of all postage. My snail-mail address is:

Tom Weddle
PO Box 7281
Bloomington, IN 47407

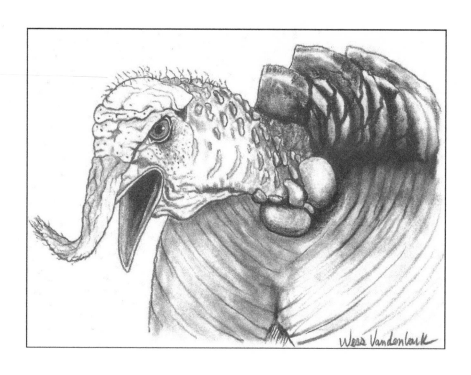

Explanations, Acknowledgements, and Thanks

This is my second attempt at chronicling the tales of my turkey hunting exploits in actual book form, and I'd like to start out with a few brief words regarding its physical appearance. Anyone possessing a copy of both works will immediately see that their covers are virtually identical except for two things: the volume number in each title, and the overall coloration schemes. The reason that I chose to stay with the same cover design for this second book is simply because I love what the original artist created for Volume 1, and I can't envision any possible way to improve upon it. Hence, I've decided to keep the artwork identical, and use unique color schemes to differentiate each subsequent Volume in the series.

You'll also note that the first illustration in each book (the gobbling tom now facing you on the opposite page) is the same, and likewise, an identical "parting shot" of a walking-away strutting turkey serves to end them both. These magnificent drawings were requisitioned from Wess Vandenbark, and then consciously placed to send out specific messages. Namely; the tom blasting out a gobble at the beginning of the book was intended to forewarn readers of exciting turkey hunting tales in the pages ahead, while the departing strutter promised more adventures in future volumes.

Besides that, I just think Wess's artwork is magnificent in and of itself, and I'm proud as a peacock (or, more appropriately, a tom turkey) that he's allowed me the use of his adroit skills with pen and ink to grace the pages of my writings. I hope that my story telling efforts are worthy of sharing these pages alongside the immense talents of Wess Vandenbark and the unknown artist responsible for my cover design, but I have my doubts...

I would now like to take a moment to thank my Editor, Tom Pero. Tom called me some time ago to ask if I would consent to being interviewed for a book that he was writing about lunatics like me who have completed U.S. Super Slams (the killing of a wild turkey in all 49 states that offer spring hunting seasons). Our collusion on that project has led not only to a successful endeavor in that regard, but a friendship. I admire Tom's expertise as both an editor and a writer, and I'm very much honored that he thought my own feeble attempts at becoming a wordsmith warranted some of his valuable time in helping to guide me through the authorship hoops. Tom's company, Wild River Press, has put out a number of absolutely incredible books, including not only the aforementioned one that I am featured in (*Turkey Men*, Volumes 1 & 2), but amazing tomes covering the Ruffed Grouse (*A Passion for Grouse*), the Civil War (*Gettysburg 1863 – Seething Hell*), and various fishing titles for both salt and fresh water. Give his wildriverpress.com website a look - you will *not* be disappointed in what's to be found there.

As for others who have helped me with this book, again I would like to single out Tom Skirvin for his assistance in the adjustment and technical manipulations of all the photographs. Tom is one of my best friends in the world and a true wizard on the computer, so he saved me immeasurable time and frustration with this process. I mentioned in my previous book that he's also an incredible chef, and following the spring shenanigans last year I brought home 30 live lobsters from Maine. After a Lobsterfest the likes of which my Midwestern hometown has never seen, we still had a bunch of meat to finish off, so a few days later Tom reaffirmed his mad culinary skills by creating an amazing and memorable dish on his old Wolff stove: Green Chile Lobster Enchiladas. Oh. My. Goodness. That was absolutely the finest food I have ever eaten!

Unfortunately, Tom is one of those chefs who create magnificent masterpieces on the fly without ever writing down any sort of recipe, so we may never again be able to exactly duplicate that unique taste. That's ok, though; while this particular meal was truly epic, the fact of the matter is that we put together frequent wild game feasts, and every time the bar gets set just a little bit higher. My belly and I both look forward to many more of these legendary events.

I'm sure that I'll now come up short in adequately acknowledging all of the other people who have influenced me or helped to guide my existence towards becoming a true Turkey Man, yet I have to give it a try. I firmly believe that each and every one of the characters and cohorts with whom I share experiences both in the field and around remote hunting camps has indirectly contributed to this book. Without them, I wouldn't have the stories which fill these pages, and without the support of family and friends egging me on and encouraging my insane lifestyle, I might not have been able to keep going at the pace and for the duration with which I have attacked the sport of turkey hunting for these past 35 years. Thank you one and all, from the very center of my heart!

Furthermore, without the foundation of love for nature and wild things that my Dad instilled in me early on in life, I might not see my place in the universe through such a prism of connectivity to the natural world. My very soul is steered by a strong pull towards the woods and hollows, creeksides and swamps, mountaintops and valleys, and every other wild place where my mind continually longs to be. Out there amongst nature is where I am the most happy and content, and only when I can immerse myself in the natural rhythms of the land and its wild denizens is my mind fully at peace.

I want to thank my Dad for starting all of that by taking me hunting when I was knee high to a grasshopper. I am likewise forever indebted to him in how and where I was raised. Having an aluminum rowboat by the age of eight allowed arm-power access to the 10,000 acre lake in our backyard, and the miles of unbroken hills and hollows surrounding those waters opened up worlds of wonderment and places to explore to my heart's content. What more could a young kid in love with the outdoors want? I know beyond all shadow of a doubt that it was those never-ending hours spent on the water and in the woods which have made me what I am today.

I can't really say that I never had the chance while he was still alive to tell my Dad just how grateful I am for all of those gifts; I can only admit and regret that I never did. I hope that he knew it, anyway.

Finally, I want to thank my Mom. I owe her not only for my very life itself, but for all of the support, encouragement, and faith in me that she's unwaveringly shown since the day I was born. She also contributed the turkey tracks drawing at the beginning of this summary, along with the feather images accompanying each chapter heading. Well done, Mom.

OK; with all the perfunctory stuff now out of the way, let's get going on Volume 2.

My Dad - the consummate Outdoorsman. He got me started down this path, even though there weren't any turkeys around for him to hunt in his own heyday.

CHAPTER 1

Here We Go Again

Welcome to my second volume of Turkey Tails and Tales from Across the USA. The mere fact that you've opened this book means that you probably weren't unduly put off by anything I had to say in my first literary attempt, but, then again, who knows?

Maybe you're just a glutton for punishment, like me. As fellow suffer-ers of this maddening turkey hunting malady, it basically goes without saying that our souls are similarly possessed by an inexplicable willingness to endure hardships, trials, and tribulations far above and beyond what other human beings would ever accept as "normal." Such toughness (read: stubbornness) is a common attribute amongst folks of our ilk, because excelling at the turkey hunting game on a consistent basis isn't easy; it takes a great deal of hard work, perseverance, and tenacity. Only a special breed of outdoors enthusiast can handle the mental and physical demands it entails, but for us like-minded souls who fully feel the passions inspired by a spring morning in the turkey woods, the rewards far surpass the pains incurred along the way.

Likewise, there are no shortcuts in the steep learning curve inherent to becoming a good turkey hunter. Getting there is a hard journey fraught with obstacles all along the path, and sitting around your man-cave reading how-to books or watching instructional videos and TV shows won't change that fact appreciably. If you truly want to improve your success rate at this game and reach a higher level of expertise, then you've got to jump right into the trenches and spend lots of time and energy in direct, close contact with our noble, feathered adversary.

Nothing less than complete emersion into the game can ever fully teach you the intimate little details of turkey behavior that you'll learn by spending excessive amounts of time in their presence, and that is one reason why so many of today's dedicated turkey hunters seek to maximize their time afield by hitting as many states as possible each spring. Doing like me and spending every available daylight hour in the woods will certainly add to your knowledge base and make you a better turkey hunter, but be forewarned that such a practice will also put untold hardships on every other aspect of life back in the "real" world – that place where we must inevitably return to live for the other nine months of the year when hunting seasons are closed. A lot of important stuff gets postponed or ignored during turkey season, and not everyone in your life will find that to be acceptable. Trust me on this!

Of course, I feel as if I can share the joys, point out the hardships, and commiserate with the pains felt by my fellow traveling turkey hunters so well, simply because we are one and the same: diehard devotees of the sport to the center of our souls. This brotherhood shares a strong allegiance; one bonded through the blood, sweat, and tears born of traversing rugged country at all hours of long days and short nights for months at a time, while being subjected to the blazing heat, bitter cold, pouring rain, and whatever else Mother Nature dishes out in between. We push our bodies to the absolute physical limits of its endurance, and drive ourselves like rented mules. We eat poorly; neglect important duties, responsibilities, and loved ones for long periods at a time; and stagger around in a daze during the entire spring season while suffering through both the physical exhaustion and mental strain of being beaten down regularly by an adversary with a brain the size of a shelled pecan. The funny part is that we do all of this quite willingly, and with unapologetic, unbound enthusiasm.

To the non-hunting populace, our feathered foe is often viewed as merely a dim-witted, ungainly bird with a pitifully ugly head and face. However, anyone who has spent time around wild turkeys knows the truth to be far different from that misconstrued perception. Not only is our quarry something to be marveled at and admired, but a tom turkey in all of his glory could succinctly be described as "wary magnificence and absolute beauty incarnate." And, since a big old boss gobbler also possesses the keen survival instincts and unyielding tenacity of a special ops soldier, bringing him to bag provides one of the ultimate challenges in all the out-of-doors. A turkey's first order of business every single day is to stay alive at all costs, so he will never, ever give up until the very last tail quiver once you've finally made that killing shot and are standing on his neck.

As I said earlier, it isn't easy to excel at this sport. Seeing a hunt turn out in our favor takes everything we possess as top-end predators, but in my humble opinion, the constant struggles are a huge part of what defines that peculiar magic found during a day in the turkey woods. The hardships and heartbreaks serve only to accentuate all the thrills and excitement. I love how difficult this game can be on any given day, and I love how frustrated and stupid these birds make me feel on a regular basis.

Writers of far greater talent than I have previously noted how easily this turkey hunting "disease" can get under a person's skin, and I would vehemently concur with their observation! After the bug has bitten and left a mark, its sufferers will forevermore find themselves thinking about their wary antagonists and eagerly anticipating the next chance to match wits with him. We poor, suffering souls will then eat, drink, and breathe the sport like junkies on smack. Any tales gleaned from cohorts and companions in either the written or oral form serve only to help feed an addiction which we are completely powerless to overcome.

Rehashing these old hunts with our comrades in arms is merely one of the many ways that turkey addicts find to keep their frazzled brains in perpetual contact with a rival who sooner or later comes to control our innermost thoughts and desires anyway, and if not forced by circumstances beyond control (i.e., a good slap upside the head), we're likely to find ourselves slipping into "turkey mode" at any hour of the day or night - particularly when we should be doing something else important, or concentrating on other things at hand. These evil birds even go so far as to invade our brains 24/7 by creeping into nighttime dreams when we try to catch up on a little much-needed sleep, but wakefulness offers no respite either, since we always seem to be searching for the latest tips, hints, or advice which might help us climb the ladder of becoming a better and more successful turkey hunter.

That right there is, after all, one of the main reasons why you're reading this book; isn't it?

- To fuel the insatiable quest for turkey hunting knowledge, and wet an appetite which threatens to consume you?

- To hear how others infected by this sickness have perhaps gained an upper hand on conquering those gobbling demons that pervade our psyches?

- To find similarities in what the rest of us have encountered in our own turkey hunting lives, and through these shared stories and tales, hopefully come to understand our paranoid, feathered opponent - and ourselves - just a little bit better?

- To get a glimpse into why these wicked, hainted birds act and react in such a maddeningly and unpredictable manner, and yet seem to so effortlessly make us look like inept fools when we attempt bringing them to bag?

Well, good luck with all that! While you might find some answers to those nagging questions here in this book, it is not intended as any type of a guide to be followed by aspiring turkey hunters. The author (me) is unquestionably a certifiable turkey hunting "nut," but I most certainly don't possess any top-secret methods which will help you become a better turkey hunter, and I would never recommend that anyone heed my advice or follow my lead. I have, after all, taken a path far astray from what ordinary, *sane* folks should ever choose. If I'd known beforehand what I now realize about the hazards of the trip, perhaps a different route would've been plotted in my life.

Then again; maybe not.

While there have been plenty of problems and difficulties encountered along the way to becoming a true Turkey Man, it's mostly been a journey filled with thrills, excitement, good times, and positive experiences. I have seen things out in the wilds of nature that would boggle the mind of any urbanite, and mere words can never adequately describe all the reasons why I count myself amongst the luckiest people to have ever lived. It's been a good life; one spent traipsing around in the beautiful spring woods and jumping from state to state at the drop of a hat, while meeting folks as whacked-out and crazy about turkey hunting as myself. To me, it simply defies logic why every person in the world isn't out there doing the very same things that I enjoy, but of course, I'm glad they aren't. The public lands where I hunt are already crowded enough!

One particular aspect of turkey hunting which I appreciate more every year is the fact that it's a lifelong learning process and not something that you try a time or two before moving on to something else. There are lessons to be learned and re-learned every single time that you step into the spring woods, and the more experiences garnered along the way, the more one realizes just how very little is truly known. This leaves an inquisitive mind continually asking itself, "what if," or "why" as we struggle onward.

Except for those spine-tingling and heart palpitating thrills caused by in-tight toms gobbling, spitting, and drumming at close range, the game of golf (yet another of my "weaknesses") bears some similarities with turkey hunting, in that you can never hope to master either endeavor completely, nor achieve ultimate victory whenever we participate. The very best of us cannot possibly birdie every single hole during a round of golf, and likewise, taking a tom each time we leave the house is totally inconceivable. All we can really hope for in either sport is to progressively work at lessening our mistakes and defeats, while hoping to win an occasional battle. That is the true essence of this unleashed beast called, "turkey hunting."

With that basic premise in mind, I'm now ready to start on another long and winding trip down memory lane, where I'll be reminiscing about past hunts, good friends, and noble adversaries battled along the way. Through my tales of errors made and sporadic victories won, you will perhaps come to better understand what makes this particular turkey hunter's heart tick faster. Furthermore, I would hope that this treatise helps to illuminate why myself and all of my brethren of the springtime woods so proudly share the strong belief that matching wits with a bird-brained adversary is the ultimate thrill in all of our lives.

My first book detailed the beginning dozen of a 35-years-and-counting involvement with (and thorough fascination of) hunting the wild turkey. It took us chronologically up through the 1994 spring season. This volume will pick right back up where that one left off, ending only after I've run out of space between its covers. No single book (or half a dozen, for that matter) can possibly hold all of the tales still rattling around in my turkey-addled brain. Any planned future editions will continue this pattern, and hopefully, I can also add enough tips, hints, and information on traveling to other states in order to give these books value beyond just the prattling-on of some old geezer with more stories than good sense.

As I warned you earlier: don't expect any earth-shattering knowledge or secret methodologies to come oozing from these pages. However, I take tremendous pride in helping out my fellow sufferers of this maddening malady, so if this book perchance inspires you to get out there and plan a trip of your own to some far away turkey woods that you've never seen before, then I couldn't be any happier with what I've triggered.

Likewise, if any of you read my tales and see the merit in writing down your own adventures, then that too would warm my heart. Just the act of keeping a simple pocket journal can provide a vast wealth of knowledge years down the road – not only for entertainment purposes as you read about past hunts, but in helping to plan future ones. Believe me; you will *never* regret the little time that it takes to put your thoughts, feelings, and adventures into print, and the more you can stuff in there, the better. I highly recommend this practice for everyone.

I also think that every single one of us has a story to tell, and which other people would enjoy reading. The burgeoning self-publishing industry has made becoming an author a fairly easy thing to do. Of course, any money generated through actual sales will probably not even come close to covering the expenses incurred in getting a book to print, but the positive intangibles are both incalculable and wonderful beyond measure. Simply put; there is no other feeling in the world like holding in your very own hands the first copy of a book with *your* name on its cover!

Please feel free to contact me if I can ever be of further help in this regard. As in turkey hunting, book publishing can be an intimidating journey with a few land mines in the path to dodge along the way. I've learned a thing or two about how to avoid the worst of them, so I'd be more than happy to help you navigate the process.

Furthermore, if you would like signed copies of my previous book, this one, or future volumes, they can be purchased on Amazon or ordered directly from me. I actually prefer to sell them from home so that I can sign each copy to its recipient. Paperbacks are $25, and hardbacks are $35. I'll take care of the shipping costs. Please let me know to whom they should be personalized, and if you want me to say anything special. Otherwise, I'll likely muck it up with some drivel of my own choosing. Checks or money orders can be sent to me in this way:

Tom Weddle
PO Box 7281
Bloomington, IN 47407

I know: these aren't turkeys. But, I like this picture, and I love my pheasant hunting! The pigeons were a welcomed bonus and warrant a story of their own – in another book. Dan Luczinski (in the picture) and his brother-in-law Mike Bramlett (behind the lens) were my companions on this hunt in South Dakota.

CHAPTER 2

A Quick Review

Wild turkeys entered my life back in 1983, and it truly was a love at first gobble. Even before my rookie season had come to an end, I realized that hunting a few days each spring would never sufficiently scratch the itch that this sickness invoked, so I made a conscious and calculated decision to completely mold my life around hunting these birds as often as possible. March, April and May were thus set aside exclusively for traveling from state to state and chasing after that ever-elusive gobble coming from as-yet unseen lands, and that has been my annual modus operandi ever since. In hindsight, I certainly don't regret that choice in the least, for it has supplied me with untold wonderment and adventure in my life. My journeys over the last 35 years can best be described as one long, intensive study session of wild turkeys and their maddening behavior, filled with all the thrills, spills, and emotional highs and lows inherent in a quest to become a true Turkey Man.

There was sort of a natural progression to my passions, as well. When I first began hunting these birds, I just wanted to kill a turkey. Once that was accomplished during my rookie season, I felt the need to shoot another tom in order to prove that the first one wasn't simply a fluke or an accident. This happened the very next year, and a couple seasons later I set out to expand my horizons by hunting somewhere other than my home state of Indiana.

I failed to pull the trigger during that initial road trip to South Dakota, but the state-hopping trend was thus entrenched in my brain and I would go on to fill my first non-resident turkey tag the following spring in the lovely state of Virginia. That very same season I also killed my first subspecies of wild turkey other than an Eastern; he was a Merriam's jake taken on a return trip to the Black Hills of South Dakota. Two years later, in 1989, I shot an Osceola in Florida and a Rio Grande in Oklahoma to complete a Lifetime Grand Slam of the four predominant subspecies of wild turkeys found in the USA. Coupled with successful visits to South Dakota, Indiana, and New York during that very same spring, I could also lay claim to my first Single Season Grand Slam. The following year saw the bar raised even higher when I achieved my first Double Grand Slam (two specimens of each subspecies, all killed during the same spring season).

After taking that DGS in 1990, the act of "Grand Slamming" sort of lost its shine for me. I felt a little bit like I'd "been there, done that; got the t-shirt to prove it." However, my desire to hunt wild turkeys was now stronger than ever, and the thrill of chasing them in faraway lands where I'd never set foot before was a powerful pull. Thus, my focus from 1991-onward in some ways became more streamlined; I wanted only to hunt on as many days as possible every spring, and in as many places as I could afford to buy a license. This resulted in trips to a number of states where I'd never been, but at that point there wasn't any particular rhyme or reason to the new places I chose to hunt. I just picked states where I'd always wanted to go, and then did enough research before the trip to help me find turkeys on their public lands.

I also hadn't as yet discovered the miracle of the plastic credit card, which would allow me in future years to delay payments on expensive non-resident hunting licenses until I was back to work in the summer. The general lack of money in my wallet forced me to keep it fairly close to home in those days, and yet I was still able to add a new state or two to my resume every spring. By 1993 I could tally a lifetime total of 11 different states hunted, with somewhere in the neighborhood of 50 dead turkeys to my credit. This wasn't a bad start for a simple man of little means - but it was nowhere near the pace that would occur in years to come.

In 1994 I joined up with Golden Hands Construction of Bloomington, Indiana. The kind-hearted owner of this small restoration-based remodeling company gave me the freedom to take nearly three months off from work every spring in order to pursue my passion for turkey hunting. This allowed me to greatly expand upon the theme of traveling to random new states and far-off locations at the drop of a hat. However, I still didn't have any sort of structured plan in choosing where my travels would lead me; it was almost a random crapshoot as to which states made it onto the schedule each spring.

All of this changed in 2001, when my good friend Larry Sharp planted the "U.S. Slam" seed in my turkey-addled pea-brain. This newly recognized form of slam entailed the taking of a wild turkey from every state which offered a spring hunting season: 49 states in all (Alaska being the only exception). Once I'd decided that this was a goal worth pursuing, then conquering it became the main driving force in my life. This gave me a sort of "template" for helping to choose particular springtime destinations, and following a lot of scheming, dreaming, hard work, and travel to places where I'd never hunted before, I completed my first aforementioned U.S. Slam in 2006.

I knew that I wasn't the first person to accomplish one of these U.S. Slams, but there surely hadn't been very many others before me, either. It felt really good to join the ranks of this rather elite group of skilled turkey hunters, and yet, almost immediately, I began thinking to myself, "what now?"

In looking over the data that I always keep in an ever-present hunting journal, I soon realized that by successfully returning to a relatively small number of states where a single bird had previously been taken, I could conceivably fulfill a second U.S. Slam fairly quickly. The opportunity to perhaps become the very first person to do such a thing provided me with the added incentive to give it a go, so off I went on the quest.

During spring of 2011 I shot the last bird needed to fulfill that dream, and once again in perusing my journals and notes afterward, I discovered that it wasn't too far of a stretch to think about doing the U.S. Slam thing yet a third time - most certainly something that nobody else in their right mind had ever been crazy enough to attempt!

As this book goes to press there are four states remaining where I've killed less than three toms. All of them are tentatively scheduled for visits this coming spring, so I anticipate finishing up my third U.S. Slam in 2018. Ultimately – and for no other reason than it's one of my "lucky" numbers – I've set my sights on taking at least five toms from each of the 49 states encompassing the U.S. Slam. Only time will tell if that ever happens, though. Life tends to get in the way when looking too far ahead, and I hate to count my turkeys before they're in the cooler. If it were all to end tomorrow, I'd still die a happy man with no regrets.

Now, before I go one step further, I want to take a brief moment here to strongly emphasize that any absolute numbers I quote in this book are *not* what I'm all about as a hunter, and the major driving force in my life is *not* concerned with kill totals and various "slams." I'm sure that probably sounds like hogwash after reading the last few paragraphs, but I can't emphasize any stronger how this is most certainly not the case. While my nation-wide accomplishments sort of give me some validation in writing these books from a rather unique perspective, I *do not* focus on numbers of dead turkeys as a measure of success. I really don't!

This kind of says it all, and I honor every single one of them.

I am simply a turkey hunting fanatic to the core of my soul, and I've done so much of it, over such a long period of time, that these numbers have added up to some fairly substantial figures. I can't help that; I can only emphasize how unimportant the actual kill totals are to my own daily motivations and aspirations. People ask me all the time how many turkeys I've shot in my lifetime. I know the answer, but I never give out that figure. I would much rather have my successes judged by the number of sunrises I've been afforded the opportunity to watch while sitting on a log awaiting that first gobble of a new day. Any subsequent trigger-pulls are merely icing on an already-delicious cake.

Even though I speak of numbers not being important, in total fairness and honesty, I do harbor in the dark recesses of my brain the thought that certain accomplishments are noteworthy. These U.S. Slams really are something of which I'm very proud. However, I don't think they should matter to anyone else in the world besides *me*. Setting and then reaching particular goals in hunting is an extremely personal thing, in my opinion, so I am always very reluctant to discuss what I've done out of fear that people will think that I'm bragging or laying claim to being a better hunter than someone else. Please believe me when I say that I am not nearly as good as many folks think I am! And, while I realize that the U.S. Slam is a difficult quest to fulfill, completing one really just means that I've sacrificed a good deal of time, effort, and money in order to hunt lots of different places, over a lengthy span of years. That's it in a nutshell.

To me, the only true measure of value for my U.S. Slams lies in proving that any ordinary "Joe" can conquer just about whatever he sets out to do in life, if he's determined, dedicated, and persistent. Yes, it takes untold toughness and resiliency to stay the course long enough to achieve a lofty ambition such as this, and a few fortuitous circumstances and lucky breaks along the way don't hurt a bit, but hard-headedness and stick-to-itiveness go more towards turning dreams into reality than anything else - in turkey hunting, and in life. The lessons learned in the turkey woods go far beyond what we take home in the cooler.

Today, I view my own continuing quest for fulfilling U.S. Slams as merely an efficient way to help organize and plot where to hunt each spring. Even without such a guide I would still be hunting as much as possible and in as many states as I can crowd into the schedule, because dancing from state to state all spring long while maximizing my days afield is how I've designed my life. I wouldn't have it any other way.

While the actual hunts themselves are undoubtedly the end prize, they aren't the only reason why I keep pushing forward; I gain nearly as much excitement and anticipation from the planning, research, and hard work necessary to make it all happen. The whole entire process is just part and parcel of who I *am*, and so long as I can figure out a way to *somewhat* afford it, I hope to continue this crazy lifestyle for as long as I'm walking upright.

In my travels I'm frequently asked, "what's your favorite state?" Although I'd love to give a simple answer to that simple question, there's simply no way to pick one – or even a top 30! Some of them I like more than others for one reason or another, but each and every state of the nation has supplied me with glorious sunrises, fascinating terrain with varied and wondrous wildlife, interesting people met along the way, plenty of hard-headed gobblers to confound me on a regular basis, and the occasional hard-fought victory to help sooth my soul.

Rather than pick favorites, I will merely say that there are a few select destinations which I tend to make return trips to more often than others. Three of these make up a short list of places that I've hunted more than 21 times apiece: Florida, Indiana, and New York. A longer list encompasses those states that have seen my return somewhere between three and eight times: AL, AZ, CO, CT, DE, IL, IA, KS, KY, LA, ME, MA, MI, NV, NH, NJ, NM, OK, PA, RI, SC, SD, TX, UT, VT, VA, and WV. I've hunted the remaining states (AR, CA, GA, HI, ID, MD, MN, MS, MO, MT, NE, NC, ND, OH, OR, TN, WA, WI, WY) only once or twice. One thing that I'd really like to do in coming years is return to each and every one of these "lesser-hunted" states in order to give them another look-see, but in truth, I would really like to go back and hunt *every* state again...and again...and again. Yes, it is a compulsion – and, yes, I am powerless to stop it!

The only other accomplishments in my turkey hunting travels which I think might be worth noting here are that I've never hired a guide or outfitter, and I've done the vast majority of my hunting while on public land. You could even say that I have a virtual U.S. Public Slam under my belt, since I've killed turkeys on public property in every state except North Dakota. Sadly, that state's regulations don't allow non-residents to hunt turkeys on public land in the spring, so I had to kill my ND birds on an Indian Reservation.

While I occasionally hunt on private land if it can be secured with nothing more than a handshake, I would rather not. I am a public land kind of guy at heart, so I would *much* rather do my hunting on ground that is open for anyone's enjoyment. Free-access properties have supplied me with quality hunts on a consistent basis throughout my turkey hunting career, and in no way do I feel like I have suffered even a little bit from being out there and rubbing elbows with "the masses." I like it there, I feel my best there, and I truly would rather have it no other way.

As this treatise moves along I'll have plenty more to say about all the individual states and their public land offerings, but for now I've had enough talk of numbers, "slamming," and stuff like that. I think it's time to get back to the hunting stories and reminiscences from years gone by. Let's first look at a few more pictures that prove I sometimes do other stuff besides hunting turkeys. Then, we'll pick right back up where I left off in my first book.

A 43 pound Wahoo caught while fishing out of Cape Hatteras, NC. We used our own boat: a 22' Aquasport. This trip was a High School Graduation present from my Dad.

An 18 pound Steelhead I caught a few years later in Lake Michigan, aboard Dad's pride and joy: his all-aluminum, hand-built "Weeble." That's him over my left shoulder, and an Offensive Lineman for the Indianapolis Colts football team to my right dwarfing both me and my fish.

This is a two man limit of quail taken with Ron Ronk, along with a rabbit, and a pigeon killed by a thrown rock. I had a pretty good arm in those days.

A ten-pound Carp on a fly rod puts up a wonderful fight!

CHAPTER 3

Back on the Road

A couple of things happened in 1994 which had huge affects on me and my turkey hunting. First, I had an operation on my eyes to correct the near-sightedness which had dominated my very existence since early childhood. I have often wondered what my life might've been like (especially in sports), if I hadn't been born in the days before corrective surgery, and I cannot overstate how much this operation changed everything in my world for the better.

This is how it came about.

At the 1993 Quail Unlimited banquet in Sullivan County, an ophthalmologist named Frank Emert purchased a guided turkey hunt that I annually donated to help raise money for the cause. Although we had never met before, I knew of him by reputation as a highly capable doctor skilled in radial keratotomy surgery: the procedure of actually cutting a person's cornea with a scalpel in order to correct vision problems. These incisions are made in a "pie-shaped" pattern for near-sightedness, which flattens out the cornea into its ideal form and thereby allows visual images to be properly projected onto the retina - thus achieving sharp focus.

I had already been researching this surgery for a couple years leading up to that banquet, because getting rid of eyeglasses had always been perhaps my very deepest wish. Laser surgery and its inherent improvements to the process were still merely a pipe dream at that point, so RK was really the only way of attaining good vision without wearing glasses or contact lenses.

I hated eyeglasses with a passion unbound, and after that surgery I went from wearing coke-bottle-bottom glasses every waking hour, to having very-nearly perfect vision. This change was profound, wonderful, and everything else I had ever dreamed it to be, but do you want to know the very best part? When Frank and I had been discussing whether I was a good candidate for RK during a lull in our first hunt, he also told me that he was willing to provide the surgery free of charge in exchange for occasionally taking him turkey hunting. Yeah, that's right; I said, "FREE OF CHARGE!"

My initial reaction was, of course, "you've got to be kidding, right?" Bartering for health care; as a poor man with no insurance, I loved the very concept of that, and I couldn't believe my good fortune in receiving this tremendous offer. Needless to say, I accepted his kindness with a hearty handshake, and except for a few minor glitches along the way, the subsequent surgery was a resounding success. In fact, there eventually came one memorable day when I slipped on a pair of protective goggles and smashed my hated-and-now-unnecessary eyeglasses into smithereens. That felt real good.

The second bombshell to happen in 1994 was the aforementioned job with Golden Hands Construction, where my new boss told me that it would be ok if I took three months off from work each spring in order to pursue my truest passions. This obviously changed my very existence in another life-altering way, for now I found myself free to pursue wild turkeys all spring long and wherever my little heart desired. Trust me when I say that my heart desired a lot of turkey chasin', and in a lot of places!

Well, the 1995 spring turkey season once again started off for me in Florida. Since I had already hunted there during five of the last seven years, its sandy soils and tangled swamps now felt like a welcome mat for a much-anticipated traditional return. I've not missed a single season of Florida turkey hunting since that time, and furthermore, I have no intentions of ever breaking that streak.

Wild, native Florida gives me things that I can't find anywhere else in America, including diverse flora and fauna, those evil, hainted Osceola gobblers who roam its jungles and swamps, and the strong sense of family I share with a whole caste of interesting characters. For me, there is absolutely nothing else like it, and I look forward to the experience all year-round. I actually miss Florida whenever I'm not there, but of course, the thought of moving down to the Sunshine State would never be an option for a native Hoosier like me (too much heat, and *far* too many people). However, I do value my time in her magical river swamps and awe-inspiring oak hammocks more than anywhere else sans the beloved deciduous forests of my Midwestern upbringing. She's so unique: lovely, enchanting, and challenging beyond measure.

That spring I again came back to hunt at Green Swamp Wildlife Management Area, which by now I considered my "home" WMA. After a very long hike deep into her darkest depths in order to escape the hordes of hunters crowding through the gate on opening day, a fine Osceola gobbler introduced himself to me late in the morning. I introduced myself to him soon thereafter, and we exchanged pleasantries till the 1 o'clock closing time. We met yet again shortly before sunup of the second day and went through the same routine. but it wasn't until the third day of the trip that we actually "shook hands," and he came home to dinner at my camp.

The battle with this tom was an emotionally rewarding three-day marathon which played out like a challenging chess game. I enjoyed our duel immensely, and felt like I had hunted both patiently, and extremely well, in order to achieve success. Unfortunately, things got very tough at "The Swamp" after that, with not a single additional gobble heard in over a week. As time dragged slowly by without any results more tangible than the mosquito welts rising up on exposed flesh, I decided to leave Florida earlier than intended and head out for my next destinations on the schedule: a short stint at the Alabama hunting lease of Zane Caudill, followed by a western swing into the panhandles of both Oklahoma and Texas.

I had met Zane during one of my first trips to Green Swamp, and he was without a doubt one of the most colorful and interesting characters whom I have ever known. Zane was a real live-wire; known for his blazing-quick wit, unquestionable intelligence, an intense, inquisitive mind, joy of life, and a complete no-nonsense rejection of fools and charlatans. You always knew where you stood with Zane, and he wasn't the least bit shy about voicing his opinion on any subject. He also had a bazillion stories from a life well-spent in the wilds of Florida, and these were often shared around our campsite and accentuated with an infectious laugh that belied his mischievous soul.

Tragically, my good friend died this past September from a stroke suffered much too young. To me, his death felt like the invincible Superman in our lives had unbelievably succumbed to a lethal dose of Kryptonite. I thought "The Zinger" would live forever.

One of Zane's truest passions was deer hunting with a bow, and he was darned good at it, too. Interestingly enough, he was red/green colorblind, which made following a blood trail *extremely* difficult! In order to compensate, Zane had begun raising Dachshunds as an aid in the recovery of his kills, carrying his little companion in a back-pack while sitting a tree stand. When a deer was inevitably shot, the two of them would climb down and trail the deer until it was found - and Buck (Zane's canine sleuth when we met) *always* found his deer!

Zane and his line of blood-trailing Weiner-dogs become regionally famous for their successes, including numerous deer shot by Hank Williams, Jr. in Alabama. Even today a good number of his many friends have descendants of that bloodline both as beloved pets and working trailing dogs. As for me, I was lucky enough to witness Buck in action a few years later while Zane and I were both deer hunting in Kentucky with Larry Sharp and his sons Philip and Kenneth. It was a sight to behold, too! The search ended with Philip's fine 10-point gut-shot buck successfully recovered after an unbelievably long and difficult tracking job across highways, deep creeks, and a couple miles of rugged terrain.

Upon finding any deer, Zane's diminutive but fearless hound would immediately attack it whether alive or already dead, and his first move was to go straight for the Achilles tendons on the back legs. Once they had been chewed-through - and it took only a few seconds - Buck instinctively knew that he had both found and incapacitated his quarry, so he would begin prancing around in a "victory dance" like he was the baddest dude in the forest. From my perspective, that is *exactly* what he was!

Well, that spring we most certainly needed feather-trailing dogs, or a rabbit's foot for good luck, or something special like divine intervention, because in four days of hard hunting Zane and I heard exactly zero gobbles. It was a frustrating trip overall, with only a couple of hens seen, and by the time it ended I was more than ready to try something else in someplace new. Pointing my 1968 Ford Econoline van (nicknamed "Petunia the Road Pig") west into the setting sun, I headed off for a scheduled meeting with Judson Holmes.

Buck and a litter of his puppies with their Momma (I can't remember her name), along with Ron Ronk, Zane, and Zane's wife Laurie.

Judd is another good friend of mine whom I have known since we were 16 year-old kids working summer jobs at Lake Monroe. As founding members of our self-proclaimed "Paynetown Assault Force," we had shared many a wild youthful adventure, intense Frisbee session, or fun time out on the lake water skiing. Judd had then gone off to play college basketball in Texas, and while there he had married a beautiful local gal named Mary Ann Proctor. Her parents owned some ground near Wichita Falls that held a decent population of Rio Grande turkeys, and since their ranch wasn't too far from where I had been hunting in Oklahoma for four of the past five years anyway, Judd and I decided to have a "go" at some of their buff-tailed toms. A couple of hours after picking him up at the Oklahoma City airport, we were welcomed into the home of Mr. and Mrs. Proctor.

Once in the field Judson wasted no time limiting out over the course of the first two mornings. Meanwhile, I struggled to get on the scoreboard at all, and when Judd then hitched a ride with another friend to catch a plane bound for home and work commitments, I found myself still in possession of all my turkey tags. However, Mary Ann's folks were kind and generous beyond measure, and they told me that I was welcome to stay for as long as I wanted. Truth be told, it wasn't hard to convince me to stick around, because Mrs. Proctor was also the best cook that I've *ever* known, and for my part, I really like to eat. Besides that, I was determined to seal the deal on at least one Texan Rio Grande gobbler before heading back north to Oklahoma.

Judd Holmes and a pair of his toms.

While it's true that I hadn't as yet pulled the trigger in those first couple of days, I wasn't exactly spinning my wheels; there had been numerous oh-so-close encounters where the results might have been different if but for chance and circumstance. One tom in particular had slipped by me just out of gun range on several different occasions. The memories of those close calls were gnawing at my guts, and I wanted revenge on this bird – *badly*.

Redemption with that scaly-legged Houdini came late the next afternoon, following a marathon morning hunt when he refused to budge from a huge, rolling pasture that also hosted a number of hens. Able to accomplish absolutely nothing from my hide in the distant, surrounding tree line along a creek, I had finally snuck away for a quick lunch with the Proctor's before hurrying back to find the tom still in the same place as before.

By then I'd already decided that doing *anything* had to be better than doing nothing at all. Using the contour of the ground to conceal my initial crouched approach, I then slithered like a snake in the wispy grass to the top of a little knoll 125 yards from the strutting tom and four of his girlfriends. It was a bold maneuver that I hadn't really thought would work, but after making it there I was definitely close enough to be considered "in the ballgame."

For the next three hours I laid there baking in that blazing Texas sun while periodically sending out yelps that generated absolutely nothing in response. Neither the tom, nor his hens paid me the least bit of attention. As time dragged on I got more and more aggressive with my calling, until finally, the hens began talking back to me. Once that happened, it was like a light switch had been turned on, and all four hens marched towards me with a purpose. A brand new kind of sweat began breaking out on my forehead.

The tom dutifully followed along like a puppy, but his constant strutting kept him trailing behind by a good measure. He was still further away than I ordinarily like to shoot by the time his girlfriends climbed the slope to me, and when they all began nervously purring and soft putting from no more than ten feet away, he took notice. As he slicked down and raised that red head to full height, I saw that he was also starting to edge away. The time had come for action on my part.

Maybe the hens thought that I was a rattlesnake coiled up in the grass. If so, they were sadly mistaken - the only venom I possessed erupted out of the end of my gun barrel and smote their boyfriend dead in his tracks at 32 yards. He was a dandy of a Rio Grande tom, too; weighing almost 22 pounds and sporting an 11- 3/16 inch beard and sharp spurs measuring a full 1- 1/4."

I was so thrilled with both this turkey, and the difficulty of the hunt, that I didn't even bother staying around to risk using up any more of my good luck. Heading north with three unused Texas tags in my wallet, there was a smile on my face and a warm pie on the seat beside me - a parting gift from Mrs. Proctor.

My first Texas Rio Grande from the Proctor Ranch.

I soon discovered that the hunting in Oklahoma was much tougher than in previous years. Although I did hear six gobbling toms in the first six days, I killed none. Four of those were safely across fence lines on private property, while another was a "super-jake" who tantalizingly strutted just like a big boy for a half-dozen hens in front of my gun barrel at 25 yards. Luckily for him, his teenage status kept him just as safe from harm as the property fences had proven for his elders, and even though I watched the show for quite some time with my sight beads aligned on his flame-red noggin', his life was never in jeopardy unless my gun had spontaneously discharged.

The sixth bird was different than the others. Although his strong preference for roosting on the public side of the fence seemed to make him killable, an annoying habit of gliding down into forbidden private lands each morning made that a challenge. He'd then stay over there all day with a noisy flock of hens, and would only wander back to his large grove of roost trees just before it was time to fly up for the night.

On our final, fateful afternoon, the tom came back across that protective boundary line much too early for his own good. I got clued-in to his whereabouts when a rapidly advancing thunderstorm provoked a shock gobble, and then he made an additional mistake by answering a single yelp from my mouth call. He never saw me tucked up against a big blown-down cottonwood, and he never noticed the muzzle end of my 12 gauge tracking his every advancing step. When he periscoped that big cotton-topped head up at 13 yards, it was the last voluntary movement of his life.

Considering all of the factors that had combined to make for a tougher than normal western journey, I was awfully happy with the two fine birds in my cooler and content to eat the rest of my tags. Then, while headed north towards another brand new state (Nebraska), something terrible happened which drained the enthusiasm from my soul; a couple of nut jobs blew up the Alfred P Murrah Federal Building in Oklahoma City and killed 168 people.

I will never forget the powerful feelings of anger, hopelessness, and despair that first overcame me when I heard the news of this tragedy on the radio, but I will also never forget the outpouring of kindness, compassion, and giving which the people of Oklahoma displayed in the days and weeks to follow. My path through the city to pick up Judd only days earlier had taken me very close to the site of that bombing, so I suppose this unbelievable act of sense-less violence struck particularly close to home for that reason alone. However, it was also a monumental moment in American history, which served to change my perception of the world.

Thankfully, my faith in the inherent goodness of the human spirit was uplifted as I paid close attention to the recovery efforts via newspaper and radio reports. My disdain for terrorists, however, has only grown deeper with the passage of time and an increasing frequency of these despicable acts. Terrorists are the lowest form of coward on this earth, and I hate them even worse than I do ticks!

As bad as that tragedy was, my trip to Nebraska bordered on the surreal in comparison. Knocking on a stranger's door gained me permission to camp on their property, and that allowed for a much shorter hike to access an isolated section of National Forest which was heavily timbered in big Ponderosa pines. Around dusk of the next afternoon, I called in a whole flock of strutting toms, and then I took my time picking out the one stud who seemed to dominate over his buddies. After all the flopping was done, I rolled him over and discovered that he was easily my best Merriam's to date, with needle-sharp spurs of 1- 1/16."

My hike to camp wound along an enchanting ridgeline, and halfway back a magnificent shooting star brilliantly illuminated the trail in front of my feet before it slowly disintegrated into the distant horizon. This was truly an amazing sight, and seemed like a fitting exclamation point to both the particular hunt I'd just experienced, and my 1995 western excursion as a whole. The next morning I headed for home brimming with confidence and a positive attitude.

My first Pine Ridge Merriam's tom from Nebraska.

Returning to Indiana did nothing but enhance those feelings. Since 1990 I had been hunting with Don Foley on a 1600-acre chunk of private land called "Tea Mountain" in Brown County. It was originally bought piecemeal by his Dad and two Uncles over a number of years, and in the late '80's they'd built a spectacular log cabin deep in the heart of the property. The overall topography of this ground was very steep and rugged, but it held a real good population of turkeys.

Don's Uncle Tom had subsequently bought out his brothers for sole ownership rights of the whole place, and every spring he invited a motley assembly of characters there for the first few days of turkey season. These get-togethers always produced lots of good times and camaraderie, along with filling the cabin with laughter – *lots* of laughter. Just about all of us there could handle ourselves in the kitchen, as well, so delicious meals were the norm, rather than an exception. Most evenings would then end with storytelling and half-truths told around an open fire pit.

Tom Foley wasn't into turkey hunting, but he's a dedicated picker of morel mushrooms. His good buddies Joe Harrod and Bill Utterback likewise had no interest in chasing gobbling birds around that steep terrain, but brothers DeWayne and Russ Feltner were there for that purpose, along with Bruce Wilson, Don Foley, and myself. In 1995 there were also a couple of new faces in the crowd: Mike Yordy was a state cop neighbor of Don, and Joe Hines was a timber-buying cohort of DeWayne. Mike planned to patrol the property's boundaries on opening day in hopes of dissuading trespassers, while Joe's intentions were more ominous in nature – he wanted to kill his first-ever wild turkey.

DeWayne Feltner is like a second son to Tom Foley, and he spends many hours every spring scouting these woods. His report of hearing over a dozen gobbling birds from the front porch of the cabin just a couple days prior to our arrival caused a lot of excitement amongst all of us. In fact, after we'd tucked in for the night I awoke at some point from a dream about a whole gang of toms charging at me and Don the next morning, and I abruptly sat bolt upright in bed so rapidly that I whacked my head on one of the ceiling rafters. Hard. In fact, it was such a *tremendous* blow that the sound of the collision reverberating throughout the cabin woke everyone else up. Well, either that, or it was the moans, groans, and loud string of profanities uttered into the darkness!

A few hours later there were some "tongue-in-cheek" comments made around the breakfast table expressing faux concern that I might've cracked the very beam itself with how hard I'd struck that cursed log.

Whatever; I suppose that since my skull and/or neck weren't shattered, it's ok that they all still laugh about that incident to this very day. I'll merely say that it was one helluva way to start a turkey hunt!

As the first hint of graying light crept over the eastern horizon, Don and I headed out for a section of the property that was known as "our" spot. Soon after sunup I called in a dandy of a tom which my partner promptly shot full in the face. Russell also killed a tom that morning, and the next day Joe Hines accompanied me into the same general area where Don and I had found success. Sure enough, Joe made good on a tom nearly identical to Donnie's – both of them weighing around 22 pounds, with beards over 11 inches long and sharp, impressive spurs on their legs. The third day I hunted with DeWayne, but we only managed to bump a few birds and look absolutely ridiculous in doing so. Such is the hunter's lot in life - one day you're a hero who can do nothing wrong, and the next day just another inept buffoon.

Joe Hines and his "Tea Mountain Tom."

27

Following those three days of fun at Tea Mountain, my next planned excursion was to guide for Lee Coulson. Lee was a big-time farmer, with lots of ground bordering Illinois on the western edge of our state. He had been the winning bidder for one of my turkey hunts that I donated to the Sullivan County Quail Unlimited banquet, but rather than hunt on familiar turf around home, he wanted to visit a buddy's place in Switzerland County – all the way over in the southeastern quadrant of the state. The seven counties in this section of Indiana had become THE place for turkey hunting in the last few years as our expanding flocks flourished, so that sure sounded like a great plan to me. Ron Ronk was also a mutual friend of Lee's, and he agreed to be my co-guide for the hunt.

Arriving at the farm in late afternoon, we took a short walk to get acquainted with its topography. A big gobbler ran out of the first field we came to, and then we saw several others in the next half-hour. Ron and I were pretty excited by the time we got back to the house, so after some scheming and planning for the morning's hunt, we hit the sack early for a good night's rest. Ha - fat chance of that! I tossed and turned all night long with restless, pre-hunt jitters.

Well, our hopes may have been high to begin with, but none of us were prepared for anything like what occurred at dawn. Literally; there were turkeys gobbling in *every* direction, and for as far as our ears could hear. I'm not exactly sure how many different birds we heard gobbling that morning, but no less than ten were within 400 yards of our initial setup. It didn't take long before we had one of them strutting almost violently in front of us at 25 yards, and while that was a very good scenario for the three eager hunters hunkered together under a big walnut tree, it was a really bad situation for the tom.

The following day was to be my first guided hunt as repayment for Frank Emert's eye surgery. He brought along a young man named Eric Coonrod, who worked for him as a gardener. I took them to one of my favorite spots in the Hoosier National Forest lands of south-central Indiana's Orange County, but the first turkey encounter we had that morning was very negative in nature - I bumped a tom out of the roost before daylight by trying to get too close.

After flydown time arrived, I did manage to call in a mouthy hen that stayed "in camp" with us for twenty minutes, but even though her nearly-constant cutting and lost yelping kept us wide-eyed and enraptured, not a single tom within hearing range was the least bit turned-on by anything she had to say. I was pretty sure that we were destined for failure at that point, and unfortunately, I was right.

Despite the lack of tangible success (i.e., a dead turkey in our hands) on this day, a good time was had by all and precedence was set for many years to come. Invariably when hunting with Frank, we'd hit it hard till late-morning, then resort to picture taking or digging plants and gathering rocks, fossils, and anything else of interest. Frank and his wife Nancy are world-class gardeners, with absolutely amazing grounds surrounding their home. They have Chinese rock gardens, English Commons-type lawns, roses and flowering plants of every persuasion, waterfalls and Coy ponds, woodland settings filled with native plants and trees - it's all really nothing short of phenomenal. Thousands of people have toured their gardens throughout the years, too; even students from the School for the Blind have come to touch the various plants and sniff their heady fragrances.

Following this "failed" hunt I came back closer to home and tramped around Greene County with my old friend Judd Holmes. Late on the second morning we succeeded in calling in a tom who rushed at us like he was mad about something, and Judd capably put him down before he could finish the attack. Only then did we discover that this tom had half of his tail fan missing. I'm not sure what happened with the other half - perhaps a coyote had come perilously close to turning him into a turkey dinner.

The first week of the season had thus far seen me crisscrossing the state like a whirlwind every afternoon, but now I was free to relax a bit by spending an extended period of time in the southeastern quadrant's Jefferson County. I had several more folks lined up to guide down there, and first up was a second cousin of mine named Bobby Torrance. Bob had been one of my favorite relatives when I was growing up, but I hadn't seen him in more than twenty years before reacquainting at my Grandpa's funeral the previous fall. He is about seven years older than me, and some of his own fondest memories are of squirrel hunting and frog gigging with my Dad in the early years of Lake Monroe. I was just a pup back then, but I can plainly remember those happy times, as well as Cousin Bob teaching me the words to songs like Elvis Presley's, *You Ain't Nothin' but a Hound Dog,* and Johnny Horton's, *Battle of New Orleans.*

When he found out at Grandpa's funeral that I was a turkey hunter, an invitation was proffered to hunt on his rented land, which was a farm of about 320 acres just outside the town of Madison. The upper half of this property was tillable ground planted to beans and tobacco, with the lower, wooded portion sloping steeply away towards the Ohio River. Its overall appearance shouted out, "Turkey Heaven" the very first time I saw it.

Bob is a big, burly guy with long hair and lots of tattoos, looking absolutely the part of your prototypical biker. In fact, that is exactly what he was earlier in life, but he's also gregarious to a fault, funny as hell, country as can be, and just a great guy to hang around with. Showing up at the farmhouse that morning to take him out on his first-ever turkey hunt, I was greeted at the door by my larger-than-life cousin dressed in blue jeans and a bright blue sweatshirt, with a shiny green baseball cap on his head and no facemask or gloves. Not exactly sure what to say, I could only shrug my shoulders and follow him out to the "back 40," because I certainly didn't have any spare camo clothing big enough to get him switched into more "proper" attire. Beside that, dawn was fast approaching.

That first morning on the Armond farm was certainly fun and very entertaining, but frustrating, as well. *Lots* of gobbling turkeys, *lots* of toms called in close enough to kill, and *lots* of birds subsequently scared shitless by that giant blue feller with the bright green hat!

That afternoon Bobby thought it might be best to make a trip to Wal-Mart, where he bought his first set of camo for the next day's hunt. Unfortunately, even that didn't work out as we'd hoped, because although we did keep from spooking any toms ourselves the next morning, a coyote helped us out in that regard by chasing off a whole flock of birds rapidly crossing the bean field towards us. The following day it was as if there had never been a turkey on that entire farm - not a gobble was heard, nor a turkey seen. It was utterly bizarre.

Unfortunately, that would be our last chance to hunt the "Armond" farm. Its owner had died earlier in the year, and although Bobby's beloved landlord had wanted him to buy the place before his death, the deal hadn't been finalized in time. New owners were now taking possession of the property - along with the rental house – so Bob had to move out. However, because my cousin is so well known and liked in that whole county, other options soon began opening up as word spread of his newfound interest in turkey hunting. Merely because I was Bob's cousin, many of these folks welcomed me, as well.

My cousin Bob Torrance and a small morel mushroom.

Frank and Eric came back down the next day to hunt on one of these newly acquired farms, with Eric finally getting his first chance at a tom late that morning. When this bird came in, all we could see was a single red head sticking up above a fallen log that lay ten yards in front of our hide. However, two toms flew away after the gun went off.

We all thought that Eric had missed the 14-yard chip shot, but then, as we stood there rehashing the events, powerful wings began thrashing the ground behind the log. Eric hadn't missed, after all! There had

31

been a trio of unseen toms coming in behind the cover of the ground litter, and what we'd seen leaving were merely the two lucky survivors.

Eric Coonrod and Frank Emert.

The next guy up to bat was a man I had never met before named Dave Pruett. Dave had read an article about me in the Vincennes newspaper the previous year, and then called to ask about the possibility of guiding him on a turkey hunt. This was to be my first time doing something for money that I love to do anyway, so I was a little apprehensive about it. And, nervous; I didn't want to fail. But, all that worry dissipated the second Dave pulled the trigger on a long-spurred brute of a tom weighing over 23 pounds.

The following morning I shot a tremendous gobbler of my own sporting 1- 1/4" spurs. That's the good part. The bad part is that this happened on the very last day of the Indiana season. Although I hunted or guided every single day, Cousin Bob hadn't been able to break free and accompany me on any of them after our initial adventures on the Armond farm. That was disappointing, and I vowed to make good things happen for him the following year. Hunting with "Cuzz" was just too much fun to put into words, and I was anxious to see him punch his first turkey tag.

A week later I headed out east for a return visit to New York. I hadn't made it there at all the previous year, so I was eager to spend some time once again with the family of Tony and Evelyn Bays. They had practically adopted me in 1988, and I felt like a reunion with them was long overdue.

Sure as sunrise, a knock on their door was all it took to get us laughing, talking, and telling stories like we hadn't missed a beat. Once I got settled-in to their son Jake's "Deer Camp," Tony and I took a tour around the farm so he could point out all the places where they'd been seeing turkeys. The following day I had the whole family over for our traditional feast of fried turkey with all the trimmings, and the very next morning Jake went hunting with me and shot a fine young "gobbler of the year."

Later that afternoon, The Jake'ster and I waded numerous Chenango County streams fishing for beautiful native brook trout. I don't know how many we caught, but it must've been nearly a hundred. We took home just enough for dinner, and released all the others. Two days later it was my turn to fill out a turkey tag. The tom I shot was a real good'un, too. Then, on the final morning of the season I had a hunt that still ranks up there amongst the finest and most amazing of my entire life. It happened like this:

The morning started off perfect, with clear skies and a crisp coolness in the air which promised to keep the blackflies down to a manageable level. A beautiful pink sliver of light was beginning to glow in the eastern sky as I hiked across a dew-soaked alfalfa field. Halfway across, I happened upon a newborn fawn lying there in the grass. There's nothing prettier in nature than a spindly-legged baby deer taking its very first steps, but I hustled away so as not to disturb either the fawn, or its mother.

A newborn fawn in an alfalfa field.

I had intended to climb a looming ridgeline before full dawn in order to gain the advantage that altitude would provide for hearing distant birds gobble, but my progress was stopped short of the crest by the sound of alarm putts coming from the treetops surrounding me. All I could do was hunker against a broad maple tree and slide down into the "ready" position with gun up and rested across my knee, in hopes that the semi-alarmed turkeys might calm down. Luckily for me, that's exactly what happened, and the dark woods returned to a place of peace and tranquility.

When gobbling time eventually arrived, that serenity was shattered by no fewer than four toms within earshot absolutely rocking it out. A cacophony of hen and jake vocabulary also began building from every direction. Even though it was totally by accident, I had inadvertently taken a position smack-dab in the middle of a whole *bunch* of vocal turkeys, and it soon became apparent that this was going to be one of those days when every bird around felt like telling the world just how great life was. Things got loud really quickly, and my excitement level grew in tandem with the serenade.

Turkeys eventually started pitching out and flying down, with most of them landing on a broad, flat shelf directly uphill from me. That was the spot where I'd originally been trying to reach anyway, and now I found myself both out of position, and out of the game, as I watched at least two big toms glide in to join the flock. I badly wanted to sneak up there and get situated where I could shoot onto their "landing pad," but it would've been foolish to try that move - there were simply too many eyes and ears still tree-bound all around me, and they would definitely alert every turkey in the flock to my presence.

The only thing that I could think to do was begin calling aggressively in hopes of firing up the competition, and lo and behold, that's exactly what happened when an angry hen started cutting wildly back at anything I said. I cut her off immediately, and she stomped all over my calls with obvious anger in her voice. It didn't take long before she was coming my way to pick a fight, and unfortunately for him, the boyfriend she brought along as backup took a good deal more abuse than she had bargained for when I smote him mightily about the head and neck with a load of copper-plated 6's.

After gathering up the tom, I sat back down at the same setup tree to write in my journal for a while. There certainly was no big hurry to leave the woods, because this bird completed my NY limit and I would be leaving for home on the 'morrow. Hence, a profound feeling of sadness accompanied the thrill of victory. I just wanted to sit there for a while and soak it all in.

Knowing that nine long months would pass by before I could hunt turkeys again, I called a little bit in hopes of getting one more answering gobble. I wanted to end the year on a good note, and sure enough, a distant tom piped up after my third calling sequence. Although he said nothing more, I didn't care – both my day's hunt and entire season now felt complete.

Then, a real hen sauntered up to my right front and began yammering away like crazy. When I turned my head to watch her, she caught sight of the movement and busted out of there putting, and cackling. Her racket immediately provoked not just one or two, but *several* toms in the immediate vicinity to go berserk!

That one burst of spontaneous gobbling seemed to be the trigger needed to break a silence that had enveloped the entire ridgeline since my gunshot, and from that point onward the woods began filling back up with so much turkey talk that it sounded like a Butterball Barnyard Convention. There were turkeys yelping over here, hens cutting over there, and a number of toms gobbling from 200 yards directly uphill of my position. I decided to go see if I could call them in just for fun, so I hoisted my tom over a shoulder and snuck in their direction.

It sounded like the closest of these gobblers was just beyond the lip of the flat-topped ridgeline. He was so close that I knew it would be impossible to get all the way up there with him, so instead, I stopped 25 yards short of the breakover and set up to call from there. The tom immediately began responding to anything and everything I said, and in very short order his gobbling grew even louder as he came closer.

Although he remained hidden from sight, I actually got to "watch" this tom's slow approach in a rather unique way. The recently risen sun was now directly behind him, and it cast his dancing shadow against the bright green leaves of the maple trees over my shoulder. It really was an amazing sight, and I was absolutely transfixed watching him strut back and forth in that way. I could plainly make out the shape of his beard whenever he turned sideways, or the cant of his head as he turned it this way and that in search of the vocal hen (me) who had promised him such devilish things.

Finally, the tom broke from his stubbornly-held "line in the leaves" and waddled into view over the break of the ridge at 18 yards. The sun's golden rays were now beaming directly through his spread tail feathers, giving me yet another absolutely beautiful visual that I can still plainly recall in detail whenever I close my eyes.

At that point the strutter must've seen me or the dead turkey lying beside my leg, because he began putting irregularly and retreating. However, he wasn't terribly spooked, and didn't go far. I continued to catch occasionally glimpses of both him and a previously unseen buddy putzing around up higher on the ridgeline, and after fifteen minutes or so they wandered out of sight. A few minutes later they began gobbling regularly at all the hen sounds which were still coming from down below me in a plowed field.

Creeping up higher towards them, I settled in on a big cherry tree which afforded a much better view of the shelf where they'd previously been strutting. I was just about to call again when a real hen directly downhill from me yelped loudly. I yelped right back at her to try and provoke an argument, and when she answered aggressively, I challenged her even more-so. Just like guys everywhere, tom turkeys love to hear ladies fighting and bickering amongst themselves, so it didn't surprise me when the recently departed pair of gobblers ripped into the squabble that the hen and I were having. It even sounded like a third tom might have joined up with them. Ferocious gobbling in the next few minutes kept me apprised of their advancing position as they retraced their route back to me.

Hearing footsteps over my shoulder, I slowly cranked my head around to the left as far as it would go to see the hen approaching. As she passed by my outstretched legs, she was so close that I dared only follow her progress through squinted eyes - eyes that certainly got much wider when they cut around to the right and saw three toms now standing like statues 12 steps away!

Those three lonely Lotharios would remain in that same exact spot for the next 75 minutes. The hen contentedly pecked around them in a half-circle of perhaps 20 yards in diameter, but she never visibly paid the slightest bit of attention to any of them. At one point she even laid down and took a nap.

Despite her indifference, the boys were obviously enamored of her beauty and had zero intentions of leaving. One of the toms never broke strut for the entire duration, while a second occasionally strutted. The third seldom did anything but stand at attention and stare at his brothers. None of them moved very much, and only then did they do so *very* slowly. It was almost like they were each afraid to make any quick movements for fear of provoking an attack from one another. Their behavior reminded me of mourners at a New Orleans funeral, dancing to a dirge.

Not one word was said by any of the participants during the entire first hour of this stalemate, but finally, the toms began gobbling sporadically at distant turkey talk still coming from the valley fields below. Several times they even thrust out their necks and shouted out in perfect unison with one another. Seeing them do that at such close range was an incredible thrill!

Eventually, the uninterested hen stretched her wings and began wandering off uphill, with all three toms creeping slowly along behind her. Once they were out of sight I finally found myself free to stand and stretch my cold, aching bones. The whole experience had been so intense as to leave me feeling drained, and now I was perfectly happy to head for home with a memory that would last me all the way through to the following spring.

Then, with no previous hint that anyone else was around, a *very* loud gunshot rang out from the direction of the tom's departure. Shot pellets rattled through the treetops to my right, followed by a second gun blast as more pellets sprayed the trees to my left. Meanwhile, I was diving behind groundcover! Immediately after this fusillade one gobbler flew right back over the top of me, and he was quickly followed by a second one running past at about 25 yards. I have no idea if the third tom made his escape, or got killed by those trespassers, because I was too busy getting my butt back down over the crest of that ridgeline in a hurry. I wanted to put as much earth between them and me as possible, just in case there was any more gunfire directed my way!

So ended an epic hunt in one of my favorite states, and so ended yet another season of chasing after gobbles and gobblers all spring long. Overall, I had hunted in 7 different states and spent a total of 53 days in the turkey woods. Furthermore, I had called 53 toms "into camp" (that term I use to describe turkeys called to within 40 yards), and had seen 16 of them brought to bag. Not a bad way to spend a spring season! However, while driving home I was already planning where I wanted to go in 1996.

New York's beautiful scenery is surpassed only by a big tom.

CHAPTER 4

Choosing New Hunting Ground

People ask me all the time how I choose new places to hunt, and I think this would be a good time to touch on that a bit. Believe me; ironing out my schedule every year is a tough task! Not only must I decide what states to include in the rotation, but I've also got to pick a particular region within their borders and then evaluate myriad public land holdings for their potential of providing successful hunts. I think about these choices year-round and always seem to be working on some aspect of planning for the upcoming season. This whole process is part and parcel of the turkey hunting game for me, and I get nearly as much enjoyment out of all the research as I do the actual hunts.

Well, that might be a bit of an exaggeration, but you get the idea.

By the time spring rolls around I will have printed out a number of different "tentative schedules" based on my goals and objectives for the year, with anywhere from 10-20 different states in the running for inclusion. Eventually I will settle on somewhere between eight and twelve, but one place that's always locked firmly into the itinerary is Florida. Part of that is because I have guiding obligations and responsibilities lined up down there for years in advance, but of equal importance is the simple fact that it's one of my favorite hunting destinations.

Once I leave Florida behind I'm free to pursue gobbling birds wherever I choose to go, but my days of dashing off to a state for just long enough to claim a tom from its soil are over; now, I like to stay put for several days, or until my legal limit of turkeys are in the cooler. Too many times in the past I would arrive under cover of darkness, head off into the woods before dawn, kill a tom soon after flydown, and then find myself back on the road heading for another destination before the sun even had a chance to evaporate the morning's dew. That's no way to fully grasp the uniqueness of an area, or discover the things that make it special, so these days I am much more inclined to take my time and not get in a hurry. However, I can't totally defy the Weddle blood coursing through my veins, and like my beloved Grandfather "Shine" before me, after a certain time in one place these itching feet are ready to get going for greener pastures (figuratively speaking only - I don't care much for field turkeys).

One factor which shapes everything else in how I conduct these hunts is money. Or, more accurately said, the lack thereof. I am *not* a wealthy man by any stretch of the imagination, and these springtime excursions put a severe strain on my wallet. The old bank account always glows a brilliant shade of red before I hang up my turkey vest in June, and then, for the next nine months I work my butt off to pay down as much of that debt as I can. However, it never quite works out as hoped-for and I slip a little further behind every year. Oh, well; that is the price I am willing to pay in order to experience turkey hunting to the degree that I do. Nobody ever accused me of having a *good* brain!

I turkey hunt approximately 70 days every year, so it's important to arrange my schedule in the most efficient and economical way as possible. Planning the route carefully is imperative, and so is saving money by camping every night in either a tent or my large van. My major expenses are thus reduced to fuel, hunting licenses, and food.

Cooking most of my meals in camp lets me cut expenses in the food category, but while I certainly do that a lot, I admittedly have a weakness for little "Mom and Pop" diners. In truth, I have a hard time passing them up. Fortunately, a side benefit to eating out is that local folks often initiate conversations with me just as soon as they see how I'm dressed in camo. A lot of valuable information has been exchanged in this way throughout the years regarding bird populations on nearby public lands, and a good number of dead turkeys have fallen to me as a direct result of these conversations. Many, many friendships have also blossomed from these chance encounters. Once in a while a particularly warm-hearted soul has even offered hunting access on their private ground.

While I admittedly struggle in saving pennies by eating-out so much, one area where I will *never* waste money is in motels. When it's time to do laundry or shower every few days, I'll either visit a truck stop along an interstate highway, or check with campgrounds, RV parks, or YMCA's to see if they offer these options to road-weary travelers. Often, I'll simply use biodegradable soap and bathe in a creek. I can't count the number of times I've done that very thing, and believe me, there's nothing to make you feel more alert and in tune with nature than wading naked into a cold, mountain-fed stream. Or, as is the case with Florida, into tepid, tea-colored rivers which you know hold a healthy population of water moccasins and alligators!

Since I do practically all of my hunting on public property, one less worry is the cost of obtaining ground on which to pursue my dreams. The types of land that I frequent are open to anyone possessing a legal hunting license and/or an access permit, and thanks to the hard work of wildlife professionals and game departments in every state of the nation, there is no shortage of places that fit the bill for what I'm seeking in terms of accessible land with good turkey populations. The simple truth of the matter is that I *prefer* hunting on public grounds as opposed to private land, and there are a number of reasons why.

First, I generally look for large tracts where I can cover lots of ground without having to worry about infringing on anyone's property rights. I don't care much for the thought of "beholding" to a landowner for the privilege of stepping on their turf, and I suppose this stems from having grown up in a much simpler time when a kid could walk forever without the slightest concern about crossing fences. Today, I still want the same freedom to move and hike for miles on end when I'm prospecting for turkeys or chasing after a long-legged "traveling" gobbler, and there are countless public land holdings across this country that are large enough in size to accommodate this.

Secondly, I don't feel like my odds of success are the least bit compromised when I'm on ground that's open to everyone else. My 35 years in this sport have produced untold numbers of quality hunts on public property, and despite the horror stories that you'll often hear to the contrary, actual episodes of hunter interference are surprisingly rare. Being willing to walk far from access points in order to get away from other hunters helps in this regard, but the basic truth is that I seldom encounter anyone else while in the field, anyway. Because I've experienced such excellent turkey hunting from coast to coast and border to border, I feel like the opportunity to hear, see, and occasionally kill gobblers is nearly as good on public property as anywhere else. So, why would I bother with all the hassles inherent in procuring permission on private land?

I've also got a danged wanderlust gene in my blood. I want to stretch my legs, see new places, walk on ground that I've never tramped before, and experience sunrises/sunsets over vistas where I've never been. The allure of finding out what's over the next as-yet undiscovered ridgeline is a tremendously powerful draw for me, and that's just not something which can be satisfied by going back to the same small pieces of real estate time after time.

Ok; back to choosing hunting ground. For all these reasons mentioned, as well as the fact that the hunting there can oftentimes be downright awesome, the first thing that I look at when researching a new state is whether it has any National Forests. Another benefit on these Federally-owned lands is that they almost always allow free camping just about anywhere you choose to do so. For me, that's an important consideration.

Other types of public ground (State Forests or Parks, Wildlife Management Areas, National Wildlife Refuges, Indian Reservations, etc.) can also support good hunting, but one separating factor is that camping on them oftentimes costs money, and it's usually restricted to designated sites (*if* camping is even allowed). I would much rather pick my own free spot, and then be able to step straight out of my tent or van in the morning to listen for the first gobble of another fine spring day from right where I stand.

Another great option is to find ground owned by large corporations like timber companies. Generally speaking, these can be vast tracts practically devoid of other hunters. I've experienced some really fantastic hunts on this type of landholding, and it can be well-worth the nominal fees that sometimes apply for a land-use permit. Depending on what part of the country you are in, an additional possibility might include private property with hunting rights controlled by the Bureau of Land Management. I've even killed turkeys on land under the jurisdiction of school districts, or other state/local entities.

The "secret" here is to do a lot of research and homework. In fact, it's vital if you want to experience the kind of out-of-state hunt that you've always dreamed of taking.

As for whether these public landholdings hold turkeys; again, it's of paramount importance to investigate thoroughly. Some of the western states with their spottier turkey populations might prove contrary to such a blanket statement as this, but generally speaking, if you can find large chunks of ground with good habitat, it will be supporting a flock or ten. With around seven million turkeys scattered across this nation, nearly all of the suitable habitat has been stocked. It's up to you to get out there and find them.

While National Forests are my first option, you should by no means overlook those other types of public land which I've mentioned. Oftentimes, their smaller sizes are a blessing in disguise, because game departments can utilize more intensive wildlife management practices on them. The larger pieces of ground are simply too big to do that economically. Also, these smaller, hidden gems of public land will often get little or no hunting pressure. Again; it can pay huge dividends to *diligently* research.

"Back in the day," that meant writing lots of letters to game departments and wildlife biologists, then patiently awaiting replies by snail-mail. However, the internet and cyberspace have changed all of that for the better. What used to take weeks can now be found at the click of a mouse button, and investigating new ground is a *much* simpler task. A veritable mountain of invaluable data is available on every state-run website, and it's a simple thing to pull up vital stats such as; the state's overall turkey population and/or density maps, County or Game Management Area kill totals, spring gobbling and summer brood counts, hunting regulations, license sales, etc.

Once I've decided on a particular state for my spring itinerary, I then start narrowing the search down with the aid of all this data found on the internet. It doesn't take much of an effort to figure out what region or counties have the highest success rates and/or the densest turkey populations, so I usually start there and then begin looking at public land holdings within these areas. Maps showing property lines and various other land features can usually be downloaded for free at this point, and it's even possible to carefully look over the actual terrain you are contemplating visiting via satellite imagery. While nothing beats scouting a new piece of property with boot leather on the ground, an actual picture from the sky runs a close second place and is an invaluable tool.

Now, let's talk about hunting regulations for a bit. Every state has their own set of laws, and they are unique unto themselves. For instance, *most* states offer over-the-counter license sales, but some still hold lotteries to determine who gets rewarded a permit. Obviously, it's imperative to know these differences before you arrive for that much-anticipated hunt of a lifetime!

Camping and fires, use of particular roads, tagging and checking-in of game taken, legal ammunition and the plugging of your gun – all of these, and many more, are examples of things that you need to familiarize yourself with prior to arriving in a new state. Legal hunting hours are another fairly complicated issue, with quitting times varying anywhere from noon to sunset depending on where you choose to hunt. I plan to address this last item in depth later on in this book, but I would like to briefly touch on it here.

In short, there is quite a bit of discrepancy between states regarding shooting hours. When I first started into this sport during the early '80's, most eastern states subscribed to a set of laws limiting turkey hunting to morning hours only. It was commonly believed that clearing the woods of mankind's presence by noon helped reduce the chances of hens being spooked off nests and abandoning their clutch of eggs.

However, various scientific studies since then have shown this foundational argument to be exaggerated to the point of being irrelevant. Afternoon hunting does *not* damage the resource, and over the last decade or so many states have relaxed their original restrictive laws. I find such a trend to be positively encouraging, because of the simple fact that it allows persons who can't get out there at the crack of dawn (for one reason or another) an opportunity to participate in this wonderful sport. I applaud these efforts. Unfortunately, there are still about a dozen states that hold firmly onto an antiquated "mornings-only" tradition, and some of them also operate under other such silly "blue laws" as prohibiting hunting on Sundays. A ground-swell of change may be happening in both of these areas, but it can't come soon enough for my taste.

Until then, every state has their own set of unique regulations, and it's the hunter's responsibility to learn them intimately before going afield. Since all of this information is readily available on the state's website or in pamphlets free for the asking, there's really no excuse for not being in compliance. I'll repeat this one final time, because it's so important: it is *imperative* that you spend time researching the rules and regulations of any state where you plan to hunt! Nothing could potentially ruin the excitement of taking a trip to a new area quite like being arrested and fined for game violations which you might not have even been aware that you were breaking, so be very diligent in learning the laws of the land.

Even though I hunt public ground almost exclusively, I think it would be remiss at this point not to mention private property possibilities, as well. Access on private land in this country can still be secured with nothing more than a handshake, so it never hurts to knock on doors and approach landowners in a courteous and friendly manner to ask for their permission. After all, the most they can do is say, "No." You really have nothing to lose, and so much to gain. Just be sure to present yourself as sincere and unassuming, and if you are lucky enough to be granted the privilege of hunting on their land, then by all means treat that property even better than if it belonged to you. Always consider yourself to be an invited guest and a goodwill ambassador of our sport, and act as if you realize that how you are viewed will be a reflection of the entire hunting fraternity. In many ways, that is exactly what you are! Lead with your best foot forward, and then follow that up with an even better effort. I have gained access on a number of properties throughout the years by applying these simple principles, and you can, too.

Ok, I've touched on some of the basics when choosing new states and I've offered a few valuable tips. I'll add more in later chapters, but for now, let's get back to hunting tales.

Some of the tools used in choosing new ground.

CHAPTER 5

Strategies and Adventures from 1996

In 1995 I had hunted a total of seven different states. Up to that point, it was the greatest number of places I'd visited in a single spring. The following year I would repeat that tally, and then go on to hit the same number of destinations in three of the next six springs. During the other three years my schedule contained six, eight, and nine states, so I was being pretty consistent from season to season.

I was also adding new states to my resume on a regular basis instead of just going back to hunt the same familiar ground, and that was contributing even more excitement and anticipation to the game for me. In 1995 those fresh destinations had included Alabama, Nebraska, and Texas. While no new states made it onto the schedule in '96, I added Georgia, Kentucky, Tennessee, and Michigan to my lifetime credentials in 1997. Illinois made the list in '98, followed by Mississippi and Ohio in '99, Louisiana and Arkansas in 2000, South Carolina and Pennsylvania in 2001, and Missouri, Maine, and New Hampshire in 2002.

From 2003 and onward I upped my game even more and started getting *real* serious about my turkey hunting by consistently hitting somewhere between nine and twelve states annually. However, since this book only covers the years from 1995 to 2000, let's get back into what was going on during that time slot.

The equipment used in that first half of my turkey hunting "career" had been gradually refined to include only those items which I trusted to perform in the clutch. I carried a Ruger Red Label over/under 12 gauge shotgun with x-tra full choke tubes in both barrels, and I shot Winchester XX shells in copper plated 6's (switching later-on to 5's in the newer Winchester Supreme loads). The particular camo I wore changed slightly throughout the years, but original Mossy Oak Bottomland had been a huge favorite when it first came out on the market and I stayed with subsequent variations until switching over to the Realtree brand some years later. My mouth calls of choice back then were either Primos True Doubles or Denny Gulvas diaphragms in double or triple reed construction, and I also used pot/peg calls that went through a rigorous vetting process from my discerning ear; eventually settling on the original poplar version of Doug Adkins' Cane Creek Pro Custom slates and glass calls as my favorite. I still use them extensively today, but in all honesty, I don't much care for the newer versions made from Mahogany. Occasionally, a Lynch Foolproof box call also found a spot in my vest, although I was always hesitant to carry one for fear of breaking it.

As far as my general hunting strategies were concerned, I strongly believed that the closer I could get to a gobbling tom before setting up, the better my odds of winning the fight. That meant listening from high points or ridgelines every evening in hopes of hearing turkeys fly up to roost or gobble, and if successful in that, I would then sneak in tight to their position long before dawn. If I failed to "put a tom to bed," I'd owl hoot with my own voice just before daylight in hopes of eliciting a response, then hustle to close the distance before the birds had a chance to fly down. Terrain and conditions dictated just how close that might be, but I was always trying to push the envelope by gaining as much ground as possible. I once heard that the difference between setting up "just right" and boogering a bird by trying to get too close is one step, and I've held onto that tenet throughout the years. I think getting close is worth the risk, simply due to the increased success which being in tight provides.

Another favored tactic perfected in those early years was to incrementally move around during the course of a hunt by switching from tree to tree. Forward, backward, or sideways didn't matter so much - I just wanted to add an impression of movement to my calling and make the tom think that I was a hen going about her ordinary daily patterns. Real hens seldom stay in one place all day. However, there are times when they don't go far for hours on end, so if the situation dictated, I could sit in one place for as long as it took. Believe me here; steadfastly remaining in one spot has proven to be the demise of many a wary old gobbler!

In spite of my early proclivity towards owl hooting before dawn in hopes of eliciting a position-telling response from a tom, as time passed I began drifting away from crow-calling or other loud and noxious means of shocking out gobbles. I know that most hunters do this with great success and I have absolutely no problem with it, but creating a lot of noise just doesn't appeal much to my sense of propriety in the turkey woods. Rather, I tend to treat the forest like I would the inside of a church; hushed tones and "stealth" mode feel more proper to me while I'm there. The "run-n-gun" style of covering lots of ground and forcing the action just doesn't fit in well with my personality, so even though I know it's a solid, proven method of finding and killing turkeys, I don't utilize it very much.

Instead, I lean more towards being as unobtrusive in the woods as possible and counting heavily on excellent ears and keen observational skills to help me interpret what the turkeys are doing at any given time. I'm constantly striving to blend-in with my environment and stay close as possible to the birds for as long as I can maintain contact, and then making a move to strike at the proper time. My general modus operandi might be succinctly described as trying to get where turkeys want to be even before they realize that they want to be there, and then using realistic calling uttered as if I had something specific to say in order to fool the gobblers into coming within shotgun range.

By studying turkey behavior thoroughly and continuously, I came to develop a rather unique theory that there was an almost physical "bubble" of space surrounding each tom encountered, and if I could penetrate this area before uttering the proper calls, there was very little chance that he could resist coming over to investigate. The problem, of course, was in figuring out just how large that ever-changing

49

bubble would be at any given moment, and for each particular tom. I envisioned it as being in a constant state of flux; changing in size and shape for reasons that only turkeys can decipher. Hence, the bubble's size could vary weekly, daily, or even hourly depending on the circumstances, conditions, and terrain surrounding the tom, as well as his mood. Sometimes this zone could be so large that the gobbler would run to a call offered from half a mile away, while at other times you might need to be within 50 yards to get the same response. However, generally speaking, I believed that the closer I could get to a tom, the better.

My basic philosophy of striving to blend in as much as possible with my environment and becoming "at one" with the woodland community focused heavily on trying not to send out any type of a signal that danger was at hand. What I mean by this is that no creature is more attuned to his surroundings than a wild turkey, and it isn't just the obvious squirrel and chipmunk chatter, bluejay and wren squawkings, or other such sounds of alarm that puts them on edge. There are many other purveyors of danger which are far more subtle in their messages sent, and they broadcast warning signals that are just as widely heard by all of the forest inhabitants. I felt like it was vitally important to pay close attention to whatever was going on around me at all times, because I most-certainly didn't want to become the pebble that created ripples of alarm in a still pond!

Similarly speaking, it's not only what's being said by the forest inhabitants which spooks game, but what's *not* being said, as well. There is an ongoing symphony of sound in the woods at all hours of the day or night, and when this is disrupted (tree frogs and crickets suddenly going silent, for example), that too can serve as a warning which is just as alarming as a siren to all the nervous creatures of the forest - especially so to a bird as paranoid as the wild turkey! Old toms don't have a very high degree of curiosity about such things anyway, and when they sense that something isn't "right," they have a slick habit of making themselves scarce by slipping away for parts unknown. Once safe and settled down again, they go back to being only marginally on edge and ready to turn themselves inside out at the first hint of danger, but panic is always lying just underneath the surface of their skin.

As hunters, we continually run the risk of spooking animals far out ahead of us that we never even knew were there, but turkeys are quite adept at picking up on this when it happens, and they don't stand for such things. Again, think of that pebble tossed into a calm pond...

Of course, it's impossible for human beings to attain total invisibility in the woods, because we are merely guests in that society - not members. A certain amount of disturbance is unavoidable whenever we enter their domain, so in those early years, when I was moving towards the first gobbling bird of the day, I didn't believe in wasting much time. Only after I got within his "zip code" would I slow down and focus on trying to figure out the best place to call him in. Still to this day I spend a *lot* of time studying the surrounding topography to get a feel for where I think the tom will be most willing to approach. Taking a direct route towards a bird is not always the best way to get into the prime position for killing him, and there is seldom a good reason to hurry into assuming an unfavorable setup spot where there's very little chance of success.

Once I get a feel for where the best "killing zone" for a particular tom is located, I begin looking for that perfect setup tree. I try to avoid potential road blocks between the tom and myself, like creek channels, fence lines, or thick brush which might cause him to hesitate or be reluctant to come closer. Another hint would be to get on the tom's same level or higher, but that isn't always possible. Many times it isn't even necessary. Our views tend to change over time if we pay attention, and since those early years I've called in many a tom who came downhill the whole way. Believe me here; if you can get set up in the right spot and say the right things to tickle his ear, a hot bird will find his way to you no matter the elevation change or obstacles lying in between.

I do, however, spend a lot of time looking for a setup spot that just feels "right," and that usually means picking a place that offers a modicum of ground cover near the tree serving as my backrest. I don't want my surroundings to be so brushy that I can't see the tom's approach, but yet, I don't want it to be so open that he can easily see that there isn't a real hen standing where those sweet nothings have just been uttered. My setup trees also tend to have fallen logs, limbs, or vines growing around their bases to better break up my human form, and I most definitely seek out shade in every setup - anything "out of the ordinary" shows up significantly more when highlighted by bright sunlight!

As stated earlier, once I get focused-in on a bird I tend to stay with him for as long as I can tell that he's still in the vicinity, but if the situation calls for it I can also be a very patient man in waiting for him to come back around. By using my eyes, ears, and brain to interpret both what's going on in the present and any sign previously found, it's possible to maintain faith and the positive outlook necessary for success, no matter how long it takes. That might mean a many-hour sit on any given day, or vigilantly maintaining a potential hotspot for several days in a row.

Of course, this is not to say that I don't cover a lot of ground in my hunting style, because I most certainly do so when it's called-for. I walk many miles and cover untold acres of habitat every year in search of my feathered antagonists. But, once I'm actually into turkeys I tend to slow down and stay put for as long as it takes to gain the upper hand. I'm nothing, if not both persistent and patient.

In 1996 all these aforementioned tactics and strategies were still being ironed out and honed to a keener edge. Florida would once again prove that there was still a lot yet to be learned, but before that could happen, I had a very scary experience that didn't have anything to do with turkey hunting.

On the day before the Florida opener I was walking around the camp-ground in my bare feet and swatting a few golf balls for fun when I heard over the radio that Stanford, Indiana (where my Mom lives) made the national news when 17.5 inches of snow fell overnight. To celebrate being in the Sunshine State instead of snowbound back at home, Rick Brown and I went fishing in a nice little pond located two miles down the main gravel road from the campground. It only took us a couple hours of wading around and casting rubber worms before we had a whole stringer of fat bass for dinner, and then we changed into dry clothes before heading back to camp.

As we pulled up to the tent, I suddenly remembered taking my wallet out of its protective zip-lock bag and placing it on top of the truck's roof while I changed out of my wet shorts. Immediately, this sent me into a panic, because I couldn't remember retrieving it from the rooftop. *Every single dime* that I'd saved up for my prolonged spring turkey adventure was in that wallet! No sooner had we come to a stop before I was out the door and looking up on the roof, but of course, the wallet was gone.

The campground road in those days was very rough, so I immediately began searching along the bumpy, circuitous route that we'd taken into our campsite while Rick raced back to the pond in his truck. We'd passed at least one other vehicle on the main road, so I was a nervous wreck when my own search turned up nothing and time dragged on by with no sign of Rick.

Finally, I saw Rick's truck turning back into the campground, and when he pulled up grinning from ear to ear like an opossum chewing on briars, my feelings of dread began to relax a little bit. As he exited the truck, the first words out of his mouth were, "you ain't gonna believe this." The rest of the story is as follows:

Rick had almost made it back to the pond at about 75 miles an hour when something tumbling towards him in the middle of the road caught his eye. Braking to a stop, he realized that it was money being blown down the road by a 30 mph wind! The first bill was a Ulysses S Grant, one hundred dollar bill, and others were following behind it. Picking them up as he walked towards the parking area, he found more hundreds, some twenty's, a couple 10's, and several 1's. Then, the wallet itself was seen lying in the gravel with my ID's scattered all around it. On his way back towards the truck, Rick found a couple more hundred dollar bills that had been blown into the roadside ditch, and when counted, the wad of money totaled $816 - the exact same amount that I had tallied earlier in the day, after I'd bought my hunting and fishing licenses at Wal-mart.

To say that I was both relieved and overjoyed back at camp would be a *serious* understatement!

In the next week I got down to some serious Osceola chasin', and it started with a difficult hunt right off the bat. However, my opening morning problems weren't so much due to the bird that I'd been listening to for the last couple of scouting days. Rather, my troubles were caused by another hunter, who had obviously been keeping tabs on the same tom.

On opening day this bozo set up 200 yards west of me in the dark and began owl hooting *terribly* at 5:30 a.m. This was at least an hour before first light, and he never shut his pie-hole until after 7:30! The tom didn't appreciate this guy's horrible owl renditions every two minutes any more than I did, and he never uttered a peep. Oh, well - so much for the trials and tribulations of hunting on public land.

When "Mr. Hooty-Hoot" returned the following day and began with the same tiresome routine, I decided that it was time to head elsewhere to get away from this idiot as soon as possible. Hopping on my brand new Klein mountain bike, I pedaled as hard as I could go.

Green Swamp WMA is very large, and with the gate not opening until 5a.m., there are quite literally thousands of acres that you simply cannot reach on foot before gobbling time commences. The mountain bike changed that, and before the first sliver of pink had risen in the east, I was deep into a place where I'd always wanted to hunt, but had never ventured because of its distance from the road.

As luck would have it, there were two gobbling turkeys close to the spot where I hid my bike at dawn. Unfortunately, both of them were across a property line fence, but I set up in a clump of palmettos to try and convince at least one of them to cross onto the legal side of the fence. When t h e y eagerly answered my first yelps from a Primos True Double diaphragm, my hopes soared. Then, as they came closer I heard a pair of real hens yelping forlornly a couple of hundred yards further down the fence line, and I knew that those hussies were trouble. The toms immediately turned on a dime and drifted away in the hens' direction.

Quickly realizing what must be done, I jumped on my bike and pedaled hard to circle their position. Then, I tossed my two-wheeler behind some myrtle bushes and quietly crept to within 75 yards of where the hens could still be heard carrying on unabashedly from private land. A thick wall of tall palmettos grew along each side of the boundary line in this spot, and although I realized that getting a turkey to cross such a barrier was nearly impossible, it was my only option.

For the second time of the morning I skootched back into a palmetto clump and began calling. Immediately, I got cut off by two strident gobbles from only 50 yards beyond the brushy fence line, and a few moments later one of the toms gobbled even closer. However, from that point onward it was as if they'd drawn a line in the sand and refused to move one inch towards me. Oh, there was plenty of gobbling, and they drummed loudly time and time again, but the feathered Lotharios remained locked in place. The hens beside them would also yelp softly on occasion, letting me know that the cards were definitely stacked against me.

We all held our respective positions for nearly an hour, and during that whole time frame I kept anticipating the mouthy hens to lead their boyfriends away. However, that never happened, and as time dragged by I could tell one of the toms was getting progressively more frustrated and angry with my refusal to join the flock. His gobbles took on a ferocious rattle that seemed to shake the very bushes between us, and the slightest hint of a note on my pot call would cause him to loudly cut me off. Then, quite suddenly, he hushed up, and a few moments later I heard the sound of wings taking flight. Then, the sun was blocked out as a big black bird powered up above a cabbage palm growing along the fence line.

A sandy firebreak paralleled this fence and ran down beside its bordering palmetto ledge. Once clear of any brush, the tom dropped almost straight down to land in the middle of disked earth exactly 20 paces from the deadly end of my gun barrel. Just as soon as his scaly feet hit sand, that bright red head shot straight up to look for the sassy hen that had finally convinced him to cave in and take flight. As they say in real books, "that was all she wrote."

This was a great hunt, with lots of beautifully rendered turkey talk coming from the unseen flock of birds, and it made me proud to know that I had somehow pulled a fine old tom away from real hen feathers standing right beside him. Likewise, it was noteworthy that he'd flown up and over a *very* serious physical barrier in order to reach me. The ride back to camp on my new Klein was leisurely and fun, with the weight of a big gobbler serving as the perfect counterbalance for the rest of my gear.

Two days later I hunted a nearby WMA which was only open on Wednesdays and Thursdays. Getting to where I wanted to go entailed making a river crossing up to my shoulders in the inky darkness before dawn; a task that proved well-worth the worry it garnered (alligators and water moccasins) when I shot an outstanding gobbler in an incredibly pretty creek bottom shortly after sunup. Cypress knees and purple lilies grew in this place in seemingly equal and untallyable numbers, while ancient live oaks dripping with Spanish moss towered high overhead. The place was simply breathtaking in its beauty, so the following day I brought Rick Brown back in there with me as partial repayment for finding my wallet. It was a great hunt, and he subsequently shot a gorgeous bird out of a group of who-knows-how-many turkeys that came in shortly after flydown to some aggressive cutts and assembly yelps.

Me, my Red Label, my Klein, and a fine Osceola.

Back at our Green Swamp camp, I then met up with my old buddy Ron Ronk from Indiana, who had ventured down in quest of his first Osceola. The next day I called in a bird for him that gobbled like an adult tom, strutted like an adult tom, and died like an adult tom. He wasn't an adult tom though - just a very confident jake who was mature in his own mind and ready to challenge the world for his right to breed hens. That attitude didn't work out very well for him, since Ron was equally as eager and willing to deny the jake of an opportunity to grow long-bearded. As our old "guru" Bill Madden would often say, "he was a fine gobbler in his first year of life."

Overall, Ron was not very enamored of the trials and tribulations inherent in hunting the wild lands of Florida. In fact, he was anxious to get another in-hand look at an Osceola just as soon as possible, and thus hasten a return home. While the quick killing of that jake seemed to foretell the promise of good things to come, the land of snakes and gators was not to be denied her sadistic pleasures - she tortured my buddy for nearly another week, and ultimately refused to yield a second bird of any age class.

My 1996 Florida excursion was a wildly successful endeavor, but the highlight of the year was meeting Zane Caudill's parents, David and

Marie. They were both native Floridians thru-and-thru, and had each grown up in families who lived off the land and thrived in what wild Florida could provide its denizens during the Great Depression era. Both of them were also very accomplished and talented hunters, as well as utterly entertaining back in camp with their many fascinating tales and stories.

Rick Brown and a fantastic tom, in a gorgeous Upper Hillsboro river swamp.

For a number of years this colorful pair had worked as a team at Fisheating Creek, back when that area was a state-run WMA. Later on it was divided into two parts, with one half being run as a private hunting camp leased by David Austin and Lovett Williams. The Caudill's had continued to work for these two men, with David assuming the position as their top hunting guide for wild hogs and turkeys. He had also been their head turkey trapper, with many of his "pole-trapped" Osceola captives being released on various properties in Florida. Many folks don't know this, but a number of them were even sent to other states – some as far away as Texas and Wisconsin!

While their son Zane had been a valued member of our camp at Green Swamp since the beginning, I had never met his parents because they were always hunting down south at the lease of their good friend, "The Judge." This finally changed one fateful afternoon when they drove up and joined us around the fire pit. David was excited to tell us about the fine old bird he'd killed the day before, while Marie was

57

equally eager to share the story of how she had shot a coyote on the same morning. Coyotes were quite the rarity in Florida at that time, and it was a noteworthy event.

Ron Ronk's first (and only) Osceola.

After the first few minutes of hearing these tales it became apparent that the gobbler David had shot wasn't just any turkey, but rather, a "King of Kings" amongst his kind. Now, believe me here when I say that most large toms in south Florida will weigh less than 18 pounds. I've killed several old long-spurred gladiators that were *substantially* less, with some of them tipping the scales at under 14 pounds soaking wet. David's tom had weighed 22.5 pounds, and furthermore, had sported a beard that was 11.75 inches long. While both of these statistics were impressive, it was the reported spur length which made my jaw drop, for David said that they each measured 1- 13/16 inches long!

The world record turkey at that time was a bird killed on the Mormon Ranch of Osceola County, Florida by Lance Vincent. This tom sported the first recorded spurs of at least 2 inches in length, so it was apparent that the giant David had killed was nearly of the same caliber. I was anxious to lay eyes on such a behemoth, but when I asked him if the bird's body was at the taxidermist, he looked at me like I was some kind of a blithering idiot. Calmly walking over and reaching into the cab of his truck, he grabbed a pair of turkey legs off the dash and said, "Well, we ate most of him yesterday, but here's his feet."

David Caudill's Behemoth.

Oh, my goodness - what feet they were! I had never seen anything like the long, needle-sharp scimitars on those scaly legs, and just as David had claimed, my flexible cloth measuring tape verified their length. Everyone at camp ogled and manhandled those spurs all afternoon, and when David told me that he'd only seen two or three turkeys in his life with daggers like that, I knew this was stone-cold truth coming from a man who had literally held thousands of wild turkeys (both live, and dead) in his hands during a long and colorful lifetime spent centered around these birds.

Marie and David Caudill.

There was plenty more laughter and good cheer shared around our campsite in 1996, with many of Zane's interesting Floridian friends making up an important part of the contingent. All of these guys were awesome hunters and seasoned veterans who had been raised in the swamps down there. Kenny Dorman was in attendance, along with Charlie Parrish, Timmy Tanner, Arlis Talbert, and Kim Locke. Joining us also were people like me; "Beetleneckers" from out of state who had shown up to hunt the legendary Osceola subspecies of turkey and then became so enamored of the whole experience that they just kept returning year after year.

Our motley crew of dedicated turkey hunters has continued to expand over the years to include new hunting members, as well as wives, children, and friends of friends. I think that I can speak for every single one of them when I say that the camaraderie shared around our Green Swamp Turkey Camp is downright magical. For my own part, I can certainly vouch that when the calendar on the wall reaches March, I begin to get jittery with anticipation and start counting the days until I can once again head south to meet up with my friends and "family."

Unfortunately, the Florida fun always races past much too quickly, and in the blink of an eye I was headed for the western edge of Oklahoma. This was a place where I had been hunting regularly since 1989, and while I didn't realize it at the time (and regret it in hindsight), it would be my last trip to the sandy hills and sparsely forested habitat where her Rio Grande turkeys prevail. That certainly wasn't done on purpose, but simply because other states began taking up spots on my schedule during subsequent years and I just haven't ever made it back. I sure hope to change that in the future. However, if I don't, at least my last trip there gave me some challenging hunts and fond memories.

The excursion started off in Beaver River WMA, where it took three days of patient, calculating observation and careful hunting before I was finally able to get the drop on the one particular tom that I was after. The greatest challenge was that he lived in the safety zone surrounding the manager's residence, and he only came outside of it on occasion when chasing after some of his wayward flock of hens. I glassed him with binoculars the first day there and thought that he was worth the effort and frustration of listening to him gobble and watching him strut most of each day while safe from harm. When I finally got the opportunity to shoot him I was right; he had long, hooked spurs that he would've easily hung from, if there had only been an actual tree limb within eyesight in that barren land outside the safety zone. The hen who led him to his death had gotten very agitated with my calling and come to run me off, and when she passed by mere yards away from my gun barrel I could tell that she was sick because she coughed and sneezed several times. Those were very strange sounds to hear coming from a turkey, but I didn't pay them much attention because I was focused on the big black ball of feathers following dutifully along behind her.

I next went to a nearby WMA that I'd never hunted (Ft. Supply), and on the second afternoon there I managed to call in a lone tom who insisted on a ride back to camp in my van. Following that trigger-pull I was still one bird shy of a three-tom season limit, but with no desire to press my luck I decided to head on up to another favored state; South Dakota. However, this was the year that I chose to start hunting on an Indian Reservation near Pierre before going over to my beloved Black Hills region, and during the very first morning there I got onto several hard gobbling toms. Unfortunately, there was a wide, deep river flowing between us, so all I could do was call loudly, stand my ground, and hope they'd fly across. Such an expectation bordered on the impossible in my own mind, but my options seemed few and far between.

Oklahoma's Wayward Son.

Well, two hours later I was no closer to making something happen with that vocal flock, so I decided to head out away from them and go find another tom on my side of the river. However, I called loudly and urgently as I left, and before I'd covered 200 yards I could tell that there was newfound interest by one of the previously reluctant toms. My apparent departure had obviously gotten him worried, for now he began paralleling my course as I moved upriver. He then began angling closer with each vibrant gobble, and I caught sight of him strutting through the willows towards the opposite riverbank. Once at the water's edge, there wasn't the least bit of hesitation before he picked right up and flew on a beeline towards me. When his feet next touched down, the toenails left an impression in the sand a mere 23 yards from where I sat hunkered against a Volkswagen-sized chunk of driftwood. Moments later turkey feathers were drifting on the wind and blowing back out across the river's rippling waves.

With my reservation limit of one tom now in-hand I headed west, and by early evening had entered into the Black Hills National Forest. This is without a doubt some of my favorite ground in the entire USA, and the times that I've spent hiking and hunting in those beautiful Ponderosa pine-studded hills and hollows are very special to me. A return there always brings with it a sense of excitement, and I always anticipate fun, action-packed hunts in beautiful terrain. I'm seldom disappointed.

However, despite my great love of that whole area and its good turkey population, I tend to struggle in the actual killing of Black Hills birds. I suppose this stems as much as anything from the difficulty of traversing that rugged ground, but the proclivity of her vocal toms to cover lots of territory in a direction most-generally *away* from my calling is also a factor. Not so in 1996; that year provided a quick and exciting successful hunt on the very first day.

Arriving at a familiar campsite well after dark, I didn't have the opportunity to roost a tom. That was no problem, though; I'd hunted this area often enough in past years to know that the odds were very good of hearing at least one gobbling tom at daybreak from right where I was parked. Sure enough, at dawn a throaty tom ripped into the stillness of the chilly morning air from about 400 yards directly uphill of my van, and it only took a matter of a few minutes to get set up in good position on the tom and a noisy hen.

Of course, just as I expected, the tom and his girlfriend began walking away from me immediately after flydown. I was forced to tag along as best I could, and when they seemed to hesitate for a bit in a saddle along the ridgetop, I was able to creep in close. The hen answered my sweet yelps with those of her own, and the tom gobbled at both of us. Then, he began following the cutting, agitated hen as she worked towards my hide against a stately Ponderosa.

By the time the sassy hen came into view my gun was already propped on a knee with the safety flipped off. The tom, however, separated from his girlfriend a bit and took a slightly different path 35 yards up above us on a steep slope. The hen kept right on coming in a straight line, and she was soon pecking the ground about eight feet from of my gun barrel. When she moved behind a covering tree I thought that I could swing my gun ahead and align its sights with the tom, but the evil-eyed hussy somehow caught movement and began putting nervously while walking away stiff-legged and erect. It was obviously now or never before the whole deal went quickly awry, so I took aim at the tom's upraised head and shot.

I'm not exactly sure what happened, but I missed. Maybe I lifted my head and looked over the gun barrel and thus shot high. That is the bad part. The good part was that the tom launched himself into the air and flew downhill – directly over the top of me. Bad mistake! Without even thinking about it, I swung upward and touched off a round as he passed overhead at an elevation of about 15 yards. At the shot he folded up like he'd been struck by lightning, but due to his angle of flight and airspeed, coupled with the steep hillside we were on, he didn't crash down for another 50 yards.

Racing downhill as fast as possible out of fear that I'd only crippled the tom, I grew worried when I couldn't at first see him in the thick undergrowth where he'd hit with a resounding "thump." Then, I heard a loud "wheezing" sound which turned my attention to a tangle of blackberry vines. Crumpled in amongst them I saw my tom, and in working down to him, I came across a two-inch thick pine that was freshly broken off about five feet above the ground. The reason I took notice of it was because the whole jagged upper end was covered with feathers and blood! When I reached the now-expired gobbler I found that his upper craw and lower throat were ripped wide open - he'd obviously snapped off that pine in his freefall, and it had ripped open the gaping wound that explained those wheezing final breaths.

I had never shot a turkey in mid-air before, and I would not recommend it even to this day. However, the situation was a nearly perfect scenario with high odds of success. It really couldn't have been an easier shot for someone who has done a whole bunch of wing shooting in his lifetime, but even still, I wouldn't have attempted it if I'd had more than a split-second to think things through. My actions were purely reaction-based, and in hindsight, I felt very lucky to have pulled it off.

Once back in camp I fixed a great breakfast of fresh fried turkey breast and "Doc's World Famous Parmesan Eggs" before heading homeward. Twenty hours of driving-time later, big raindrops began splattering on the windshield as I neared St. Louis. I had no sense of foreboding at the time, but during the next 19 days of our Indiana turkey season there would be only two days when rain didn't fall. Most of that moisture came down as torrential monsoon-like deluges during prime hunting hours. Any ordinary fool might've been dissuaded from going out at all in such "inclement" weather, but not me; I ended up hunting or guiding every single day.

Two days' worth of exciting results in South Dakota.

Opening morning found me out with Don Foley at Tea Mountain yet again, but when I called in a gobbler shortly after dawn, my hunting partner refused to pull the trigger and let the turkey walk off unscathed. When I asked him why, he simply said that he wanted to hold out for a really big bird. At that point I distinctly remember thinking to myself, "Donny's done gone bat-shit crazy." I mean, really, who in their right mind would pass on a strutting tom in chip-shot range? Fortunately, there were still turkeys gobbling in every direction, so I shrugged it off and away we went to seek something "bigger."

Well, we soon got onto another hot tom and began working him. A second bird then piped up and was approaching from behind us as the first one arrived on the scene and stuck his huge head up above a line of greenbriar at 25 yards. It looked like a wide-open shot to me, but Don told me later on that from his angle there was just too much brush in the way. Suddenly, the tom putted loudly and vanished, so I wasted no time in nudging my partner in the ribs with an elbow and saying, "Damnit, Donnie…you boogered him."

65

Well, that made two toms called-in to within killing range in the first hour of opening morning without any gunpowder being burned. I feared that we might've used up all of our allotted good luck for the day, but I shouldn't have been worried - we weren't done just yet. After some loud, insistent calling on a D. D. Adams slate, the tom that had been approaching from behind us fired back up, and a few minutes later he came walking past us at about 35 yards. Unfortunately, this bird never stopped moving and his bobbing head offered no good opportunity to make a killing shot.

At that point we were 0 for 3, which ain't a good day in any ballpark! However, good hitters keep right on swinging the bat, and it wasn't long before we had yet another pair of toms fired up. They were close too, but just out of sight on top of a round knoll. We were set up on a hillside "bench" below them, and after twenty minutes of stalemate I decided to slip downhill around Donnie in an attempt to convince the toms that I was a whole flock of feeding hens. Scratching loudly in the leaves, I also yelped, purred, and clucked a lot. The toms loved it, and absolutely tore into anything I said with booming gobbles.

My ruse eventually did the trick, and their heart-shaking gobbles were soon getting closer. By that time I had snuck back to where I was just a few yards below Donnie, and while the tree he was sitting against kept me from actually seeing him, I soon spotted one of the toms circling in from the right. The bird was only 20 yards out, but when no gunshot ended his day he finally saw something that didn't please him and he ran off down through a ravine, putting loudly the whole way. I figured the gig was up – yet, again.

What I didn't realize at the time was that Don had honed-in on the other bird, which was still standing to his left. Right about the time his gun's trigger was about to be pulled, I stood up unawares and came walking back to ask Donnie just how many danged turkeys he intended to scare into the next county before lunchtime. Of course, the gobbler that I hadn't seen didn't think too highly of my ill-timed appearance, and he wasted no time in flying off into the wild blue yonder. I felt really small at that moment, and thought better about opening my pie-hole. Don gave me an exaggerated scowl before hanging his head in mock disgust. That made us both laugh.

During this whole encounter there had been a pair of toms gobbling their brains out in the hollow below us. They must've gobbled 300 times. We were standing there contemplating how best to go after this fire-cracker-hot duo when it was decided for us; they piped down and never said another word. In fact, although it was only 8:30a.m., from that point onward every turkey in the woods shut up like their beaks had been sewn shut. Long hours passed with nary a turkey sound heard of any kind. Then, a gobble finally rang out to the south of us, and not very far away. I glanced at my clock and saw that it was 11:15.

After another answering gobble to a long string of lost yelps, the tom rushed in from our right side. Since Donnie shoots right-handed, getting into position for the shot entailed a bit of contortion, and the keen-eyed rascal spotted his final adjustment. Putting loudly, the tom long-stepped away from us, and I thought the show was over. However, when he heard me cutting hard on a diaphragm, the tom calmed down and began strutting. He even gobbled a time or two, before easing back towards us.

Time was now our worst enemy, as in those days Indiana hunters had to leave the woods at noon. The tom, meanwhile, was operating on turkey time, and didn't care one iota about the hands on our human clocks. He wasn't in any hurry to die. Then again, maybe he actually did know what time it was, because he continued to dawdle about and take his sweet time in doing so.

Before he could ever get close enough for the killing shot, we got whistle-bit and had to walk away from a hot tom dancing tantalizingly close to lethal range. Oh, well; rules are rules.

Despite this ending, our hike back to the cabin had a lighthearted feel to it. At one point Don told me that this had been the best hunting day of his life. I knew exactly what he meant, for Mr. Foley and I are of very similar mindsets when we're turkey hunting. We both understand that bringing home meat is far from the only way to measure victory, and it's really all about the experiences encountered, and the level of fun and excitement produced. By all weights and measures, April 24, 1996 had been a rousing success.

The following morning was the complete antithesis of the proceeding day. While rain wasn't actually coming down at dawn, there was a heavy feeling of moisture in the air. You knew that it was just a matter of time before the skies opened up. Whereas we had heard no fewer than eight gobbling turkeys 24 hours earlier, there were now exactly two within earshot. The one east of us gobbled only a single time, and the other wasn't exactly on fire, either. Then, as we finally reached a good setup spot near his roost tree, three deer spooked from practically underneath our feet and went tearing off straight at the tom. He never uttered another peep.

By 9 o'clock we were basically just walking around looking for morel mushrooms and setting up to call every now and then without any discernible success. Our wandering route had taken us off of one tall ridge line, down through a broad bottom, and up the next steep climb. Once there I cranked out a long, lost-yelp series of calls and was promptly answered by a tom gobbling from right back on top of the ridge that we had just left. However, neither Donnie nor I was particularly interested in retracing our footsteps back up that steep slope. Instead, we decided to make a stand right where we were at and see if we could let the turkey do all the work.

Well, the tom answered my next loud yelp and began sporadically gobbling on his own as he drew closer. There wasn't as yet a single green leaf of any kind on the trees around us due to the colder-than-normal spring weather, so we could actually see the entire slope below us and all of the hollow's bottom. It wasn't long before I spotted the strutting tom as he came off the opposite ridge. Then, he turned at the rapidly flowing creek and wandered off downstream until he was out of sight. I suspected that he was just looking for a shallow place to cross.

Rising to readjust our setup, Donnie and I made a quick hundred-yard parallel move and settled in at the base of a huge red oak that had snapped off about 15 feet above ground level during March's 17.5-inch freak snowstorm. This was a really great spot to work the tom from, with good cover and an even more splendid view of the hollow down below us.

The next answering gobble confirmed that the tom had already crossed the creek and begun climbing upward. I didn't need to call much from that point on to draw his interest, and when he subsequently waltzed into view twenty minutes later in full strut at 26 yards, Don was already looking at him over the vent rib of his shotgun. A sharp cluck brought the toms head up into the perfect, "shoot me now" pose, and a swarm of hot lead bowled him over into a heap.

Unfortunately, the tom's flopping death throes then took him right back down that long, steep slope he had just climbed to reach us, and when I say "long and steep," I really mean it! By the time he finally stopped rolling, all we could see was a tiny black speck *waaaaay* down at the base of the ridge. Turning to me, Donnie asked if it wasn't the guide's responsibility to go fetch a dead turkey. My reply went something along the lines of, "You killed him; *you* retrieve him!" Ah, yes - hunting with "Teresa" Foley is always good fun!

A heavy, cold rain began falling later that afternoon, and as I said earlier, the next two weeks-plus would see this type of weather become a persistent, unwelcomed trend. All of the vertical flood water made for challenging, difficult, and very uncomfortable hunting conditions, but my buddies and I stuck it out and hunted hard nonetheless. Once in a while our perseverance and tenacity were actually rewarded with a hard-fought victory, and one of those successful hunts happened during a memorable pair of days afield in Jefferson County with my second-ever set of paying clients: the vice-president of Vincennes University (Gary Shepherd) and his dear old friend Louie Rusch, who was a farmer from Knox County.

Gary, Louie, and I were into turkeys from the very first moment of the very first day hunting on a new piece of property that my cousin Bob had secured for me, but at no point was the outcome ever a sure thing. You see, Louie was heavy-set, 70 years old, and deaf as a stone. Gary really wanted Louie to kill his first wild turkey, but to say that I had my guiding-hands full in getting that mission accomplished would be a serious understatement.

I came to realize this on Day One when we spent all morning working birds and coming oh-so-close on numerous occasions, before I finally convinced a big tom to waltz up within spittin' distance. Louie never did hear me say to kill the gobbler standing statue-still in front of his gun barrel at 22 yards, and even though I repeated the order several more times in increasing volume, the only action my words caused was for the turkey to finally putt loudly and run off into the brush. I was disappointed and frustrated, but I tried my best to assure an equally broken-hearted Louie that we'd get another chance. He dejectedly told me that at his age and health every opportunity was a precious thing, and we needed to make the most of each one. I vowed in my mind to try harder and hunt smarter by paying attention to Louie's limitations, and that meant making sure that I was sitting right up next to his ear at all times so I could hoarsely whisper instructions in a way that he might actually hear.

That's Don and his bird down there in the "holler."

Torrential rains poured all night long, but they abruptly stopped at about 4 a.m. The sky then remained heavily overcast for a couple more hours before the clouds cleared away and the wind calmed. I was confident that good things were going to happen for us with this turn in the weather, but of course, that was before Gary missed a big tom sneaking in on Louie's blind side. The sudden and unanticipated gunshot didn't seem to faze Louie any more than its shot pattern had harmed the gobbler, so I wasn't even sure if he had heard it, at all. Then, the old fella grinned widely and started giving Gary a serious razing over his marksmanship skills.

These two guys had been close hunting companions for many years, and they obviously enjoyed each other's company immensely, because there were always plenty of laughs and good natured jabs being exchanged between them. This was good for me as well, because I'd been feeling a great deal of internal pressure to produce results; that's just part of who I am and how I'm wired. Louie and Gary's constant ball-bustin' and jocularity helped to squash all of that stress, and I felt assured that no matter what happened, we were going to have fun.

Within the hour we had another tom gobbling at us from out in the middle of a large horse pasture, but he was taking forever to come our way. Luckily for him, a quartet of jakes then walked up behind our setup, and this time Louie actually heard me alert him to their presence. Getting my gunner turned around to face the turkeys was a whole 'nuther ballgame though, and with all of those eyes upon us, Louie encouraged Gary to go ahead and make one of the jakes pay dearly for their attempt to sneak off with the yelping hen (me). The shot rang true, and we finally had feathers on the ground.

This was one of those days when turkeys seemed to be gobbling in every direction, and all day long. Once the jake was secured in Gary's vest we promptly went towards the closest tom within hearing range, but before we could get set up on him a real hen came racing across the pasture with evil, illicit intent in her heart. The things she promised that gobbler effectively put an end to his interest in us.

Since it was now nearing 11 o'clock and we only had a single hour left to hunt, at that point it was beginning to look like the odds were stacked against us getting a bird for Louie. Still, we had heard at least half a dozen toms, and most of them had gobbled long and hard all throughout the morning hours. The weather forecast for the next day was dreadful, but as I said, this had been a good day with plenty of action, and both of my clients were happy and content. Of course, we had full intentions of giving it one last Herculean effort on the 'morrow, but the results of our first two days afield made everything OK if things didn't work out in our favor.

Then, halfway back to the truck I yanked a response out of a distant tom with some really loud cutting. We hustled to cross a raging creek just as fast as the old, crippled fella leaning on me could go, and then we immediately got set up in what sparse cover we could find on the other side. It wasn't good though, with only a thin veil of young saplings available to shield the three of us.

Subsequent calling on my part garnered absolutely nothing further from the original bird, but when a completely different gobbler hammered out an answer off to our right side, we swiveled to face his approach. A half-minute later another gobble let us know that he'd already cut the distance between us in half, and in another few moments I heard the loud and unmistakable, "Pffft…dmmmMMM" of a spitting, drumming turkey - a very *close* spitting and drumming turkey!

The sound that I so love to hear had come from directly behind a series of folds in the earth that looked like old grown-over bulldozer spoil piles. I instantly leaned all the way up into Louie's left ear and gruffly whispered for him to not move a muscle. His gun was already on a knee and pointed exactly where I thought the drumming had originated, and I felt to the center of my soul that the tom was going to pop up into sight at any second.

I was staring hard, trying to pick up the first hint of the tip of a tail that would alert me to his strutting presence before those beady black eyes might pick us out, when suddenly, a bright white orb began rising up over the closest little hill. Luckily, it was almost directly in line with Louie's gun, and when the tom's head then dropped back out of sight as he pecked at the ground, I grabbed Louie by both shoulders and physically swung him the necessary couple of inches to line up his sight beads with where the turkey had been standing. No sooner was this move completed than the tom's bright red head topped in white stretched straight up to full height, and Louie immediately lowered the boom. The range was 14 yards, and while most of the shot column took out a 2-inch tree trunk at the six-yard mark, enough of the pattern got past this heretofore unseen obstacle to smite the gobbler dead in his tracks.

Time of kill was 11:11 a.m., and for the next few minutes I watched a 70 year-old man turn into a 10 year-old boy right in front of my very eyes. Louie jumped for joy, whooped and hollered, and even did "snow-angels" of happiness in the leaves.

Gary Shepherd and Louie Rusch got it done.

Later that afternoon more torrential rains arrived, but despite the weather I continued to hunt and/or guide in Jefferson County. By season's end I had tallied 16 days in that part of the state, and while the soggy conditions made 1996 one of my worst seasons on record statistic-wise, we still managed to put a few gobblers in the cooler. Included in that tally was a dandy of a tom for myself, and a second-ever bird for Frank's gardening employee, Eric Coonrod.

There were other hunts that didn't end as well. Some of the characters and cohorts I shared them with are people you've already met: folks like DeWayne Feltner, my cousin Bob Torrance, and Dave Pruitt. Too much rain and too many vocal and annoying hens made for challenging conditions and stringent results overall, yet good times were had by everyone involved.

Once the Indiana season ended, it was time to make a return trip to West Virginia. I still vividly remembered striking out there in 1989, and the quest for revenge was strong in my heart. However, this beautiful state once again proved not ready or willing to grace me with the hidden wonders of her ample bosom, and six days of hunting in those gorgeous hills and hollows produced no meat for the cooler, and not a single beard or spur for the trophy wall. Oh, I could've shot a jake on the second morning out, but once identified as such, I was perfectly content to let him live to see another day. Maybe he'd still be around the following year as a longbeard willing to die a glorious warrior's death for me...

The only positive takeaways from that hunt were hearing a couple of gobbling toms. That's not much to go on after you've bought a non-resident license and spent a week of time working hard to make something good happen, but the weather was terrible from the onset. It was either raining heavily, or intensely hot and humid, and total leafout conditions made either seeing or hearing turkeys extremely problematic. Oh, well; I still had fun, and vowed to keep coming back until I got better results.

Next up was New York, where I'd been ending my turkey season almost yearly since 1988. The black flies up there can occasionally be so horrendous as to make any outdoor activity almost a dreaded experience, and 1996 would prove to be one of those times. Of course, staying relatively safe from their swarming multitudes by holing up in Jake's deer camp was certainly not any kind of an option for someone like me, so I was out there in their bailiwick every day for the last

13 days of May. I had to wear a tightly-meshed head net at all times while afield, because any exposed skin or the slightest entry hole into your clothing drew the despised black flies like a magnet. They were relentless, and maddening; absolutely awful, really!

Sometimes things don't work out as planned, but the day is never a waste. Here Dave Pruitt takes a break amid phlox and twinleaf in the Indiana hardwoods.

Despite the buggy difficulties, I heard turkeys gobbling nearly every day and worked a number of them into range. Unfortunately, on the third day of the hunt I did something really stupid. It was raining hard that morning and I was tucked back into a thick grove of hemlocks when a pair of toms answered my calls and crossed a plowed field on their way to find me. I'm not sure why I didn't wait, or what I was thinking when they appeared over my gun barrel, but I pulled the trigger when they were at a subsequently paced-off distance of nearly 60 yards. Man, I would've *sworn* that they were right about at the 40-yard mark, but I was grievously wrong.

All I can say in defense is that it was dark back in the rain-soaked hemlocks, and the turkeys were seen through sort of a tunnel out into that open field. I don't know why that might make them appear closer than they really were, or how someone who is so adamant about killing his birds at less than 30 yards could make such a terrible mistake in yardage estimation, but that is exactly what I did. I must've laid awake for most of that night worrying about whether my targeted tom was reduced to coyote poop because of one fraction of a second worth of brain fart on my part, and I felt horrible.

The next morning I returned to that same area behind Jake's newly built house and promptly called in a pair of toms just after sunrise. Shooting the trailing bird at a much more respectable 18 yards, I was perplexed when I then discovered that his beard was caked together with dried blood. At first I suspected that he'd been spurred in a fight with another tom, but a necropsy on him back at camp found a single pellet wound at the base of his beard. It was quite fresh, too; in fact, I much-more-than-strongly suspected that it had been made approximately 24 hours earlier, when I had taken that ridiculously long shot from the hemlocks. I slept a lot better that night, knowing that I had sort of made amends for my previous screw-up by finishing the job of killing this tom.

A few days later I watched a bunch of turkeys scratching around all afternoon in a freshly plowed field. Right at dusk they began flying up to roost within a hundred yards of the field's back corner, so after dark I eased in and built a brush blind beside a tree that stood 30 yards from where they had entered the woods. Then, I went back to camp and told Jake that even though there were not a lot of "sure things" in turkey hunting, if he didn't kill a tom with me the following morning it would have to be either because he was too lazy to get up and go hunting, or he screwed things up once we got there. I didn't realize at the time just how prophetic the last part of that statement might prove to be, nor how my words would come back to haunt both of us.

The next day was May 29, and at dawn the woods beyond the field sounded like the barnyard at a turkey farm. Hens were yelping, cluck-ing, kee-kee'ing, and cutting nearly nonstop from the roost, while nearby a tom gobbled often in answer to all their carrying-on. Once that first hen pitched out and glided into the disked field in front of us, six of her sisters/cousins immediately did likewise, and all of them landed within easy gun range of our hide. Then, the last bird to take flight from the roost was obviously bigger and heavier, as witnessed by the crashing of tree limbs and the heavy sound of its wing beats. Following the same flight path as the hens, a tom glided into view and promptly touched down exactly 26 yards from us. What happened next? Jake missed. I don't know how or why, but he missed. Obviously, such a dreadful occurrence can happen to any of us (some, seemingly, more than others), but it's *never* a good feeling when it happens and Jake felt miserable for having blown such a golden opportunity. Of course, I knew exactly how he felt...

The following day found us right back out there on the ridgeline above the plowed field trying to gain redemption with this tom, and when a raucous pack of crows began cawing in the dim light at 4:51 a.m., a pair of eager birds north of us began gobbling in answer. This was by far the earliest gobbling that I'd heard all season, but these two birds sounded like jakes to me. When a *real* tom finally blurted out a challenging call at the more respectable time of 5:10, they hushed up and never said another word.

Turkeys began pitching down within sight of us a few minutes later. Following lots of answers from both hens and gobblers to my aggressive cutts and yelps, they began easing in our direction. Soon, there must've been 15 or more hens within 30 yards of us, and then the first adult tom in full strut arrived on the scene. Working his way in front of Jake, I expected to see him fold up in a puff of feathers at any moment, but the gunshot never came. Jake told me later-on that he'd been worried about screwing up a second time, so he was waiting on the "perfect" scenario before pulling the trigger.

Finally, the strutter began easing out of Jake's swing angle and more in front of me, so I whispered that it was time to kill this tom when he next came out from behind a tree that was shielding his head and neck. In my peripheral vision I saw Jake make a move to get his gun out ahead of the tom's path, but then I heard a loud "thunk" sound as his barrel ran into a dead snag that hadn't been noticed beforehand. The tom and several other turkeys around us also heard this noise, and they began putting loudly with heads craned up.

At this point it was quite obvious that our hunt was about to go south in a hurry, and although I wanted Jake to kill the tom instead of me, time for drastic measures had arrived. With Jake's gun hung up on the stob and the tom high-stepping away, I took hasty aim and touched off a round myownself. The gobbler promptly picked up and flew off totally unscathed.

Talk about frustrated; one second everything had been peachy-perfect, with lots of contented and unaware turkeys feeding and loafing all around us. The probability of Jake getting a nice revenge-tom had merely been a matter of waiting for the right time to pull the trigger. Then, in the blink of an eye everything had turned to Hell in a hand basket! In hindsight, I knew that I'd also made a serious mental mistake by panicking in the pinch. I should've just let the tom go, or waited to see how everything panned out for Jake. It was foolish of me to take that shot.

Like Jake only one day before, I felt hangdog and miserable at the unexpected turn of events, and I spent most of the afternoon moping around like a beaten pup. This had been a textbook example of just how quickly a turkey hunt can go from good to bad, and I was really upset with how I had handled myself.

Still; despite feeling terrible inside, the hope that springs eternal in a turkey hunter's heart kept me looking for a bright spot in the doom and gloom. After some deep thought, I began to see that the day's misadventure could serve as a learning experience. I needed to figure out a way to slow everything down at the moment of truth, and act in a more calculating, lethal manner at all times; focusing more sharply on what was happening in the big picture. I had to resist the urge to act first before thinking everything through.

Of course, telling myself what needed to be done was the easy part; actually *doing* it would be much, much tougher. Turkey hunting does strange things to the human brain!

I still felt like I should've killed that tom outright. He had been plenty close, and with his head held high, I couldn't understand why he wasn't sent sprawling at the shot. I'd also found a few small neck feathers at the spot where the tom had taken flight, and that left me feeling exasperated and frustrated. Over the course of the last couple years there had been several instances where I felt like good shots had failed to produce dead turkeys, and I'd begun to think my choice of ammo might have something to do with that. Could it be that the size 6 shot which I'd been using for so long wasn't carrying enough lethal energy to finish off turkeys every single time? This latest incident drove a tangible wedge of doubt into my brain, and it also bruised my self-confidence more than just a little. As turkey hunters, we all know that there is no room for doubt or lack of confidence in the turkey woods...

On the final day of May I ventured back out for one last try at making amends on this tom, and just after the crack of dawn I heard him gobbling from out on the tip of a narrow hogback ridge. In very short order I found myself leaning up against a tree in what I considered an ideal position - about 80 yards uphill of the tom, with a flat spot on the ridgetop separating us. It seemed like the perfect place for him to parade about for any available hens after flydown. When a couple of his ladies began softly yelping from close-by, I answered their morning's greetings with some of my own.

Now, I usually don't like to call while turkeys are still in the tree, and here's why: since I hunt public land almost exclusively, I don't want the birds to stay in their roost any longer than necessary, or gobble any more than I need to get myself set up nearby. Excessive gobbling does nothing but give other hunters a chance to arrive on the scene and booger everything up. I want that bird on the ground just as soon as possible, and only then do I ordinarily start calling.

However, today I gave a few muted tree yelps of my own and the hens eagerly answered back. The girls were in no hurry to fly down, but a couple minutes later I heard the tom pitch out and land on the slope below his roost tree. It was still quite early and very dark in the woods, and although no additional gobbling was uttered, I soon heard drumming as he worked up towards the flat. At one point the tom seemed to be fading away, but some excited yelping on my part brought him drumming right back towards me and I soon spotted a white-topped head peering intently from around a tree at 26 yards.

Not able to positively identify whether it was a jake or tom in the dim light, I held fire for the longest time until, finally, he gobbled and I caught a glimpse of long whiskers when he thrust out his neck in song. As soon as he stood back upright with head stretched high I let 'er rip – only to watch in abject horror as this now seemingly invincible tom took off like his tail was on fire. Blinking unbelievingly, I could only sit there in perplexed, slack-jawed shock and confusion as I contemplated how in the world I had blown such a picture-perfect opportunity.

Not only was I broken-hearted and disappointed, but even more so when I once again looked around where a "missed" tom had just been standing and found a few cut neck feathers. This discovery made me feel like puking right there on the spot, and my attitude immediately took a nosedive as I thought back to the aforementioned toms in my past that had supposedly been "missed" while shooting 6's, but which further investigation had determined to have been more aptly termed, "hit, but not recovered." Right then and there I vowed to switch over to size 5 shot. Whether this was the right or wrong interpretation of the evidence before me was perhaps questionable at the time, but I reasoned that the smaller-sized pellets didn't pack enough "umph" to kill the biggest of turkeys every single time, and such a scenario just wasn't acceptable to me. To this very day I still continue to shoot the larger-sized pellets, and I feel like they truly do outperform 6's.

Well, despite the 1996 season ending on an unprecedented three-peat of failed opportunities, it had been a very good year overall. I'd spent 58 total days afield in seven different states, and called in 45 toms to under 40 yards. Of those birds, 18 had stayed behind - killed either by myself, or other hunters whom I had guided. Still, it was those last three misses in closing out the year that most haunted my daydreams whenever I thought back on the entire campaign afterwards, and I was bound and determined to do better in 1997.

At least the trout fishing was good.

CHAPTER 6

Scoring Turkeys

As you have probably come to figure out by now, I tend to keep rather detailed field notes of my hunts. These records include various data about the day's happenings, as well as a plethora of information about the individual birds taken, such as body weight, beard length, and spur size. I'm not sure why I like to put all of this information down on paper, but I do know that years after the fact I can take one glance at what was recorded earlier and remember the hunt like it happened yesterday. That right there is reason enough for my nearly-compulsive record keeping.

For any of you who don't know about such things, the National Wild Turkey Federation has a system in place which puts those physical measurements into a formula used to compute a final score. This was developed by Colonel Dave Harbour, and he designed it with the intention of treating those three parameters listed above as basically equal in value. Many turkey hunters couldn't care less how their turkeys score in this system, and in all honesty, I really can't find fault with such a position. After all, we really need not spend too much time worrying about how any one turkey ranks over another, since *every single one of them* are worthy of pride.

However, a lot of us do indeed like to see how our turkeys compare, just as we enjoy seeing how an exemplary specimen of any big game animal stacks up against others of their species. It makes for an interesting aside to the hunt, and there's nothing inherently wrong with paying attention to such detail - so long as the quest for shooting "trophy" animals doesn't rule our actions and behaviors during the hunt. In other words, the ends should never justify the means. Nor should killing a so-called "trophy" tom be used to elevate ourselves above other hunters. Shooting a bigger tom than the next guy doesn't mean that you're a better hunter than him. Longer beards, sharper spurs, or heavier toms will always be more a matter of luck than a display of exemplary skill on the part of the trigger-puller.

Despite some misgivings for those reasons, I do see value in keeping a nationally recognized record book of the top scoring turkeys. However, I'd like to see it done in the right way. Back in 1992 I wrote a letter to the NWTF in which I claimed that the three parameters used to score turkeys should *not* in any way be equal. Rather; I strongly advocated how they should be given point values which better reflected their true relative worth to any total score. My basic premise was that body weight should carry the least importance, with beard length having a somewhat greater value, and spur length being honored above any of the others.

My position on this topic had been percolating for several years as I'd read and re-read Colonel Dave Harbour's fabulous book, *Advanced Wild Turkey Hunting and World Records*. In studying the scores of toms listed therein, it had become quite clear that a serious disparity existed in the rankings, whereby heavy two year-old toms oftentimes outscored birds with longer beards and/or spurs.

In my mind, it was a complete "no-brainer" that older, longer-bearded and sharper-spurred birds should score higher than their younger and sometimes heavier brethren. In fact, as far as I was concerned a bird's body mass shouldn't carry much weight (pun intended) at all towards the total score. Think about it this way; is weight a parameter used in scoring deer or other big game animals?

It's a documented fact that a dominant wild turkey tom can lose up to 30% or more of his weight during the course of a spring breeding cycle, simply due to spending the majority of his daytime hours strutting and breeding instead of seeking out nourishment. How could it be fair to compare him with toms lower on the pecking order that spent more of their time feeding instead of breeding? Furthermore, how would certain subspecies that are inherently of smaller stature (Osceolas) ever be able to compete on a level playing field with big, corn-fed Easterns?

Now, please believe me that as someone who has experienced both difficult hunts for young birds and easy ones for older toms, I know that their physical attributes don't have anything to do with the quality of the hunt itself. They truly don't! However, bragging rights are bragging rights, and the words, "limbhanger" and "longbeard" are both colorfully descriptive terms that we proudly use when telling our hunting tales to friends and cohorts. Old warhorses with long spurs and ground-dragging beards are revered and hold honored places in our memory banks. In a nutshell, it's my sincere belief that *these* are the very toms which should be getting top scores in the record books - not those fat two-year olds who waddle around feeding on sweet clover all spring long while their superior elders are fending off competitors in brutal fights for the right to breed more of the hens and thereby pass on their genes.

In carefully perusing the Colonel's book, it became plainly apparent that the older, dominant toms were most-definitely not always getting their just rewards, so I made a few tweaks to the system in order to fix this discrepancy. It was really quite simple to do, since the basic formula already in place was sound and worked fairly well. I merely increased the value of spur and beard measurements, while keeping body weight the same. These simple changes gave each trophy parameter a better reflection of its respective level of importance in the grand scheme of things.

Here are the changes that I made:

A tom's weight would continue to be scored at one point per pound, rounded to the nearest 1/16. Each ounce would thereby be equivalent to .0625 of a point. An example tom weighing 20 lb., 1 oz. would thus score 20.0625 points.

Beard value was then doubled to four points per inch, so each 1/16" would now equal .25 of a point. That same example bird with a 10- 1/16" beard would tally 40.25 points in this category.

Finally, spur scoring would be raised to two points per each 1/16-inch, so a tom with matching one inch spurs would total 32 spur points per leg, or 64 total points. In the Colonel's NWTF system, spur length was multiplied by a factor of 10, resulting in this same example bird scoring only 20 points.

By adding all these parameters together in my adjusted version of the official NWTF scoring system, a hypothetical "trophy" tom of 20 pounds, with a 10-inch beard and matching 1-inch spurs would thereby achieve a total score of 124.0 points (20.0 + 40.0 + 64.0). In the Colonel's system, this same tom would tally only 60.0 points (20.0 + 20.0 + 20.0).

Even at first comparative glance of these scores, the impact of my system vs. the NWTF's becomes plainly obvious. Most notable is that each of the three scoring parameters immediately assumes their rightful place of hierarchy, with spurs becoming the single most defining measurement, followed by beard length, and body weight reduced to the very least important factor. A tom's mass would now have approximately half the value of his beard length, and somewhere around a third the value of those long spurs which old birds earn by staying alive for at least three years - not an easy task when you're an animal near the bottom of the food chain!

Once I administered this new formula to a sampling of toms in the official record book, it became even more crystal clear that several advantages could be found in using my "tweaked" system over the one already in place. First and foremost is that "trophy" status would forevermore be based primarily upon spur scores, with older toms alway finding their way to the top of the record books. Since most trophy animals are judged by the headgear they have grown over time, it just seems fair that turkey scores should likewise be reflective of bone growth (even though spurs are actually made up of a keratin outer layer growing over a bony core).

Secondly; body weight could never again take such an important place in scoring as to override normal beard and/or spur measurements.

As I've said before, this happens quite often in the current record book, but in my adjusted formula it's nearly impossible for fat two-year-olds to top their older brethren. In "world-class" turkeys such as the current record holder shot my James Lewis (a monster of a tom weighing 33 lbs., 9 oz. and which also had a 13.75 inch beard and spurs of 2- 1/4 and 2- 1/8 inches), even this tom's incredible body weight would only factor in at about 24% of the total projected score in my system of 227.5625 points (33.5625 + 54.0 + 140.0). This tom's bulk alone accounts for more than 32% of his 104.8125 score in the current NWTF records.

Thirdly; my improved method of scoring turkeys would give values approximately equal to those of typical whitetail deer. At first glance this comparison might seem unrelated, unimportant, and capricious. After all, any turkey hunter knows that shooting a danged hooved-carp could never be equal to besting a wild turkey! However, if you think about it, there is a method to the madness of somewhat equating their respective scores. Herein is the case I outlaid in my letter to the NWTF:

Even those of us who don't care much for deer hunting know that a "trophy" typical whitetail will score upwards of 140 points, with anything over about 180 points being considered an absolute monster. A deer that tops 200 points is truly "world class" and worthy of challenging for the title of biggest deer of all time. For instance, both the "King" and "Hanson" bucks score over 220 gross points as typical whitetails, and although there is some ongoing dispute of whether the King buck should be scored as a typical or non-typical (and depending upon whether you support Boone and Crocket or the Northeast Big Buck Club), each can legitimately vie for the title of "World Record Holder." In either case, that 220-point tier is a tremendous score, and it sets a mighty high standard for others to follow.

As I stated earlier, most of us view a typical "trophy" tom to be in excess of 20 pounds, with at least a ten-inch beard and spurs over an inch long. A tom matching these three minimums would score 124 points by my method, and would thus be approximately analogous to an "entry-level" whitetail score of 130 points into Pope and Young's archery record book. Boone and Crocket entry scores for whitetails are set even higher due to many factors including the greater number of specimens in their record books, so their entry standard is also set at a greater value of 160 points.

Here's where the comparisons between the NWTF's and my system get interesting: a really great turkey weighing 20 pounds and sporting an 11-inch beard with matching 1- 1/2" spurs would likewise score 160 points. Mr. Lewis' record tom would score 227.5625 points in my system, while the top scoring whitetails top 220 points. Are you starting to see any similarities here?

Turkeys and whitetail deer are the two most widely pursued big game animals in America. Scoring them similarly would make sense for another important reason, and that is because in these difficult times when hunters of all persuasions are finding themselves under attack by the "anti's," it would be an opportunity to close ranks and better relate to one another. Since hunters make up such a low percentage of the general population in today's world, the only way we will ever be able to coexist in the future is if we support one another. There is too much in-fighting and bickering about this method or that, or hunters of one variety of game vs. hunters of another, with each trying to elevate themselves above their "competitors." What we need is to find our similarities, instead, and support one another. We must fight as a cohesive unit on common ground. It's really the only way our precious lifestyles can continue to exist in the coming decades, as less and less of the non-hunting population has any connection whatsoever to the ways of wildlife, nature, game management, and hunting. That's a sad testament to the human condition in this world, but it's true, nonetheless.

As for "non-typical" birds possessing multiple beards and spurs, or birds having broken or missing accoutrements; they can still be easily included into this new system. Merely score these toms by the longest measurement of what's there. A separate category could be set up to better reflect their uniqueness, but they can continue to compete in the typical ranks, as is.

Well, such was generally the case I presented to the NWTF in a six-page letter dated February 29, 1992. Another five pages of graphs and charts supported my position, and I also offered to help implement and administer these changes free of charge. Since the official scoring system hadn't been in place for very long, I felt like the benefits of changing over to a better way would far surpass any difficulties which might come along with the territory.

My only motivation for all this effort was to create a system which could be viewed as more fair and equitable to the resource - the wild turkey. I didn't give one hoot about taking credit, and I actually thought that my hard work on this project would garner positive dialogue and change from within the NWTF. However, the response I received was rather lukewarm. In a one-page, 10-sentence letter, Rob Keck thanked me for "my time and positive effort to improve our program." He did admit that I "may have even a better plan than the original Dave Harbour one," but he claimed that "there would be more problems than benefits to make the change."

That was it. In other words, "thanks, but no thanks."

Oh, well; I tried as best I knew how to make a positive contribution, and got absolutely nothing accomplished for the effort. That wasn't the first time such a thing has happened to me, and it probably won't be the last. Such is life.

To this day I still continue to use this enhanced scoring system without any further adjustments when ranking turkeys killed by myself or others, and I still think it is far superior to the system in place with the NWTF for all the reasons listed above. There are others which I haven't even touched upon here, as well, such as level of accuracy and ease of use. Feel free to try it out on your own birds and see how they stack up with one another. Maybe someday my vision of a changed system might find favor amongst the NWTF, but probably not.

Please remember this, though – scoring turkeys is just for fun, because *every* gobbler is a trophy!

National Wild Turkey Federation, Inc.

Wild Turkey Center, P.O. Box 530, Edgefield, South Carolina 29824 (1-803-637-3106)

July 30, 1992

Mr. Tom Weddle
P.O. Box 7281
Bloomington, IN   47407

Dear Tom:

Please excuse the slowness of response to your suggestions regarding Wild Turkey Records. Your letter arrived just after our February board meeting in Indianapolis and was held for discussion at our recently completed summer board session.

Staff reviewed your proposal and feels that you have some excellent points and obviously you've put a tremendous amount of thought into the system. You may have even a better plan than the original Dave Harbour one, but at this time, changing the system would be tough.

Considerations on what would be done with present listings and re-scoring and re-entering the entire computer file is more than we can manage at this time. Economics and staff would pose a large challenge to us that at this time we cannot undertake. Bottom line is that at present there would be more problems than benefits to make this change.

I do appreciate your time and positive effort to improve our program. At present the foreseeable future, I think we'll continue as is.

Many thanks and best wishes in the great outdoors.

Sincerely,

Rob Keck
Executive Vice President

RK/pt

Dedicated to the wise conservation and management of the American Wild Turkey.

Rejection letter from the NWTF.

CHAPTER 7

Setting the Bar Higher in 1997

The 1996 spring turkey season had been a very good year; both for me, and the people with whom I had shared time in the woods. Together, we had set all-time high marks in total days afield (58) and overall kills (18), while calling "into-camp" the second-most toms of my career (45). Unfortunately, there had also been a record set in the number of misses (6), including four in which I had been the triggerman. Even more distressing was the fact that Jake Bays and I had combined to miss the final three shots of the year, and that did not sit well with me as I began planning for 1997's itinerary. I wasn't at all sure how to go about getting better results in the marksmanship category, but changes definitely needed to be made.

Another area where I was looking to shake things up a bit was in which states got included on the schedule. For seven of the past eight springs I'd been hunting out west, but the simple truth was that her wide open spaces and grand vistas didn't thrill me nearly as much as the rolling hills and deciduous forests closer to home. Since there were still quite a few eastern states where I had never even been before, I felt like the coming year was a good time to concentrate my efforts in the types of habitat which I most preferred. Of course, Florida' place on the schedule was never in doubt, but after leaving there I planned to work my way northward with the season and see how everything panned out.

The weather started out very fickle in the Sunshine State in 1997, and her confounding Osceolas which I so-much love to hate proved to be even finickier than normal. This subspecies seems to be more influenced by climate than all the others; they're prone to remaining hush-mouthed if everything isn't "just right" at dawn. Cold temperatures and cloudy skies especially seem to shut down their ardor, and both of these conditions were unfortunately the norm for my entire 9-day stay. However, it actually rained only once or twice in that timeframe, and because it had already been a very arid winter prior to turkey season, the swamps were drier than I had ever seen. This allowed me to wander further back into places where I'd never been able to explore before, and by hiking far and working hard to get away from any roads, I was also able to avoid other people. Not once did I have an instance of "hunter interference," despite the fact that Green Swamp WMA is just about the most hard-hunted piece of real estate in all of Florida.

On the second morning out, in one of those new secluded spots set far back away from anywhere, I heard a total of five gobbling toms. Never in my wildest imagination would I have anticipated hearing that many birds on public land in Osceola country, and after subsequently calling in a pair of them strutting up through a thick stand of cypress knees along the edge of Devil's Creek Swamp, I focused on the lead gobbler and shot him dead as a doornail from 26 yards out. He ended up being a dandy of a bird sporting long, needle-sharp spurs. At that point things definitely looked promising for a banner year, or at the very least, a prognosticator of good things to come in the land of snakes and gators.

Returning to the very same area the very next morning, I anticipated the gobbling action to be similarly good. However, the weather had turned gray, overcast, and quite cool overnight, resulting in only one distant bird heard at dawn. With nothing else going on nearby, I took a compass bearing and began working my way through the crispy-dry swamp lying between us. It didn't take long before the terrain turned into a thick, gnarly mess of downed logs and briar tangles, leaving me hot, sweating, frustrated, and mad at myself for once again making the fateful mistake of taking a direct line towards a gobbling bird in Florida -

something that I'd supposedly learned a long time ago to not even *attempt* in this state.

By the time I fought my way through the mess and emerged in a real pretty burned area on the other side, it had been quite a while since I'd heard any gobbling. I had no idea if the tom was even within a hundred miles of me when I yelped on a brand new Cane Creek Pro Custom glass call, but there wasn't any hesitation before he jumped all over the first note from about 200 yards away.

This hunt quickly turned into an intense cat & mouse chess game as we each maneuvered and counter-maneuvered around the burn. Then, I either said something right, or set up in the right spot (probably a combination of both), and the tom's gobbling began drawing near. Actually, I'd already determined that it was a pair of birds eagerly answering my calls in tandem, and as they first came into sight at about a hundred yards out I could see that one of them was hurrying to stay ahead of the other and reach me first. Periodically he would fly 20 yards closer to gain the upper hand, but then he'd pop into strut and focus so hard on displaying that his buddy would simply walk right on by and take the lead. The strutter would then realize that he'd fallen behind again and repeat the fly-ahead maneuver. They did this time after time, and it was kind of comical watching their routine. Long before they'd reached gun range, I'd already "graded" them out to evaluate which one was the better bird.

Then, a thought popped into my head and raced through my brain like a vision. It was totally unexpected, but in that brief instant I simply decided to let them go. I'm not even sure why I did it; I just made a conscious decision to pass on the shot. At the same time there was a nagging little voice inside of my head saying, "Dude, have you lost your mind?" After all, I had just called in a pair of adult Osceolas, on a very hard-hunted WMA, way back in the brutal swamps of public-land Florida, and then let them walk away unscathed. It's a hard thing to explain *or* understand (even now, in hindsight), but for some reason it just didn't feel right to kill one of those clowns. A part of me afterwards was mad at myself for doing such a crazy thing, and yet, at the time I actually felt real good about the decision.

For the last half-hour of this hunt I had been hearing another tom gobbling far off to the east, so once "Lowell & Hardy" wandered away I began working towards him. This time I circled out around the swamp

90

lying between us instead of fighting my way through on a direct route, and before long I had closed to within 150 yards of the loudmouth, who was still gobbling real well on his own from the middle of another burned-over area. If I so much as touched a call he would gobble back heartily, but despite several incremental movements on my part, he refused to budge an inch closer until I once again found a "sweet-spot" where he was willing to approach at a quick march. However, upon reaching a position approximately 40 yards away from my gun barrel, he drew his own personal line in the sand and refused to cross it.

For more than an hour this gobbler pranced, whirled, and twirled around in full strut; never being more than 40-50 yards away from me. I wanted him at less than 30 yards, so I refused to pull the trigger until he cooperated. Eventually, he tired of the silly game I was playing and drifted off through a cypress head, leaving me to retire back to camp empty handed. That was alright with me, though; I'd called three adult toms into killing range, and let all of them go free. The day had been a resounding success!

Another thing which I seem destined to relearn every year is that in turkey hunting, there can be a very fine line between riding on top of the world, and being run over by it. It's easy to find yourself feeling like a hero one day, and a total heal the next; confident in every move you make one minute, and soon-after questioning whether you've ever done anything right in your entire life. That's what these infernal birds routinely do to a hunter's psyche, and for the next few days that is exactly what they did to mine. I hunted hard, and overall felt like I hunted well, but every time I'd find myself on the verge of pulling the trigger, some blunder or simple miscalculation on my part would jump up and slap me across the face. I made errors in judgment, errors in technique, and errors in perception - and they all resulted in hearing the audible, dreaded "PUTT" of an alarmed tom as he ran or flew away to safety.

Of course, with each new failure I would think back to the second day of the season when I had intentionally passed up multiple chances to fill my final tag. Had I perhaps tempted fate and toyed with the turkey gods too much by doing such a foolish thing? I feared that the answer was a resounding "YES," and the feeling of dread that caused became particularly acute during a foggy morning of the second week, after roosting a pair of toms the prior evening on a long, narrow pine island way back in the swamp.

My personal "mantra" since arriving in Florida had been to go easy, try not to pressure targeted toms, and call sparingly. I didn't want any bird that I was working to have the slightest hint of me being within their zip code until they wound up flopping in the sand at my feet, and even though I'd been failing miserably with that plan for the past week, it was how I *intended* to approach the birds this day, as well. However, I got a little turned around in the dark as I approached their location, and somehow I walked right up underneath the roost. This obviously caused them a great deal of mental anguish, which they demonstrated by flying out of there like scalded dogs. They scared the holy bejesus out of me in doing so, too! "Damn," I thought to myself, "so much for my supposed minimal-impact hunting strategy."

In talking with my local hero David Caudill the previous day, he had opined that blind luck often made a man seem to be a better turkey hunter than he really was. Perhaps that was what happened next, because after working my way through a series of small burns along the swamp edge, I leaned up against a good setup tree beside another burned-over area and then cut lightly on my sweet-sounding Cane Creek glass. Immediately, a tom shattered the air with a loud gobble from only 60 yards away, so I slid down the tree trunk and got my gun up and rested on a raised knee. No sooner was I adjusted and focused-in before the tom's flaming red head appeared over the top of my gun barrel. The range was only 35 yards at that point and rapidly dropping as he came on in a steady walk. Although this fine old gobbler never quite made it under my previously-designated 30 yard range limit, he was certainly close enough when I pulled the trigger.

So ended another great trip to Florida, and whether it came as a result of blind luck or just from being tenacious, this last hunt served to buoy my bruised confidence. Once again I felt sure of myself and eager to hit the road in search of turkeys where I had never stepped foot before.

My first stop heading north was Alabama. I had actually hunted there in 1995, but that had been a brief and unsuccessful trip to Zane Caudill's leased ground near Troy. This time I planned to explore the state's public land possibilities in earnest, and for the next week I tried numerous spots where their turkey biologist had personally recommended I go. All of the countryside I hiked looked good, but contrary to what I'd come to expect from reading countless tales about Alabama's famous turkey hunting, there wasn't really a gobbler hiding behind every tree. In fact, I struggled to even hear an occasional bird sing out at dawn, and failed to put one in the cooler.

Finally, on the very last day of my scheduled trip I called a bird in by utilizing a late morning tactic which I'd been practicing all week without any measure of success - setting up in places with lots of sign and rhythmically scratching leaves in a pattern typical of a feeding turkey. The tom that warily snuck into gun range two hours later never uttered a peep, but he was definitely looking hard for the source of my subtle ruse when a swarm of Winchester Supreme 5's smote him mightily about the head and neck.

Alabama's dogwoods were more numerous than her toms in '97, but this one eventually found me.

The Appalachian mountain range can be subject to temperatures that fluctuate widely in the spring, and that was exactly what I experienced the next day in another new state. Whereas central Alabama had been nearly ideal with crisp mornings followed by beautiful spring-like days, that first sunrise in northern Georgia found me shivering in my boots as a howling, below-freezing wind cut right through my clothing. I never heard or saw anything to make me think that there was the first wild turkey within the same zip code of that rocky crag, and as I sat there shivering while assessing the situation, I remembered an old adage that said the peak of gobbling occurs when the leaves of oak trees are about the size of a squirrel's ear. There wasn't the slightest hint of green anywhere, so perhaps I had arrived in the mountains of Georgia a little bit too early.

That afternoon I decided to move further southwest and drop off into the foothills, where the change in both climate and foliage was not only dramatic, but welcomed. The dogwood and redbud trees were already fully flowered down there, and the temperature was also more spring-like, with leaf cover about halfway grown out, as well. However, the most important difference was that I began hearing gobbling toms, along with lots of hen talk. I spent nearly all of that first day in close proximity to a big flock of vocal turkeys, and although I never got the drop on them, I came close a number of times. Walking back to camp that night I felt victorious despite an empty game bag, because I'd been able to "talk the talk" with wild turkeys for practically the entire day.

For the next week I continued to find myself in amongst turkeys regularly, and even though I did manage to shoot a couple of them, things did *not* exactly go swimmingly. Each day started out with tough, mentally draining battles against toms that completely ceased gobbling soon after flydown, and it seemed like they were continually surrounded by hens running interference. The girl turkeys were just as reluctant to answer my calls as their tight-lipped boyfriends, continually hurting my feelings as they refused to answer anything I said. Both successful hunts happened only after I'd put a tom to bed the night before, and then set up tight to the roost the next morning. Neither bird had uttered a word after flydown; they'd merely drifted in silently to a few soft yelps.

Having now spent the last two weeks enduring henned-up toms who were reluctant to answer a call, I was both eager and willing to go somewhere else – hopefully, to a place where the birds would at least respond to the sweet renditions of hen talk coming from my new Cane Creek glass and slate calls. I'd just added these to my arsenal, and felt like they were the very best pot calls I'd ever owned. That opinion was further bolstered one afternoon by a good 'ole boy encountered in Alabama. This fella had tried to sneak up on me while I was blind calling from a spot shredded by turkey scratchings, and after seeing me waving my hands to alert him of my presence, he came over to talk. The first thing out of his mouth was to ask whether that was really me making those "purty" hen sounds. After I pulled out the glass to run a few yelps for him, he slowly shook his head and proclaimed, "Son, son, son - it jest don't get no turkier than that."

Georgia was also a challenge, with very little gobbling.

The next two destinations on my itinerary were new places where I'd never hunted before (Tennessee and Kentucky). I had very high hopes for both of them, because reports had been coming in from friends and acquaintances that the whole Midwest was currently on fire with gobbling. Turkey populations across the region had exploded in the last few years, and there were now turkeys seemingly everywhere.

My first stop was at a big WMA in Tennessee called Catoosa. This property was comprised of some 80,000 acres of rugged ground in the eastern part of the state, and I was hopeful that its large size would allow me to stretch my legs and get away from other hunters. However, I hadn't counted on the pressure this place received!

Opening day was a madhouse, with people tearing up and down the roads. Every time I started working one of the several birds heard gobbling at daylight, some fool would invariably move in and run him off. The traffic calmed down considerably after the first couple hours of dawn, but so did the gobbling and I never heard anything else all day. I did, however, find more scratchings in the woods than I'd ever seen in my life, so that kept my spirits up.

The second morning I didn't hear quite as much gobbling, but a three-some of longbeards came running up to me right after flydown. Unfortunately, they never broke stride and kept going right on going before I could fire a shot. Then, they got into a terrible tussle with another pack of unseen gobblers on the adjoining ridgeline. I held my ground, hoping to call in either the winners or the losers of the skirmish after it was settled, but none of the combatants were ever seen or heard again.

Catoosa's management practice back then was to divide the season into a series of six 3-day hunts. On the final day of the first hunt period I once again witnessed behavior which seemingly indicated that the local toms were more interested in hanging out with one another than in seeking out girls. They obviously hadn't fully broken up from their winter flocks, so a change in tactics was called for if I wanted to fill a tag.

That afternoon I once again set up in the middle of a scratched over area raked almost bare. However, instead of hen talk, I tried to sound like a gobbler by using slow yelps and deep clucks. My strategy was centered on a belief that these birds were more interested in feeding than breeding. I guess it worked, because at 4 o'clock a trio of longbeards came slowly scratching their way towards me. I shot the first one to present a good, unobstructed view at 17 yards, and back at camp I opened up his craw to see what he'd been eating. The contents were so interesting that I recorded them in my journal. Here's what I found:

> 47 beetles of some genus I couldn't identify; each about a half-inch long
> 45 clover leaves and/or blossoms
> 33 blades of grass
> 19 acorns
> 11 June bugs
> 11 soft red worms about 1 1/2 inches long
> 10 mealworms

9 dandelion leaves
8 "flip beetles"
5 other beetles that were kind of flat
5 spiders
4 moths
4 ants
3 tubers
3 pebbles of about 1/4-inch diameter
2 big yellow and black centipedes
2 snails
1 unidentified beetle about an inch and a quarter long
1 pretty blue/purple beetle about an inch long
1 wild cherry seed
1 stinkbug
1 flying ant
1 mosquito

A brand new 3-day hunt period began the next morning. After hearing a bird gobbling very early, I snuck in tight to his roost tree before he even thought about flying down. I didn't call at all while he was tree-bound, said very little after his feet touched ground, and merely waited. It didn't take long; soon thereafter I heard drumming as he approached my hide. The tom's final resting spot was 31 yards from the working end of my shotgun.

My season limit for Catoosa was now filled, forcing a move to another piece of public property nearby. When I pulled into their parking lot the next morning it was raining hard. The weather threatened to dampen my enthusiasm, as well as my clothing, but since I wasn't due to meet up with DeWayne Feltner in Kentucky until the following afternoon, I couldn't think of any better way to pass the time than exploring new ground.

The rain suddenly cleared off about 8 o'clock to find me standing on a high ridgeline projecting up above a sprawling creek bottom. Cutting hard on the glass call brought no response, but when I repeated the effort a half-minute later, a tom answered from only a couple hundred yards away.

I quickly halved the distance between us and set up on a tree that offered good concealment. Then, I issued another cutt sequence with my glass pot. Not only did I get a gobble in response, but also some broken, rough-sounding yelping that I interpreted as coming from a jake. I wasted no time in yawking out my own rendition of a slow gobbler yelp, and that immediately brought forth something sounding very similar. When I once again butted in with yelps of my own, it was the tom who answered this time with a gobble – a *close* gobble! I gently placed the Cane Creek in the leaves at my feet, leveled the Ruger over my knee, and flipped off the safety.

The varied contents of a hungry gobbler's craw.

A jake immediately popped into view before me, followed by a strutting tom. As they neared my position they split up; the jake going left, while the tom swung over to my right. I'd already aligned my gun ahead of the gobbler by then and planned to kill him after he came out from behind a big poplar tree at 27 yards, but just as I started squeezing the trigger the jake rushed over and stuck his head up directly between the tom and myself. If I'd shot right then, I would've killed them both.

I held fire and waited for some separation. Instead, the tom turned back around and stepped behind that poplar. After a tense minute or so he eased out from behind its sheltering cover again, although this time only his head and neck were visible to the right side of the tree as he stood there in a half-strut.

I really should've waited for him to come on into the open completely, or at the very least, held fire until he stretched out his neck good and proper. Unfortunately, rational thought processes right then were being directly and negatively influenced by the actions of that nervous jake, who was now standing only twelve yards away from me and starting to get very "hanky." Knowing that the whole scenario was about to take a nosedive, I leaned out to my right a bit and pulled the trigger.

I shoot left handed. My right eye apparently told the left one that the tom was totally clear of the tree, but it was a lie. Big chunks of bark beside the turkey's head flew into the air when I shot.

It wasn't a total miss, though. The tom also went down - just not for long. By the time he got back to his feet they were already churning, and when I attempted to finish off the running tom with my second barrel its shot pattern pulverized a small tree between us. This made the crippled tom take wing, but he was real wobbly in flight and only went about a hundred yards before banking sharply and coming down on the other side of a deep ravine. Although I never actually saw him hit the ground, judging by his air speed and angle of descent a hard crash landing seemed inevitable.

Digging into my pants pockets for additional ammo, I found none. When I realized that they weren't there, it suddenly dawned on me that I had done my wash at a Laundromat the previous afternoon. Obviously, I had forgotten to put my spare shells back in their designated pocket, and that realization made me utter a long string of curse words under my breath.

As I trudged the mile and a half back to my van, I had plenty of time to think things through. Yes; I felt bad about blowing the initial shot, but the way that tom struggled to fly away also gave me reason for hope. I knew without a shadow of a doubt that he was badly hurt, and in fact, I thought the odds were pretty good that the bird might already be dead as a doornail right where he'd hit the forest floor.

However, I wasn't going to begin the search for him with an unloaded gun – just in case!

After changing into dry cloths and making sure that both my gun and pants pockets contained fresh rounds of Winchester Supreme 5's, I went back out to the scene of the crime. I'd initially taken careful note of the tom's exact flight path, so now I tiptoed along that route while scanning the ground both ahead, and to all sides. As I came up out of the ravine and leveled off onto a brushy flat, I quite suddenly found myself staring eyeball to eyeball at a tom lying in the leaves with his head held high about 25 yards from my feet.

The very moment our eyes met he jumped up and ran for cover, masterfully putting a big tree between us before I could even raise my gun. A short sprint angling to my right provided a brief chance to anchor him for good, but then he juked at just the wrong moment and I knew even before hearing my gun go "boom" that its shot charge had missed the mark.

Back in pursuit I went, with all the speed my legs could muster. The thick brush and green-brier tangles covering that ridgeline shredded my clothing and skin as I raced to keep the tom in sight, but I didn't care. Then, I sensed that I was actually beginning to gain ground on him, and that gave me even more of a reason to believe that the tom had been badly hurt by the initial shot. How else could any mortal man ever hope to so much as keep up with a running turkey, let alone overtake him?

At that point the crippled gobbler tried to fly away while cackling wildly, but he failed to gain any altitude and came crashing right back down to earth. The exertion of that effort to escape by air seemed to sap even more of the tom's waning energy, and this allowed me to further gain precious ground. When he then took a wrong turn around a big oak tree and got himself briefly tangled up in a briar patch, I suddenly found myself close enough to make a flying tackle that pinned him on the ground.

Man; was I one happy hunter as I carried this tom back to camp! A necropsy when I cleaned him found two pellet wounds in the middle of his neck - either of which I would've thought to be lethal - along with several others that were more superfluous. Although I felt lucky that enough of my shot column had missed the tree to strike a semi-lethal blow, the kill hadn't been either swift, or pretty, and that left me feeling a bit disappointed in myself. If I'd only been more patient, and waited for a better shot…

Patience was something that I'd been consciously working on all year. Obviously, I still had a ways to go. Things happen fast in the heat of battle, and it's easy to make mistakes. Even still, I knew that the whole ordeal of having to chase this tom down could've been avoided if I hadn't initially pulled my trigger in haste.

I mean, really; so what if the tom had heeded his jake buddy's warnings and used the cover of that sheltering tree to run off unscathed? Such a scenario wouldn't have been the end of the world, and I could've always come back to hunt him on another day. Instead, I'd been hurrying to get him killed so that I could hit the road, and I let that inner, self-imposed pressure override good common sense.

Fortunately, things had turned out for the best and I walked away not only victorious, but having learned a valuable lesson. I have a tremendous respect for the wild turkey, and absolutely no desire to let coyotes and other scavengers win a free meal by leaving one crippled in the woods to die a slow, lingering death. Screwing up also makes me lose a lot of much-needed sleep at night, and that's a commodity I'm already running low of during the entire spring season. It behooves me personally to free my mind of worry and dark thoughts, because restful sleep and peaceful dreams are products of an unfettered brain.

A hard-fought victory in Eastern Tennessee.

Well, it was a much more humble and somber hunter who met up with his old buddy DeWayne Feltner in Kentucky the next day. Even though I had three dead toms to show for my brief Tennessee excursion, I was feeling a bit melancholy due to how the last one had come to pass. However, it didn't take long before DeWayne got me fired up with reports of just how good a piece of property we would be hunting for the next four days.

One of his buddies in the timber buying business owned this ground, and in a word, it was simply amazing! There were turkeys gobbling everywhere we went, and during our brief stay I called in a couple of birds for the land manager (both of which he m...m...missed) before killing one of my own that is still to this day the heaviest turkey I've ever taken; he officially tipped the scales at 26 pounds. That tom was a brute in every sense of the word. As I was standing there admiring him after the shot, I kept thinking to myself how he looked like the Shaquille O'Neal of his species - just *huge* in every proportion.

The crew in that camp was also top notch, and some of the best folks I've ever been around. They treated DeWayne and I better than royalty, and we had a blast every single day. We also ate like kings for breakfast, lunch, and dinner, and shared many a laugh around the fire pit. However, one instance will live on forever in my mind, and it happened like this:

We were sitting on the front porch one afternoon drinking a few cold beers when a young woman in a long purple dress came riding down the paved road in front of the house on a horse at full gallop. This wasn't exactly something that you see every day, so we were all quite curious about what it meant. Twenty minutes later a sheriff's car came speeding by from the same direction, further piquing our curiosity. Another twenty minutes went by, and after I'd crossed the road to retrieve some more beers from the cooler in DeWayne's truck, the cop came back again from the opposite direction.

Seeing me standing there beside the road, he slowed to a stop and rolled down the passenger-side window to ask if I'd seen an Amish woman on horseback. I confirmed that I had indeed seen her, and gave him the details as told herein. By now my curiosity was absolutely palpable, so I asked him why he was looking for her. This is what he said to me, and I relay it here verbatim; "Oh, she hasn't done anything wrong. She's just come of age in the Amish village down the road from here and has decided to abandon their way of life to head for the bright lights of the nearest big town. Her Dad is ok with that decision, but he wants his horse back."

My Kentucky Goliath.

I swear upon my most sacred copy of Gene Nunnery's, *The Old Pro Turkey Hunter* that this story is 100% truth!

After leaving this private land honey-hole I headed west to Higginson-Henry WMA (which is archery-only) to meet up with my longtime turkey hunting buddy, Ron Ronk. Two days earlier he had arrowed his first bow-killed gobbler; a brute of a tom weighing 23 pounds, with an 11 inch beard and spurs of 1- 1/2 inches. Now, we planned to hunt together in one of Leroy Braungarte's "portable" ground blinds, which measure about six feet in diameter and stand 7- 1/2 feet tall; they look like big camouflaged beer cans when erected. It also takes about seven minutes to put them together in the woods, so choosing a good initial spot is of paramount importance. These blinds aren't exactly made with the "run and gun" hunter in mind.

Higginson-Henry WMA was full of gobbling turkeys in those days, and on the first morning I called a hen in so close that I could actually see her *through* the cotton material of the blind! Her boyfriend trailed along about a hundred yards behind, and as he came towards us I looked over to see that Ron was kneeling on one knee, with his head bowed and a hand up covering his eyes. At first I thought that he was praying, but in reality, he was just overcome with emotion and trying to calm his nerves before the tom arrived. That's always been the case with Ron; turkeys quite simply turn him into a hyperventilating, jittery wreck.

Then, at 11 yards he rushed the shot a little bit and nicked the window of the blind just enough to send the arrow deflecting up over the tom's back. Talk about sick - my poor old buddy was a basket case for the remainder of the day, until Larry Sharp and I got a few beers into him while commiserating around the campfire. That seemed to work for a while, but I knew his pain would return after the hangover subsided.

The rest of the trip was very interesting, to say the least. Despite hearing who-knows-how-many gobbling toms and calling in several of them to ranges perfectly acceptable for gun hunting, yet too far away for the bow, I failed to run an arrow through any of them. This was the first time that I had ever hunted turkeys with archery tackle, or out of a blind, and to be perfectly honest, the whole ordeal left me feeling rather nonplussed.

When hunting with a gun I am apt to move around the woods incrementally as tactics and conditions dictate. I feel like it adds realism to my ruse, and gives the tom an impression of natural hen behavior. However, in that big immobile blind I felt trapped and unable to hunt the way I wanted. It also seemed like the blind stifled my vision and hearing to such a degree that I felt like I was missing out on the true essence of the hunt.

Shooting Stars - one of my favorite springtime plants.

While my overall impression of bowhunting for turkeys may've thus leaned towards the negative side, there was certainly no denying the excitement that it generated. Plus, as I said earlier, this archery-only WMA was absolutely loaded with birds that gobbled hard and occasionally even acted right. I vowed to return in future years with hopes of actually killing one.

After all of the gobbling action experienced in Tennessee and Kentucky, I couldn't wait to see how things were going back home. Unfortunately, the Tea Mountain toms hadn't yet received any memo dictating how they were supposed to be performing during the spring of '97, and as unlikely as it sounds, Don Foley and I heard only one gobbling bird during our too-brief, two-day stay. Guiding duties prevented me from sticking around until things had a chance to change (as can sometimes happen overnight during turkey season), so I headed on down to see if the birds in Southeastern Indiana knew what spring was really all about.

The Tea Mountain Crew in '97; Tom Foley, Don Foley, and Joe Harrod in back, with myself, Russ Feltner, DeWayne Feltner, and Bruce Wilson up front.

My cousin Bob Torrance had moved out to a house in the most rural part of Jefferson County by then, and he had gained permission for us to hunt various farms in that vicinity which were owned by an Amish family with the last name of Wickey. There were 9 boys in this family, and each of them was given a farm by their father Soloman when turning 21. The two youngest boys were still under-age and living at home with their parents, but every one of their brothers' properties ended up being prime hunting ground. For some time I was given access to turkey hunt on those farms whenever I wanted, and with whomever I cared to bring. However, I would eventually come to learn an important truth about the Amish; that they tend to favor their fellow clansmen over any "English" acquaintances.

I called in numerous turkeys for those Wickey boys over the course of several years, and did innumerable favors for them like driving their families into town for supplies. But, once they realized just how much fun the turkey hunting game was, I gradually found myself

106

more and more restricted on access to their farms. Eventually, I was edged out completely in favor of their Amish friends and neighbors, and by then I felt more than a little bit taken advantage-of and used. The experience left a lasting impression on me that I haven't forgotten, but it also fortified some beliefs that I've always held regarding my preference for hunting on public property; namely, that when I'm on public ground I am beholding to no one else, and nobody is beholding to me. I like it like that.

Well, back in 1997 I was just beginning the string of years hunting those Amish farms, and Cousin Bob broke the ice when he shot his first-ever tom on the second day out. That was an especially sweet victory because of how hard we had been trying to get it done over the past couple of years. Dave Pruitt also came back and took a double bearded gobbler, while Gary Shepherd and Louie Rusch returned victorious, as well. A couple of the Wickey boys (Jake and Ervin) likewise killed birds with me, while a third (Joe) missed a big one.

Cousin Bob Torrance's first tom.

Similarly, Frank Emert's hunt with Eric Coonrod and Christine Gerace spiraled downward when Eric crippled and lost a huge tom. We all searched long and hard for that bird, but came up empty handed. Fortunately, the day brightened up a little bit when Christine was then able to successfully pull the trigger of her beautiful, gold-inlayed Winchester 101 Over/Under 20 gauge just a few minutes before the noon whistle. She'd bought that gun at the Sullivan County Quail Unlimited banquet the previous fall – an event which also led to another victory for spring of '97. Jeff Bell had won high-bid honors on my donated turkey hunt at the banquet, and the two of us had then received valuable help when Marvin Harris took us to some of his prime local ground.

Dave Pruitt and I doubled a few minutes apart.

Frank Emert, Eric Coonrod, and Christine Gerace exploring a creek with me after our hunt.

After that whirlwind Indiana season I once again decided to venture out to West Virginia – a beautiful state that had captured my imagination from the very first time I'd visited there. I was bound and determined to finally find success in her heavily forested hills, and it almost happened immediately upon my arrival when I blundered onto a tom and his lone hen during a heavy dawn rainstorm. The 38-40 yard range was longer than I'd wanted, however, so I decided to pass on the shot. Admittedly, that decision was internally questioned over and over again for the next couple of cold, rainy days as I hunted hard without so much as a single gobble to show for my efforts. Even still, I held firm in my belief that letting a turkey go free was a far better option than risking a crippling loss. I didn't have any idea what fate had in store for me...

The next day started out on a positive note with the sound of a distant gobble. Things went progressively downhill from there, though - both literally *and* figuratively - when my mad scramble to close the distance took me off the mountaintop several hundred feet in elevation, only to discover that the tom was both across a road, and on private land. All I could do at that point was backtrack up the steep slope to where I'd begun the hunt at dawn, then listen for a different bird on legal ground.

Luckily for me, the next bird heard was on WMA land, and I was able to close the distance between us. Then, I made a hurried, ill-advised setup in poor position, and the sneaky rascal circled around to pop into view 10 yards over my left shoulder. That worked out far better for the gobbler than it did for me, and he immediately skedaddled on out of there to safety.

After hiking back to my van, I decided to drive over to another parking spot deeper into the WMA. On the way there I stopped to talk with a young fellow walking down the road, who for some reason felt the need to try and impress upon me just how much turkey *mis*-information filled his head and overflowed through his pie hole. There was only one thing said which rang true during our too-long conversation before I could finally wriggle free and get gone, although with his heavy West-by-Gawd accent it took me a few times hearing it to understand exactly what he meant. "Ah'm a tellin' ye, it's the WAY-ther," he kept insisting. "These he'ah toms ain't a actin' rat 'cuz o' the WAY-ther. " Oh, yes; indeed - the *weather* was being problematic at best, with lots of cold, biting rain and wind keeping the birds quiet. However, there were certainly turkeys around, as evidenced by scratchings found in the woods, tracks seen in muddy spots, and droppings scattered here and there.

About 8:30 a.m. some crows on a far ridgeline started giving a hawk or owl some serious grief, and their racket fired up a tom much closer to me. I hustled to get in position on him, but before that could happen I felt a pressing need to answer the call of nature and feed the bears (so to speak). Even though this bird was easily within 150 yards of me, there was quite literally no time to put things off, so I found a debarked, horizontal sitting-log, kicked back some leaves and toed a hole in the dirt with my boot, and commenced taking care of business. Wouldn't you know it? At the worst possible moment I suddenly heard loud drumming and sticks cracking directly in front of me. The tom must've heard me rustling those leaves and come to investigate its source, and he was about to catch me at a *very* bad time!

Raising my gun, I anticipated having to shoot this tom from a rather unorthodox position. But, before his full fan could materialize over my gun barrel, a low-down, scurvy hen popped into view about 10 yards off of my right shoulder. She was NOT amused by the sight of me sitting on a log with trousers bunched up around my ankles, and she burst into flight with a loud and obnoxious cackle. I neither heard another peep, nor saw a single feather of her boyfriend after that.

As I said earlier, this day had begun spiraling downward just after the crack of dawn, but it hadn't as yet reached its low point. That was soon to come.

The current list of miscues and outright screw-ups had me feeling a little bit underwhelmed, so I hiked on out the looping trailhead another mile to a small, oblong wildlife foodplot that I'd found a couple days earlier. It was only about 30 yards wide and 45 yards long in size, but there had been a number of fresh turkey turds scattered around in it. More than a few of them were J-shaped!

Standing at the center of this green patch once again, I let out two long and loud lost yelps with my Cane Creek slate call. Then, I hustled over to the southeast corner and picked the only sizable tree that offered both a view of the field, and good shade in which to sit. The clock said 10:30, so I was planning to just hang out there until the noon quitting time in hopes that my siren calls might've lured in a curious tom.

I hadn't heard any turkey sounds at all since spooking that hen and gobbler nearly two hours prior, and after twenty more minutes of nothing but silence I decided to abort my original plan and venture on back towards the van. My attitude wasn't very good at that point, and I just felt like walking it off. Directly on the other side of this little field was a steep drop-off of perhaps 40 feet in elevation before the ridgeline leveled out again. I wasn't paying nearly enough attention as I popped over the top - immediately blundering upon a tom that was silently headed up my way from that lower shelf. He wasted no time in busting out of there like a rocket.

It was only then that I saw a second gobbler behind the first, which hadn't as yet seen *me*. Quickly throwing gun to shoulder, I took aim, but before I had a chance to shoot, the tom became alerted and began high-stepping away with his head and neck bobbing and weaving. Forgetting everything that I'd been preaching to myself previously about waiting for the right moment, I pulled the trigger. The gobbler went down in a heap as the 12 gauge roared, but to my dismay he jumped right back up and ran behind a group of trees. I took off running in pursuit, only to be stopped in my tracks by the sound of wing beats powering the crippled tom up and away. I never even caught a glimpse of him.

When I got to where the tom had initially been standing 36 yards from my gun barrel, there were feathers *everywhere*. It looked like a turkey had exploded in that spot. I could even track the initial 50 yards of his flight by the feathers that had drifted back down to earth. It was a wonder that the bird could even fly with so many feathers missing, so I felt sure that he had to be severely hurt. Although his downhill flight hadn't been seen, I had every confidence of finding this tom tucked up underneath a brush pile somewhere along the line indicated by those lost feathers.

Immediately, I commenced searching in earnest. I only stopped many hours later when it finally became too dark to see. By then I was just miserable with anger, and sick to my stomach with angst and frustration. I felt certain that this tom was dead or dying; it didn't even seem feasible that he could've taken such a heavy load of Winchester Supreme 5's without something vital being hit.

After a restless night of worrying and stewing instead of sleeping, I didn't much feel like hunting the next morning. Instead, I came back to look for my crippled bird again and subsequently spent the entire day doing just that very thing - with absolutely no positive results to show for it. The following day was yet again spent unsuccessfully combing that whole area before finally admitting to myself that I wasn't ever going to find this tom. Believe me; that was a very bitter pill to swallow, and I felt absolutely terrible about it.

While West Virginia was one of my favorite places in the whole country aesthetic-wise, I had certainly struggled to kill any of her turkeys. In fact, over the course of the last three seasons I had tallied seventeen days of hard hunting with zero tags punched. What had I done now, when finally given the chance to kill a bird? I'd crippled and lost him. To describe my mental state as brokenhearted would be technically accurate, yet it can't come close to adequately describing just how rotten I was feeling.

For the next five days that attitude did nothing but get progressively worse due to a series of additional blown opportunities. By then I was in a terrible-foul mood and mad at the world - especially-so at myself. It seemed like I was boogering turkeys every single day, and whether I was moving or sitting still trying to remain undetected didn't seem to matter one bit; they *all* honed-in on my human form and left the scene with loud alarm putts echoing in my ears. The weather wasn't helping things either, continuing to be windy, cold, dark, and rainy, with some snow thrown in for good measure. Self-doubt was my constant soul-mate, and with only four days left of the season my bruised and battered brain was down to thinking, "Maybe next year."

Finally, the eighth day of my trip dawned clear and cool, with no wind whatsoever. This was definitely an improvement. Despite the case of recurrent doldrums weighing me down, I actually woke up thinking that perhaps this weather pattern was a good sign, and things might even make a change for the better.

When the first tom heard at daybreak rattled off seven consecutive gobbles in answer to one gentle yelp from a Primos True Double diaphragm, those good feelings began growing more pronounced, and as his approaching drumming grew louder and louder I dared to think things might go my way. Then, another damnable hen stuck her head up over the contour separating me from seeing and killing her boyfriend, and she busted out of there like I had jumped up and shouted, "BOO!"

I wanted to bang my head against the tree at my back in frustration, but with another tom gobbling in the distance, I headed towards him at a trot, instead. As I neared his position atop a high knob, I had to climb through an entire slope of ground that looked like street sweepers had driven over it the previous day. Obviously, the turkeys in this area were finding something of keen interest here, so rather than press the issue with a tom that had by now quieted down, I decided to hunt smart. Pulling a little surrounding brush together to create a crude blind, I would try to lure the tom in to a place where he had been spending some time anyway.

Occasionally throughout the next hour I would hear drawn-out, hollow-sounding single yelps, or lyrical, plaintive kee-kees and lost yelps coming from up on the knoll. However, it wasn't until some nearby crows got belligerent with a hawk that the tom finally ripped out a gobble. A hen beside him then began answering my periodic 3-4 note yelps with two-note yelps of her own, and I began copying her in tone and cadence. It wasn't long before I saw her little brown shape coming my way at 30 yards. I could also faintly hear the tom drumming as he trailed behind.

When she began veering off to the left, I two-note yelped again and she immediately turned back my way. On she came - much quicker than I'd anticipated - and was soon standing ten feet from my make-shift hide. I thought at one point she might just walk on by and ignore me, but I should've known better; the rotten skank took one hard look with an evil black eye and practically turned herself inside-out heading for parts unknown. As she thundered off into the heavens I could only shrug my shoulders under the resignation that yes, of course I had failed again; it was inevitable, because I was living out an episode of "The Twilight Zone."

With no compelling reason to do anything different, I decided to just hang out amongst all these scratchings in hopes that their makers might return. After all, the tom following that hen certainly hadn't seen me, and perhaps in his mind she had simply been spooked off by a predator. Periodically I would utter contented purrs and inquisitive clucks on the mouthcall or glass, and about every half-hour or so I would send out a longer, louder, and more-plaintive 6-8 note yelp.

At 10:15 a tom up on the knob gobbled in answer to one of those louder calls, but then he said nothing more until 11:20. With a noon quitting time looming large and the tom unmoved from his last known locale, it didn't seem like staying put in my brush blind was the best option, so I got up and hustled towards him. Two more gobbles echoed out as I quickly maneuvered into position, and another greeted a yelp from my diaphragm after setting up on a broad red oak. Then, a previously unheard hen chimed in to our next exchange of calls. Of course, I immediately thought back on how many times the fuzzy-headed ladies of West Virginia had proven to be my Achilles' heel during this trip, and I cursed her under my breath.

Sure enough as day follows night, I soon spotted this hen snaking her way towards me. Every single time she would yelp or say anything at all, the tom behind her would gobble, but there was enough separation between the two of them that I couldn't see him. Just like so many of her kind before, this little hussy was soon standing 20 yards away from me and yelping inquisitively to try and find the source of my calls. I hadn't said anything else once it became apparent that she was on the way, and after a couple of minutes standing there erect and turning her head back and forth to gaze in every direction, she turned around and began retracing her path towards the tom. A sharp 2-note cutt from me turned her right back around though, and this time she hustled on over to within 10 feet of me. Can you guess what happened next? That's right - for the *third* time in the same day a leading hen spotted me and took off into the ethrid like a rocket, cackling as she went. I was so mad that I felt like shooting her!

Instead of that, as soon as she blasted out of there I cutt hard at her departing protestations, and then I let out a long, excited sequence of yelps. At first I didn't think my attempt to overload the tom's brain with hen talk had worked, and I figured that I was destined for failure, yet again. But, twenty seconds later I yelped once more, and the tom gobbled back at me. HOT DAMN; I was still in business!

During the next 10 minutes we exchanged three or four racy promises as the loverboy slowly eased my way. Then, I finally saw that
beautiful sight which I had been waiting oh-so-impatiently and for
oh-so-long to see in this state - a strutting tom 27 yards in
front of my gun's muzzle! When he periscoped up that long neck
to full height at 11:49 a.m., I bowled him over with a load of
Winchester Supreme copper-plated 5's. As soon as he piled up in
the leaves, it felt like the terrible spell that I had been hunting
under was finally broken. Life was good again, and I could now
unconditionally confirm that West Virginia's toms weren't really
armored and immortal, after all!

A long-awaited victory in West Virginia.

My emotions had certainly run the gamut during this trip, with
incredible highs and terrible lows. Putting that bird in the cooler rejuvenated my self-confidence, and with improving weather conditions,
I began to hunt smart once again. Oh; the numerous vocal hens still
kept trying to steal toms out from underneath me, but I wasn't letting
that bother me as much. I figured it was only a matter of time until I
got the better of them, and a couple of days later I filled my
second tag. Soon thereafter I was heading on up to end the season
with Jake Bays and his extended family in New York.

In 1996 this annual trip had produced fantastic results, with turkeys seemingly gobbling everywhere I hunted. Not so in 1997; it was nothing like that at all, and we struggled to find birds on either the Bays dairy farm or surrounding public properties. There was also a lot more pressure on those State Lands, with hunters' vehicles parked in places where I had never encountered them before. Gobbling toms were few and far between, and those that we did find seemed to further support an old axiom that had long been one of my most basic of tenets: the one that said you'd better go toward the first tom heard gobbling, because you never know if he'll be the last one you hear all day.

Despite tough conditions and mostly silent toms, Jake and I hunted hard. After eight days we had each managed to fill a two-bird limit, with the first one I shot weighing over 23 pounds. This is really heavy for turkeys in that area. When I headed for home on the last day of May, my van also carried something of great value besides turkey meat - ten gallons of Jake's maple syrup, in various-sized bottles. These would be distributed over the coming months to friends and family, as well as being used for "thank you" gifts to landowners like the Amish farmers who had allowed me to hunt on their ground.

In reflecting back on the season after arriving home, I realized that I had hunted in nine different states. Included in this list were successful first-time visits to Georgia, Tennessee, and Kentucky. I'd also killed birds in two states were I had previously been skunked (Alabama and West Virginia), and squeezed in a brief two-day trip to Michigan in the middle of our Indiana season. That hadn't gone very well. In fact, I'd failed to get a tom while there, and would have to go back at some point for redemption.

Between myself and all of the people I took hunting in 1997, we had accounted for a whopping 25 dead turkeys – a total far surpassing the previous annual high of 18 set just one year prior. However, the statistic that I was most proud of was that by carefully lining up my schedule in an efficient manner, I had managed to hunt on 75 of the 78 days that fell in between opening day of Florida and the closing day of New York. That meant I had wasted very little time doing anything other than hunting turkeys all spring long. By the parameters that I considered to be most important, it had been one helluva fine year!

Jake Bays and I in New York.

CHAPTER 8

Morning vs. Afternoon Hunting

There is absolutely nothing in this world like sitting out in the middle of nowhere as dawn breaks over the horizon, listening for turkeys to start gobbling. Nothing!

Watching the whole world wake up and come alive provides such a thrill as to be simply indescribable in its glory, and those magical moments of breathless anticipation before the King of Spring belts out his first call of the day are priceless beyond measure. I get so excited just thinking about the promise and possibilities lying ahead that I absolutely cannot wait to jump out of bed each and every morning. It doesn't matter how late I stay up the night before. By the time summer rolls around I will be worn to a frazzle from too many long days of hunting, followed by too many short sleepless nights, but that's ok - I really wouldn't have it any other way. Spring is when I most feel alive.

The next few hours following sunrise are also a special time, filled with action-packed adventure and excitement. For the birds we pursue it may be just another day of normal living and breeding routines, but as hunters, this is when we shine. It's a time of breathless anticipation; a time of thinking, theorizing, plotting, planning, and implementing strategies that will help us become victorious in the battles against our feathered foes. This is when adrenalin courses through our veins like water blasting from a fire hose, and when our hearts beat so loud and hard that it seems like they will surely explode.

For all these reasons and more, it could very easily be said that mornings most clearly define what turkey hunting is all about. I'd be hard-pressed to argue the point. To me, it's as if the magic of the sport is condensed into its purest form as the sun comes up. Afternoon hunts can certainly supply similar breathlessness and wonderment, but it's different. There's definitely something unique about the emotions felt early in the day. Maybe it's because our brains are fresh and rejuvenated soon after awakening. I don't really care why; I just love the way mornings in the turkey woods make me feel.

In previous chapters I've tried to convey just how much I hate to miss even a single sunrise during the entirety of turkey season (the months of March, April, and May), as well as how hard I try to maximize my hours afield by carefully plotting an itinerary that minimizes the miles and drive times in between states. In order to reach these goals, I usually do most of my traveling after dark.

I can't even begin to count how often I've driven hard all night and pulled into a new destination just prior to the first hint of dawn, or if lucky, arrived a couple hours earlier than that and then slept while sitting up in the driver's seat until the first hint of a graying sky awakens me. Simply put, I don't think there is anything more important in turkey hunting than just being out there as the sun cracks forth over the horizon. In my mind, it's the only way to fully and completely experience the utter euphoria that accompanies the first gobble of a new day.

Besides, turkeys usually sound off more often in the morning, and it's hard to deny that most of the successes in actually bringing birds home with us will also occur before the noon whistle. However, while those first few hours of daylight are a wonderful time to be hunting, it is not the *only* time to get things done. No; after the "morning rush" is over there are still many valuable hours left before the sun finally sets, and afternoon hunts can often be just as exciting and productive as those happening earlier in the day.

In this chapter I want to talk a little bit about what each of these time-frames can offer, and I also want to discuss why I think every state should enact laws which allow afternoon hunting. While times have certainly changed over the last few years and most game departments are now permitting all-day participation in this sport, there are still a few holdouts that make us leave the woods around noon or 1 o'clock. I'll try to lay out some valid reasons for why I think this is the wrong approach.

Ok; following an initial flydown after sleeping in the treetops all night, turkeys begin wandering around their core area and feeding as they go. Subsequently, they spend a whole lot of time doing just that very thing – eating. Of course, sex-driven toms are more inclined to forego food and focus instead on displaying and following their hens around in hopes of finding one willing to breed, but generally speaking, that is how a turkey's waking hours are spent. There will be periods of loafing around, preening, and other stuff, but the major expenditure of their energy is in looking for something to eat.

Hence, one of your first priorities in scouting an area is to figure out what the turkeys are feasting on. This isn't as easy as it sounds, because turkeys are opportunistic feeders and will generally gulp down just about anything that looks the least bit edible, is small enough to swallow, and is immobile or slow enough to catch. That last sentence is to be taken quite literally, because their diet can encompass anything and everything from vegetable matter to insects, and even small vertebrate and invertebrate animals. Grasses, forbs, nuts, berries, seeds, tubers, flowers, spiders, worms, caterpillars, snails, lizards, etc.; you name it, and a hungry turkey will probably eat it.

One telltale sign that they often leave behind in searching out these food items are what's called, "scratchings." This is where turkeys rake back the leaf cover with their feet to expose the bugs and other delicacies hidden underneath. It doesn't much matter where turkeys live, either. They are internally programmed to scratch, and they just gotta do it. I've seen them scratching in all type of habitat, too; from forested land to muddy swamps, grassy prairies to desert sands, and everything else in between. Furthermore, they scratch in a very pre-determined manner by first reaching forward and scratching back towards their body with one foot, followed with two quick strokes of the opposite foot, and usually ending with another swipe of the initial foot.

120

The sound this creates is very distinctive, and the rhythm is easily identifiable if you're paying attention. It goes, "scratch...scratch-scratch...scratch," and on a still day in dry woods you can hear it for quite a long distance. I've found turkeys literally hundreds of times throughout the years by merely easing along and listening for this telltale sound, and on many occasions I've then been able to set up and successfully call the birds to me. Sometimes they never utter any vocalizations at all as they come in, and at other times they might get fired up when they hear my calls, start gobbling, and head towards me fuzz'n and buzz'n for all they're worth.

Turkey scratchings in the snow, under a dogwood tree. Dogwood berries are a favorite food.

Another deadly tactic is to simply mimic these scratching sounds of a feeding turkey - either in addition to vocalized calling, or all by itself as if a bird were quietly feeding along in silence. Both methods add realism to a setup and increase your odds of success. A turkey's hearing is absolutely amazing, so it goes without saying that they can tune in to these scratching sounds from much further away than you can even imagine. Hopefully, their curiosity and/or innate flocking instincts might then cause them to come investigate the source. I discovered early-on that actual turkey calls themselves weren't the only way to bring birds into a setup, and this scratching tactic has been a staple in my bag of tricks ever since.

As I said, wild turkeys are generally generalists in what they eat on any given day, but they sometimes hone in on food sources that appeal to them during a particular time period or weather pattern. For instance, an Alabama biologist once told me to be on the lookout for a type of sedge that was seeding right then, and which the local turkeys were feeding on heavily. After he pointed out the plant I began actively looking for it as I scouted around, and soon found that it grew plentiful in low-lying areas throughout the public ground where my buddy Tracy Deckard and I were hunting.

By focusing on those areas we were able to kill three big gobblers in very short order, while everyone else around us was struggling to even find turkeys. The birds weren't being very vocal at that point of the season, so our strategy following an initial roost gobble or two at daylight entailed setting up to call and scratch in the leaves where the sedge grew thick. Upon opening up the craws of our dead birds to see what they'd been eating, guess what we found in great quantities in all three toms? That's right - black sedge seed.

Tracy Deckard and I with big toms, and even bigger grins.

Now let's delve further into some of the reasons why I so strongly support afternoon hunting. First of all, I believe that any argument either for or against the practice must be based primarily on biological reasons. It's vital that we trust our trained wildlife professionals to set the season dates, bag limits, and hunting hours according to their learned knowledge, and politics or social pressures should never, under any circumstances, influence those decisions. What's best for the resource itself needs to be of paramount importance above anything and everything else.

People far more intelligent than me have conducted lots of thorough studies in the last couple of decades, and these regularly conclude that afternoon hunting does no harm to the flock. If we abide by the research and believe in its results, then why do some states hold onto the stale morning-only edict that makes us quit hunting around noon?

An early theory which drove game departments to enact such laws was the belief that hunters wandering around in the p.m. hours were bound to inadvertently spook hens off their nests and thereby cause them to abandon the eggs. This sounded perfectly logical "back in the day" when we were first trying to restore turkeys to habitats devoid of them for nearly a century. As lovers of the wild turkey, we were more than willing to follow whatever steps were deemed necessary in order to help those rejuvenated flocks grow and prosper. Restrictive rules like this were thus enacted in good faith, and there wasn't much questioning by the hunting public. It was only later on that we learned how things are not always as they seem to be at first glance.

For instance; while spooking a hen off her nest is never good (and something we should certainly try to avoid), the real truth of the matter is that wild turkeys have evolved over eons of time to handle this scenario quite well. In the first place, that hen is going to be very reluctant to abandon her clutch of eggs - especially if she's already begun the actual incubation phase of sitting on them both day and night.

Think about it in this way; hens have a lot of time, effort, and energy invested in their nest. Why would they be willing to give up on it merely because of someone walking around in the woods? Turkeys are indeed nervous by nature and constantly dealing with predators trying to eat them 24 hours per day, but the way they handle that pressure is by fleeing until safe and then going on about their business as usual. Hence, there is a high degree of probability that a spooked hen will come right back to the nest site after she calms down.

However, if perchance she does decide to abandon that clutch (and it most definitely happens), the wild turkey's amazing biology then comes into play. Check this out: she still carries enough viable

sperm in her oviduct from one initial breeding in order to successfully re-nest several times, if need be. How cool is that? So, most
hens that lose or abandon their first nest will try again. This is an
important point, because that fact alone greatly lessens the impact
which hunters might have when a hen is disturbed. It is also one of
the main reasons for invalidating the original justification for setting
restrictive hunting hours, but that's far from the only one. Read on:

Both turkey vocalizations and hunter movement tend to slow down
as the day progresses. Along with that comes a lessened potential for
hen disturbance, simply because less ground is being tramped upon
by hunters. Once afternoon arrives, the turkeys will have gravitated to
a much quieter existence focused more on feeding rather than breeding, and successful hunters take advantage of that fact by spending
far more time setting up and calling in likely areas, rather than racing
through the woods trying to get birds fired-up. Naturally, the chances
of spooking hens off the nest are greatly lessened by a more sedentary
style of hunting - exactly like that which is practiced in the p.m. hours.

Conversely, a substantial percentage of people out hunting in the
morning employ a style that can best be described as "run-n-gun."
In other words, they cover lots of ground in hopes of finding a bird
willing to play the game. Studies have shown that most hens lay their
eggs sometime around mid-morning, so if anything, these more-ag-
gressive tactics actually present a greater risk of disturbing hens. If
game departments were overly worried about nest disturbances, then
it would seem like morning hunting hours should be the ones subject
to restrictions. Afternoons spent sitting around and gently calling in
areas where your scouting has shown that turkeys like to hang out and
feed presents a much-lessened risk of bumping hens off their nests.

Yet another reason why afternoon hunting inherently holds a lessened potential for hen interference (and this is *huge*), is the simple
fact that hunter numbers in the woods drop quite low as the day
progresses. Anyone who has spent much time as a public land turkey hunter knows that there is a sharp decline in competition as the
morning progresses, and by nine or ten o'clock you're likely to have
the woods all to yourself. Most hunters who don't take this sport
seriously have had enough frustration by then and are headed for the
house to eat a biscuit. This is especially true in today's atmosphere of
instant gratification, because if things don't happen quickly for the
rather spoiled hunter of today, they tend to go do something else.

A turkey nest of 14 eggs.

The hen came back, and 12 of her eggs hatched.

Personally, I rather enjoy this strange quirk of human nature, because I am just the opposite; I'm one of those guys that stays out in the woods till the whistle blows. When other hunters quit early it drastically lessens my own chances of having to endure "hunter interference" while I'm working a bird. I also kill lots of turkeys after most folks have headed home, but that's beside the point.

OK; this drastic drop in hunter participation during late morning also carries over to afternoons. Even in states that allow it, there will be *far* fewer people traipsing around in the woods post-lunchtime, as compared to the crack of dawn. Local folks may be busy at work making a living by then, or doing yard work and "honey-do's" back at home, or perhaps be off fishing, mushroom picking, or a million other things. The lion's share of the hunting pressure in afternoons will thus come mainly from the most fervent turkey-chasers, and that's not a very large percentage of the hunting population.

Non-residents are of course included in the group of hard-core devotees, since they've got so much invested in the proposition. They've traveled far and bought expensive licenses for the privilege of hunting turkeys, so they're usually more intent on getting their money's worth by staying out during every available daytime hour. However, I believe these die-hards who hunt all day are also the guys that will be the least likely to bump hens, because they know what they're doing and aren't just running around the woods helter-skelter. They will be hunting with a purpose, and focused on blending-in with their surroundings to create minimal disturbance.

Afternoons are certainly a good time to be out "scouting with a gun in your hands," but I try to be low-impact and careful with how I move about and search for hot turkey sign during those hours. I would much rather fail on the side of conservatism in my approach to scouting, rather than risk running a tom out of his core area late in the day. I take it easy and spend more time watching and listening than I do covering ground. The goal is to keep any gobblers in the area calm, undisturbed, and at peace with the world. Hopefully, that might lead to seeing or hearing them go to roost – a tremendous advantage for the next morning's hunt.

Like I've said before; spooking hens off the nest is undesirable and something that should be avoided, but the cold hard reality is that hunters just don't kick them up very often. When they do, it's usually not that big of a deal. In all my years and thousands of miles hiked while hunting, I've probably only found 15-20 nests. Oftentimes, I've snuck back to check on them at a later date and found the hen safely sitting on her eggs. I would venture to say that mushroom pickers disturb far more hens than turkey hunters ever do, but you'll never see restrictions placed on what time they can be out filling their Wal-Mart bags with tasty fungus. I just don't think it's necessary to limit turkey hunters, either.

So, now that we've established how scientific studies show no sound biological reason for outlawing afternoon hunting, then the question is why aren't all states rushing to change the rules? I believe the main reason is simply a general reluctance to disrupt the status quo. One time a biologist actually told me that, "this is how we've always done things, so it must not be broken." I can somewhat understand and empathize with a cautious approach in regards to making changes that could affect the overall turkey population, but afternoon hunting has been studied a *lot* by now, and there are many more reasons to allow the practice than there are excuses not to.

Currently, we have 33 states that permit all-day hunting. Only ten states strictly adhere to a ban of all hunting past noon or one o'clock, and of the six remaining, one of them (FL) unfathomably restricts public land hunters to mornings-only while allowing all-day hunting on private land. The other five states are now "experimenting" by having an early closing time in the front half of their season, followed by an all-day policy in the last part.

As someone who travels extensively every spring in order to hunt turkeys (almost exclusively on public land), I find two things particularly annoying: these antiquated laws that make me quit hunting at noon, and the equally-as-silly rules set up by the ten or eleven states that won't let me hunt on Sundays. Both of these unnecessary and capricious restrictions are even combined together in a few of the same states, and I personally think it's high time that they got their shit together and brought themselves into the 21st century. These rules serve nothing but to limit opportunities for good people to hunt, and neither of them have any basis whatsoever in biology or science. We are living in a difficult time period right now, when hunters not only need to band together in support of one another, but also actively recruit new members into our fold. Overly restrictive rules accomplish neither.

For instance; what is gained (or more to the point, what is lost) by noon closures? First of all, any hardworking man or woman in this country can relate to either losing hunting time in the woods because of having to get to a job, or being too tired from working all the time to go hunting. If morning hours are the only legal option, but their job interferes with being able to participate in the sport during those hours, then something is bound to be sacrificed - and earning a paycheck sure ain't gonna take a backseat to hunting for most people! It becomes a totally different reality if that same guy or gal can slip out in the afternoon and fit in an hour or two of hunting during the long hours of a spring day.

Let's put this in another way. Everyone's situation is different, and we all have our own priorities and schedules in today's harried world. What's good for you might not be nearly so for someone else, and the rules that fit your own life might place undo hardships on others. As far as I'm concerned, no life is complete without turkey hunting in it, so I think it's vitally important to set rules that will allow hunting opportunities for anyone who desires to be out there in the woods. Not all of us are lucky enough to have the luxury of being able to hunt whenever we like, and far fewer are as crazy as me and refuse to let work get in the way of hunting, but that shouldn't mean those less fortunate souls get no chance to enjoy the most wonderful sport in the world.

Now let's bring kids into the argument. There is absolutely nothing more important to the future of hunting in this country than the recruitment of our youth into the shooting and hunting sports. Think about this; if your state restricts hunting to mornings-only, then just when is a kid ever going to get an opportunity to discover the magic that is to be found in turkey hunting? They've got school all week long, and with Sundays off limits in some of these states too, that leaves only Saturday mornings for them to go hunting. Anyone who has ever raised kids knows that there are a million other activities vying for their attention on Saturday mornings. Hunting is usually not at the top of the list. I'm serious here when I say that these states which put restrictions on hunting are totally blowing it for these kids, *and* for our future! The rules need changed immediately, if for no other reason than this.

I can't even begin to tell you how many afternoons of my own youth were spent out fishing, or hunting, or just kicking around in the woods after school, and my love for the outdoors and nature are a direct result of how much time I spent there. Period. The more opportunities these kids are given to explore the wonders of the natural world, the better it will be for both them, and our country as a whole. Please, please look at hunting hour rules from this angle, and encourage these backwards facing states to turn around and help us help our own future by enacting more liberal laws!

As important as those last couple of paragraphs are, they are not quite the entire reason for why I want these rules changed. Like I said, I travel and hunt extensively across the country every spring, so there is a certain element of selfishness involved. However, despite the fact that I would gain field time if all-day hunting were enacted nation-wide, I know in my heart that the stance I take comes from an altruistic point of view. Once I came to realize that these restrictive rules only served to unnecessarily limit the hunting opportunities for certain people without impacting the overall turkey population, I became a staunch objector. These laws make no sense, while contrarily, it makes *perfect* sense to be able to hunt all day (and on Sundays, too) if a person wishes to do so.

Furthermore; what else is a traveling turkey hunters supposed to do with themselves after driving across the country to hunt turkeys in a state that unduly limits what days and times it can be done? The hours spent scouting without a gun in hand are just wasted time, in my opinion, and being forced to sit out an entire day of every week-end because of religious beliefs is just ludicrous.

Personally, I don't travel in the spring to go fishing, or sightseeing, or shopping at the mall. I am there to *hunt,* and during the latter part of spring it might be nine hours or more in between a forced noon quitting time and sunset. That's an awful lot of time to spend catching up on sleep. Besides that, I would much rather take my naps in the woods while I'm set up in the middle of some fresh turkey scratchings. I mean that quite literally, for there is no place in the world where I sleep better than in the turkey woods. Trust me, here; I can supply a long list of accomplices and cohorts who will swear to my prowess at that skill!

Me catching up on my sleep in the turkey woods.

Now I'd like to say a few words about the success rates of morning hunting as opposed to afternoons. I've often heard people say that mid-morning is the very best time to call in a bird, because the hens have already left their toms to go lay an egg - thus resulting in suddenly-lonely toms becoming more receptive to calling. Many people go on to claim that the majority of their kills happen after 10 o'clock, with some even asserting how there is little excuse for failing to call in a bird if he's found gobbling during those late morning hours. Toms are "easy" to call in, then. Or, so they say!

Well, first of all; utmost care should be taken in putting anything about turkey hunting into the absolute. If you make some bold, definitive statement as a cold, hard fact, some old longbearded tom will soon enough make a fool and a liar out of you. While those "truths" illustrated above may be quite accurate at times, they can also be patently false, as well. That's the nature of the game we play, and of the opponent we're trying to best.

I've had a hard time calling in turkeys in the late morning hours *many, many* times, and one reason is because toms don't always lose their hens like they are "supposed" to do. More and more these days, it seems like gobblers are *always* in the company of their girlfriends. In some regards this can be seen as a good thing, since it signifies a strong and robust turkey population. That wasn't always the case across this country, and whereas a flock of birds "back in the day" might mean a tom and half a dozen hens, today that same group might number upwards of 20 members. Some of those hens are bound to be barren, or just on different laying schedules, and so long as the gobbler has real feathers in view he'll tend towards hanging tightly with them, rather than seeking out some unseen vocal promise in the bushes.

As for the 10 o'clock statement; I have lots of trouble with that one. First of all, turkey season stretches to over three months in duration across the United States, with daylight hours getting progressively longer the whole time. An early-March sunrise in Florida might occur at 7:30 a.m. before the clocks have "sprung forward" to account for Daylight Savings Time, but in the first week of June in Maine, that same sun is popping up at 4:30 a.m. That's a three hour difference! Rather than making some blanket statement claiming that turkeys are easier to fool after 10 a.m., I think it's much more relevant to correlate a perceived mid-morning increase in success rate with how long those birds have been on the ground after flydown. The hands of a clock mean next to nothing - 10 o' clock in one instance is the very same thing as 7 o' clock in the other.

I have been keeping detailed records of all my turkey hunts since 1983, and these journals have included statistics for a number of things that I consider to be important. One of these items has been shot times; not only for the turkeys I've killed and missed myself, but also for those shot at by people in my company.

I've grouped this raw data into one-hour time slots, and under two different headings: "Clock Time" is, as you might assume, the actual time on a clock, while "Real Time" refers to when the shot occurred relative to official sunrise/sunset. Turkeys usually fly down from, or up to their roosts approximately ten minutes either side of official sunrise/sunset, so a hypothetical turkey killed at 10a.m. will have been on the ground for different lengths of time, depending upon the date and place where he was shot. Rather than using the hour hands on a watch, I think it's far more relevant to know just how long that tom has been parading around for his hens on the ground before I called him in and took the shot. That's why I think the "Real Time" heading holds greater value.

The internet has made determining how a shot relates to actual sunrise or sunset a simple thing. I always record the actual clock time in my journal, and once the season is over I then go online to look up the official sunrise/sunset tables for the specific date and the nearest town to where I was hunting when the trigger was pulled. Then, I do a little math and enter the results into a spreadsheet which helps me figure out the percentage of shots taken in each hourly category, and under each of the headings. Here are morning results from my journal that you might find interesting:

Clock Time			Real Time		
4:00 – 4:59 a.m.	=	1.3%	Sunrise + <1 hours	=	30.6%
5:00 – 5:59 a.m.	=	7.5%	Sunrise + 1-2 hours	=	19.0%
6:00 – 6:59 a.m.	=	18.8%	Sunrise + 2-3 hours	=	12.0%
7:00 – 7:59 a.m.	=	18.5%	Sunrise + 3-4 hours	=	9.1%
8:00 – 8:59 a.m.	=	13.6%	Sunrise + 4-5 hours	=	9.4%
9:00 - 9:59 a.m.	=	11.7%	Sunrise + 5-6 hours	=	4.5%
10:00 – 10:59 a.m.	=	7.0%	Sunrise + 6-7 hours	=	3.6%
11:00 – 11:59 a.m.	=	7.1%	Sunrise + 7-8 hours	=	0.3%
		85.3%			88.5%

I do the same thing for afternoon hunting, except that I use official sunset as the starting point in my "Real Time" category, and count backward from there. Hence, the breakdown looks like this:

Clock Time			Real Time		
12:00 – 12:59 p.m.	=	2.9%	Sunset – 6-7 hours	=	0.2%
1:00 – 1:59 p.m.	=	1.1%	Sunset – 5-6 hours	=	1.8%
2:00 – 2:59 p.m.	=	0.8%	Sunset – 4-5 hours	=	0.3%
3:00 – 3:59 p.m.	=	1.0%	Sunset – 3-4 hours	=	1.3%
4:00 – 4:59 p.m.	=	2.1%	Sunset – 2-3 hours	=	2.3%
5:00 – 5:59 p.m.	=	1.8%	Sunset – 1-2 hours	=	3.1%
6:00 - 6:59 p.m.	=	2.9%	Sunset – < 1 hour	=	2.5%
7:00 – 7:79 p.m.	=	2.1%			11.5%
		14.7%			

There are now well over 600 entries in my log, and I think that's a pretty good base of data from which to make some observations. For instance; while the actual time on the clock doesn't seem to tell me much, I can say with a very high degree of certainty that 30.6% of the recorded shots have been taken in the first hour after official sunrise, and 61.6% have been in the first three hours. I don't know what other hunters do during their own time afield, but for me, this is far and away the best timeframe for actually *killing* turkeys.

Another conclusion based on these figures addresses the aforementioned claims of increased success after 10 o'clock. My charts show no substantial midmorning jump to support that, so I can't really say with any degree of confidence that birds found gobbling in late morning are more likely to end up in the game bag. Sometimes they do, and sometimes they don't, but the impartial data in these tables doesn't lie. Maybe my own results have more to do with how I hunt, or some other unknown factor, but midmornings for me are most definitely not even close to a "sure thing."

Of course, raw data is also open to interpretation, and it doesn't necessarily give you all the information needed to make hard-and-fast conclusions. For instance; if I'm hunting in a state with a one-bird, or one-per-day limit and shoot a tom early in the morning, it goes without saying that I won't be out hunting later-on to potentially add a kill in another timeslot. There are a lot of these types of unseen factors which can skew the results of statistics, so perhaps it's best to say that nothing found in these charts should be considered as cold, hard evidence of anything; it's all merely interesting data to observe, which *might* show certain trends and tendencies - or not.

I would, however, like to point out that only approximately 15% of our total shots have been taken in the afternoon. Most of those happened during the last three hours of daylight, but again, some of that might simply reflect an increased presence in the woods at those hours. First of all; not every state allows me to hunt in the afternoon. Shots can't be taken if you aren't there. Secondly; over the years I've come to determine that there's often a general lull in the action following midday, so I sometimes take a break myself to eat lunch back at camp, run errands in town, or maybe take a nap to catch up on the general lack of sleep that accompanies my very existence during the entirety of spring. I might even opt to go fishing every once in a while.

Anyhoo; for whatever the reasons involved, I can see no particular time in the afternoon that is statistically more likely to produce results than others. Judging by the apparently low success rates reflected in these charts, some people might even wonder whether it's worth hunting at that time of day. All I can say in defense is that it's a helluva lot better to be out in the woods hunting than doing anything else. Whether that leads to a "successful" endeavor, or not, I'll always opt for time afield when given the chance.

Another thing that the data couldn't possibly show – but which I know without a shred of doubt in my mind to be true - is that there would be many more shots taken and kills recorded in the afternoon hours if every state allowed me to hunt all day long. Like I said a couple of paragraphs back, I sure can't kill turkeys if I'm sitting around camp!

One final reason for my staunch support of afternoon hunting involves the topic of hunter interference. All of us hate to have a hunt messed up by someone else, but it's bound to happen once in a while. The best way to lessen that chance is by lowering hunter numbers in the field, so think about it in this way; the sooner I kill my bird and get moving on to another state, the better the situation becomes for other hunters in the area that I've just vacated. The opposite is also true; I want that "other guy" who's hunting in the same area to get his bird and get out of there ASAP, so that my own chances of having an unmolested hunt increase.

133

Similarly, if someone kills their bird in the afternoon, then they won't be in the woods to mess up another guy's hunt the next morning. Hence, allowing afternoon hunting is yet another way to lessen hunting pressure.

OK, I've said enough about this subject for now; it's time to get back to tales from 1998.

If you can't hunt in the afternoons, there's always mushroom picking. Here are a few morels Kenneth and Larry Sharp found with me.

CHAPTER 9

1998 - A Year of Contradictions; Good vs. Bad

Weather-wise, 1998 was an El Nino year, which is when the Gulf Stream dips far south of its typical path and brings with it more-than-usual amounts of warm, moist air. To the west coast, Texas, and the Florida peninsula this means severe weather patterns and rain - lots of rain. Florida's Green Swamp WMA can be a totally different place depending upon the amount of water it holds during turkey season, and in a wet year those 55,000 acres become practically impenetrable unless you are particularly fond of sloshing around in water all day long and running into lots of cottonmouth water moccasins and alligators.

In a dry year you can at least move around in the formidable swamps and thickets of that heavily hunted public property, but 1998 was *not* a dry year.

The state had already received large amounts of "liquid sunshine" all winter long, and then two weeks prior to my arrival a broad band of vicious thunderstorms accompanied by multiple tornadoes had swept through the area and further inundated their saturated soils. As if that weren't bad enough, a total of six more inches of rain fell on the Thursday before they opened the gates, which caused flooding so bad that erecting a tent in the campground was simply out of the question. I ended up sleeping in my van for the whole duration of the trip, and that was a bummer because of how much I enjoy lying in a tent at night and being serenaded to sleep by tree frogs, whippoorwills, and other such "jungle music."

Another negative factor encountered in 1998, and which made Florida one of the worst hunting trips of my career, was the bugs. Of course, Florida is known for their bloodsucking mosquitoes, and it's true that they can be absolutely horrendous. Another pesky pest are the deer flies, whom I truly hate with an unbridled passion. However, in certain years there is another flying insect which is *far* worse than any others, and these are called Buffalo Gnats – a name usually preceded by any number of colorful adjectives. I don't know where these critters originally came from, but I strongly suspect that they were released out of the very gates of Hell, itself!

Exposed skin is hungrily sought out by these devious and diabolical minions of the devil, and while they may be diminutive in size, their attack is both vicious and relentless. Their bite causes immediate swelling and itching far beyond tolerable, and they have an especially annoying penchant for finding their way into any open seam of your attire before biting without the first sign that they were even there. Another place they love to attack is the soft, moist flesh surrounding eyes and lips; if caught in the field without a fine-meshed head net to protect these tender areas, your face will likely swell up to the point where your own mother couldn't recognize you.

In 1998 these tiny but terrible beasts were so thick that I felt pity for all the wild creatures in the forest that had to endure their painful and incessant attacks. Several times I actually witnessed turkeys flying up into the highest reaches of tall pines in the middle of the day and just sitting there, and I am quite certain that the reason for this odd behavior was simply an attempt to get away from the hordes of biting gnats. The only turkey I shot that year provided further proof of this theory, since every bit of exposed flesh on the bird was crusted-over with scabs. At first I thought that he was diseased, until Zane told me of putting out a decoy one day and watching the entire head region immediately turn almost solid black in color from all the gnats descending upon it!

136

Unfortunately, this was also the year when Frank Emert chose to make a try for his first Osceola. By the time I picked him up at the Tampa airport on Monday I had yet to hear a single gobble, and three days later when he headed back home to his ophthalmology business in Vincennes, Indiana we still hadn't heard a bird. Anyone else might've been disappointed by those results, but not Frank – his eternally positive attitude allowed him to thoroughly enjoy his stay and look forward to a return trip in the future.

My good friend Larry Sharp was also in camp that year, and after Frank left I tried my best to get him onto a bird before his duties as property manager of Kentucky's Higginson-Henry WMA demanded his presence. Try as we might, those fickle Osceola toms were so messed up by the marauding bugs and a prolonged heat wave that they refused to cooperate. The two of us heard just three total gobbles during seven additional days of hunting. The only redeeming factor seemed to be that nobody else was doing any good either, so at least we had lots of company with whom to share our misery. Generally speaking, the attitude in camp was pretty somber and dour when I headed out to scout on the final afternoon before Larry's last hunt.

The torrential rains of early spring had washed out a series of culverts along one of the main thoroughfares through Green Swamp, thereby forcing a road closure that virtually eliminated a huge chunk of property from anyone other than the hardest-working of hunters willing to walk or bike in. Although I'd sold my mountain bike the previous year and would thus need to hump it on foot a total of about twelve miles to reach the back portion of this piece and then return to my van, I felt like the hardships inherent in such an effort might very well be worth it. After all, this area had been extremely productive in years past. I was also confident that few (if any) others had been brave enough to venture into its furthest reaches. Most folks that year were hunting close to their vehicles so that they could make a quick escape from the bugs and blazing heat. I certainly wasn't looking forward to the trip myself, but I did feel like it could give us just what we were looking for.

Low and behold, at around the five mile mark of my scouting mission I spotted a tom strutting down the abandoned main road ahead of me, and after watching him follow a couple of hens off to the west, I circled out east of them to intersect another old logging road where I'd traditionally found lots of turkeys. After about a mile down that two-track I began seeing wing-tip drag marks in the trail, and not just a few, either! Obviously, there were several toms working this area, and I even found some hen back feathers and scuff marks in the sand at one place - leaving little doubt as to what kind of scurrilous event had happened there previously.

Giddy with excitement, I hot-footed it back to camp before dark with the news that I had finally found fresh turkey sign and there was still hope for Larry to get an Osceola before he had to leave for home. Larry is as good a people as you'll find anywhere, and after thirteen days of torturous hunting that had been hard on all of us, I really wanted to see him find success. The decency of full disclosure dictated that I tell him exactly how far we had to go to get back into this new area, and just how tough it was likely to be with all the bugs, but I figured correctly that my Kentuckian buddy was up for the challenge.

The next morning we were first in line when the gate opened, and after a nerve-wracking high-speed drive over pockmarked roads in the dark, we slid into our parking spot before anyone else. Immediately, we began the long hike to try and reach my newfound hotspot before gobbling time. I didn't really think we could get all the way to the strut-marked fire lane before daylight, but we had to try. Our second option was to stop short of there (where I'd seen the puffed-up tom), and I was pretty sure we could be in that vicinity by sunup if we force-marched our way at a steady pace.

Sure enough, the sky was already pinking up in the east as we closed in on the nearer of the two targeted areas, and soon thereafter a gobbler only a couple hundred yards away greeted the rapidly advancing dawn with a loud shout-out. Easing off the road into calf-deep water, we started creeping towards the little "island" of high ground (the *only* dry spot for hundreds of yards in any direction, except for the road) on the other side of a long cypress strand where the tom was roosted in a copse of tall pine trees. I felt like our best chance for success hinged on getting up there with him ASAP, but we encountered belly-button-deep water the further we went, and before we could maneuver through the tangled strand I caught a glimpse of the gobbler pitching down to several hens that were by now yelping and kee-keeing below him.

As we finally exited the strand and slogged up out of the water onto relatively dry land, I could hear the tom loudly drumming directly ahead of us beyond a green wall of palmettos and cabbage palms. However, we were in a terrible spot to call from, with coffee-colored water behind us, and an impenetrable jungle of vegetation blocking our path to the turkeys. Luckily for us, the thick palmettos formed sort of a ring around the spot where the tom and his hens were conducting their morning rendezvous, so I told Larry that it might behoove him to creep ahead of me on all fours, and then ease up to see if he could spot anything over the top.

As Larry inched forward to the edge of the brush line and slowly arose to a crouch, I could soon enough tell by his tensing body posture that visual contact had been made. The gun at his side inched up to shoulder height, followed by his head coming down to meet the stock, and then the morning calm was shattered by the explosion of gun powder. Turkeys flew off in all directions as Larry turned to face me with a look of such obvious disappointment and sadness in his eyes that there was never a doubt about the results of his errant shot.

"What happened," I incredulously asked?

After what can best be described as a "pregnant pause," my dear old friend slowly shook his head and simply said, "shot well...nothing fell."

I felt terrible for Larry, because I knew how hard he'd hunted since arriving in Florida, and how badly he wanted an Osceola. I also knew that with 14 hours of driving time ahead of him, his brain would think back and replay what had just transpired a million times before the pain might ever subside. Memories like that are something which nearly every turkey hunter must endure at some point, and it doesn't get any easier on your twentieth miss than it was on your first; it hurts - and it hurts *badly*. But, we somehow find a way to go on, and by the time Larry and I got back to camp the laughter and good feelings that steer our friendship had returned. He left for home shortly thereafter, but we planned to meet up later at his archery-only WMA in western Kentucky.

The next morning I headed out alone to try and reach the fire lane containing all of those strut marks, but once again that first gobble of the day came when I was still a mile short of my goal. It had originated from basically the same general area as the previous day, so I was sure that this was the very tom Larry had missed. However, I made a strategic error in judgment regarding just how close I could get before setting up, and his hens spotted me en route. They immediately started putting loudly, the tom ceased gobbling, and then they all flew away. I was left angry at myself for getting in too big of a hurry and blowing the whole deal after working so hard just to get there.

There was nothing to do but back out and go someplace else, so I hiked on down the main road until reaching the enchanted fire lane. I knew from this point on that it was 1834 counted steps to where the strut marks had begun in earnest, so I hustled to cover that ground as quickly as possible. Three hundred yards short of my destination I eased around a bend in the trail and spotted what looked like two black bears standing in the middle of the lane ahead. No; wait - those weren't bears - they were strutting toms!

Slowly sinking to the ground, I rolled to my left far enough that I wound up laying prone a couple of feet into the edge of the palmettos with my gun pointing down the roadway. The thick vegetation blocked any view of the gobblers, but one gentle yelp on a mouthcall brought forth a sweet-sounding answer of the feminine variety. I then caught a fleeting glimpse of the hen who made that call as she sauntered my way, and I could plainly hear her subsequent soft, inquisitive perts and clucks as she advanced.

Although I still couldn't see her boyfriends, their spitting and drumming was getting louder and louder, and left no doubt that they were following right behind. Then, I caught another flicker of movement in my peripheral vision, and realized that it was the hen standing six feet to my right! I dared not even blink or make eye contact with her at that range – all I could do was remain frozen solid and stare straight down my gun barrel in hopes of catching sight of the toms before they were on top of me, as well.

Suddenly, a gobbler's bright red head popped up directly in line with the double sight beads of my Ruger. The range was extremely close – 13 yards – and a quick trigger pull put him down for keeps. Meanwhile, the hen and surviving tom blasted off into space like rockets.

This flash-kill had proven yet once again just how quickly things can go from bad to good in the blink of an eye during a turkey hunt. The next day would demonstrate just the opposite. First of all, I started out by getting lost. Zane and I were trying to access this same area from a different direction in order to find a short-cut through the swamp, but things did not work out exactly as planned and it was 8 o'clock before we finally bumbled into the "honey hole." Any gobbling for that day was already far behind us by then, so we separated in order to double our chances of encountering turkeys.

Judging solely by the number of tracks and droppings along the section of sandy lane where I chose to set up, I should've been perfectly content to sit there calling blind for as long as it took to find success. But, the morning's frustrations in losing my way had gotten under my skin, and after twenty minutes I was jittery and anxious to further explore the area. When I abruptly stood up, a tom 15 yards behind me turned and ran off - putting loudly. My hurried shot at his rapidly departing head and neck absolutely centered a 12-inch pine tree between us, shielding the tom from harm.

Talk about feeling stupid; I had committed at least three sins of turkey hunting by not having enough confidence, not showing enough patience, and not exhibiting enough awareness and due diligence when I finally decided to make a move. It was a long, hot, buggy walk back to the van – made especially so because I was also dragging my pride behind me. Back in camp that afternoon, Zane told me how he had whispered, "Yes!" after hearing the first shot, but changed that to, "Oh, no!" following the second.

Two frustrating weeks of tough hunting at Green Swamp had left me feeling not only willing, but eager for a change of scenery, so I headed out that afternoon in hopes of finding success at another WMA to the east. Four days later I still hadn't so much as heard or seen a tom. In hindsight, the prudent move would've been to stay the course on my home turf and hunt where I *knew* there were turkeys. Admittedly, the hard access to reach them at Green Swamp had factored into my decision to leave for "greener pastures," but that was just silliness on my part – I'd traded in a sure thing for the total unknown. In short; I got exactly what I deserved.

Resigning myself to defeat and tucking tail, I headed away from Florida's persistent, withering heat for the cooler climes of Alabama.

I had been researching that state's public land offerings ever since my moderately successful 1997 excursion there, and this time I thought that concentrating my efforts in the north might provide better options. As mentioned in a previous chapter, in talking with the local wildlife biologist for that region I found out that the birds were feeding heavily on a type of sedge that was seeding out right then, so I was determined in my scouting mission to focus on two things: finding where this sedge grew in abundance, and hiking far into the National Forest in order to avoid other hunters.

One of my oldest and best friends (Tracy Deckard) drove down to join me for a few days, and we had a large time of it in those beautiful Alabama hardwoods. I killed a good bird on the morning before he arrived, got lucky with an even better tom during his second day in camp, and then the following dawn proved to be Tracy's time to shine when he shot a gobbler that ended up being the heaviest one ever recorded on the Management Area where we were hunting. It weighed 22 pounds, 6 ounces.

These last two turkeys ranked first and third in a contest at the local sporting goods store, so with only a few days of the season remaining, its proprietor wrote down our addresses and assured us that he would send the winnings by mail. Strange as it may sound, no prize money ever arrived back at home. I guess there must've been some real bruisers brought in to knock our toms out of contention, even though my third-place bird and Tracy's "record-setting" tom had been the only ones checked in during the past two weeks. Rack that one up under the heading of "things that make you go, "hmmmm…"

Tracy Deckard's big 'ole Alabama gobbler.

And one of mine.

Larry Sharp's WMA in Kentucky was next up on the schedule, and as he had done the previous year, Ron Ronk joined us there for a few days of turkey hunting shenanigans and fun-filled jocularity. Ron may've been a "seasoned veteran" with the bow (having killed his first archery tom the previous spring), but for a year I'd been giving him a ration of guff for missing a second bird when his arrow had nicked the side of our blind and caromed over the turkey's back. Now, he was anxious to atone for that slight mistake, and on the second morning of our hunt Ron's arrow found its mark. Although the tom flew off after the shot, he subsequently folded up 50 yards out and dropped from the sky stone-cold dead. High-fiving and grinning like village idiots, we gathered him up and headed over to Larry's house for a celebration.

The next day I shot a gobbler at only 9 yards that had an incredibly long beard. This was the first arrow that I'd ever released at a tom, and even though the shot felt good and the impact point looked "right," the bird simply jogged about ten yards away from us, putted twice, and then walked off into the forest. I was so shocked by his low-keyed reaction that I didn't know what to do, so we talked it over and decided to wait a half-hour before getting out of the blind.

Immediately upon beginning our search we saw several feathers and quite a bit of blood where the tom had been standing when I shot him. Then, we found a few more drops about a hundred yards away, but no matter how hard I wished for it, there wasn't a dead turkey anywhere nearby. A very bad feeling of dread came over me at that point, and when the sky subsequently opened up with rain as heavy as my rapidly sagging heart, I felt even worse. We searched and searched for hours without finding another clue as to where this bird went.

Ron Ronk's Kentucky bowkill of '98.

While I had certainly endured many mishaps and misses in the turkey woods while using a shotgun, losing this arrowed tom left me feeling more thoroughly disappointed, distressed, and generally bummed-out than any of the rest. I knew for a fact that my Draathar Snuffer broadheads always left a huge wound channel in deer, so I felt certain that this magnificent tom couldn't possibly survive what had appeared to be a solid hit. It made me sick to think about him becoming coyote poop, and the resulting anxiety kept me tossing and turning in my sleep all night long.

By the next morning I had come to some conclusions that I didn't like, but which I had to accept if I wished to continue bowhunting for turkeys. First and foremost on that list was the inevitability of crippling losses; while these were bound to happen regardless of weapon choice, there was no getting around the fact that it would happen much more often with archery gear. Try as I might to improve my accuracy and make every shot count, the very nature of this primitive weapon, coupled with a gobbler's small kill zone, made future low points like this a certainty which didn't sit well with me. Missing turkeys with a gun was bad enough, but crippling them with an arrow was far, far worse, and I wasn't sure how much of that I could take. I mean, really; after the trigger is pulled I want to see a turkey flopping in the leaves. Anything else is unacceptable!

My overall goal in those years was to eventually hunt in as many eastern states as possible. Towards attaining that, I had applied in Illinois' lottery and subsequently been successful in drawing a tag. With that Pope County permit now burning a hole in my pocket, I quite willingly laid down the bow and picked up my trusted Ruger over/under shotgun for the two hour drive west into the beautiful Shawnee National Forest. It only took a couple of hours the next morning to call in my first Illinois tom, and then I shot him in the face from a range of 26 yards. Believe me; the Winchester pattern centered on that tom's head left no doubts about it - *this* turkey wasn't going anywhere besides back to my van!

I had actually called this bird in three different times before taking the shot, and he ended up being a bruiser with long, hooked spurs. It was a great hunt overall, with numerous gobbling turkeys surrounding me on all sides. The scenery where I shot the tom was also spectacular, with unbelievably huge timber in a valley rimmed with really cool overhanging limestone bluffs. I vowed to return at some point in the future, just because it was such an awesome-looking place to hunt turkeys.

Then, I started finding morel mushrooms - *lots* of morel mushrooms! The more I picked, the more I found, until not only was the Wal-Mart bag that I carry for just such emergencies overflowing with big grays and yellows, but so was my hat, the entire game pouch of my vest, and a t-shirt with the arms and neck tied shut. It was absolutely some of the best mushroom pickin' I had ever encountered *anywhere*. There are very few foods in this world as good as morels rolled in ground-up saltine crackers and then fried in pure butter until golden brown, and I was eager to share this bounty with Larry Sharp's family and Ron back in Kentucky.

Returning to Higginson-Henry with a couple ziplocks full of fresh turkey flesh and a cooler stuffed with fungus, I resumed trying to actually *kill* my first turkey with a bow. It seemed inevitable, because the place was slap-full of birds. But, three days later I once again made what I felt was a good shot, only to see the tom fly away with my arrow sticking out of his hide. After conducting a long and fruitless search, I was once again left frustrated, angry, and full of angst over the fact that I had probably "filled" my two Kentucky tags with dead turkeys, yet I possessed no meat, beards, or spurs to show for it. My brain was so frazzled that I didn't know what else to do short of arming my arrows with sharpened spade trowels in hopes of cutting these tough birds in two. Even then, I felt like the front half would probably fly off, while the back would exit running.

Morel mushrooms - is there anything finer?

What I really needed at that point was a positive experience to rekindle my broken spirits, and I couldn't think of any better tonic for what ailed me than a trip home to hunt on Tom Foley's 1600-acre Tea Mountain property. Opening day with that same old gang of hooligans who always showed up was a tradition dating back to 1990, and we always had a great time hunting, eating delicious meals, and yucking it up around camp.

Now in hindsight, those were definitely some special times for all of us. It seemed like every year there would be one particular event which stood out above all the rest to become "legendary," and in the spring of 1998 that occurred on the third day when DeWayne Feltner returned to the cabin shortly after noon to find Don Foley and myself already there eating lunch. As soon as he walked through the door DeWayne asked if we wanted to see a rattlesnake, to which we both replied, "Hell, yes!"

"Well," he said, "come on - there's one just down the road a piece."

We don't have a lot of Timber rattlers in Indiana, but the rugged counties surrounding my home turf have always held a moderate population. As a youth I can even recall my Dad catching them fairly often when Salt Creek was first flooded to form Lake Monroe in the early 1960's. As the Property Manager of that big reservoir, he would occasionally hold parties for all of his employees, and sometimes rattlesnake served as the food source for those gatherings. My Mom was a hunter's wife who cooked whatever Dad brought home to eat, so she certainly remembers those days, too; vividly, if not so fondly! Mom grew up as a city girl...

I've thus been around these critters quite a bit during my life, and while I respect them greatly, I'm not particularly scared in their presence. I've even handled several live ones over the years, so when DeWayne took us to where he'd found this particular snake (having gently placed a big leafy branch overtop of it to try and keep him there long enough to go get us at the cabin) and explained that he wanted to now catch the critter to show his brother Russ, I suggested that we pin its head down with a forked stick while I reached down to grab him.

What I didn't yet know was the proportions of the rattler lying underneath that branch – he was absolutely *HUGE*! That booger's head was big around as my closed fist, and the body must've been six inches or more in diameter in the middle. He stretched out to about six feet in length. In short, it was an absolute *beast* of a snake!

Once DeWayne had its head pinned down and I saw how strong the serpent looked in writhing around, I had to admit that this was simply too much snake to even think about handling. Frankly, I was worried that it might be able to wrench free from my

147

grasp whenever he damned-well felt like it and bite the shit out of me! After mulling things over for a bit, we decided to place a big cooler onto its side with the opened lid on the ground, and by poking and prodding the snake we finally got him to slither into it. Then, we tilted the cooler upright, slammed the lid shut, and wrapped four big bungee cords around the whole thing to keep everybody safe.

Speaking of sound, that snake was one mad dude. I don't think he ever stopped rattling during the whole day and a half that we had him confined in the cooler. Then (in spite of some strong objections to the contrary), we released him. He kept right on rattling while slithering out of sight over the ridgeline.

There's no telling how old a snake of that size is, and I personally think it's wrong to kill one just because he's alive. In fact, I find them to be rather fascinating. My opinion might be different if I lived someplace like Texas where rattlesnakes are so prolific as to be a legitimate danger to kids and dogs, but here at home they are more of a curiosity which most Hoosiers have never even seen. I say, "live and let live."

Later that month DeWayne ran into a fellow walking around on the property wearing headphones and carrying a set of hand-held antennae. When asked what he was doing, the guy offered up that he was a herpetologist from IU studying rattlesnakes. He went on to tell DeWayne that they'd recently been catching snakes in the area, making a small slit in their skin, sliding in a radio transmitter, and then super-gluing the slit closed. They could then track and relocate each individual snake by dialing-in its unique frequency. Being able to quickly find previously tagged snakes allowed the scientists to more easily gather valuable information about rattlesnake behavior.

In talking with the man further, DeWayne learned that these snakes are very much home bodies, and if you took one away and released him someplace else, it would soon die from not knowing where to eat or find shelter from the elements. He also told DeWayne that there was a winter snake den about 300 yards from the cabin which held the largest concentration of Timber Rattlers ever found east of the Mississippi River. Could that be why topographic maps of the area list this particular section of the property as "Rattlesnake Ridge?"

Well, after three days of fun at Tea Mountain my attitude was much better and I spent the rest of Indiana's season guiding on my Amish farms in Jefferson and Switzerland Counties. Overall, I called in 30 toms to less than 40 yards during those next 15 days, with eight of them being killed during the first nine days alone. The weather had abruptly turned cold and rainy at that point, with only one more tom brought to bag in the final week.

Despite the difficulties endured during that second half of the season, I was awfully pleased overall with how everything had gone. Highlights included another big tom for my cousin Bob Torrance, along with birds for a quartet of folks who I had successfully taken hunting in previous years: Don Foley, Eric Coonrod, Gary Shepherd, and Louie Rusch. That made three in a row for Louie, which was a feat I proudly considered to be greater than the building of the Egyptian pyramids! Louie was in failing health and died the next year.

Three of the Wickey boys (Alvin, Jake, and Ervin) also shot turkeys that spring, but there were also some hunts when things didn't go quite like we planned. For instance, Frank Emert missed a huge gobbler on the very last day of the season. As bad as that felt, it was a far better result than when Judd Holmes had crippled and lost a tom by trying to shoot through too much brush. A long search had turned up nothing but feathers and blood. Another "shot well…nothing fell" incident involved Louie missing a bearded hen. Now, I personally don't believe in killing your breeding stock, but Louie had badly wanted this unique trophy for his wall and insisted on taking the shot. Although the beard made her a legal target in Indiana, I was very happy when she flew away unscathed.

Then, there was an interesting day that started out worrisome before ending in our favor. I was hunting with Ervin Wickey that morning when a vicious thunderstorm built up around us while we worked a gobbling tom out in a horse pasture. The leading edge of the front arrived just about the same time as the tom strutted into killing range, but before Ervin had a chance to pull the trigger its powerful rain squall suddenly hit us like a hurricane.

The tom immediately stepped over to the lee side of a big multi-flore rose bush seeking protection against the huge raindrops that were being blown sideways, and for 15 minutes he squatted there with his head tucked in tight against his chest, looking nothing less than miserable. Finally, the gale passed on by and he stood back upright, shook like a wet dog, and walked towards us. I'm not sure why Ervin's forthcoming shot didn't kill him outright, but instead, the tom took off labored and flew crooked for a ways before setting his wings and gliding about 300 yards. Then, he angled steeply downward and vanished over the top of a low knoll.

Louie Rusch and longtime pal Gary Shepherd pose with Louie's last turkey.

This tom was obviously hurt badly, so we raced over and began searching every nook, cranny, crack, and crevice on that entire hillside. I was sure that we'd find him, and it wouldn't have surprised me at all to see him just lying there stone dead, but after more than an hour things were looking bleak. Suddenly, Ervin pulled up his gun and shot the 24 pound tom, who wasn't tucked up under a briar thicket or brush pile at all, but rather, was doing a marvelous job of making himself small in a wide-open patch of green grass only six inches tall. Finding this bird was an extreme thrill for both me and the youngest of the Wickey boys, and so was hanging the giant from a nearby limb with those sharp spurs of 1- 5/16 inches.

As you've no doubt come to learn by now from reading so many of my accounts, I *hate* missing or crippling game! It always leaves me feeling ill, and bothers me so much that I toss and turn at night replaying the events over and over in my mind. I had originally hoped that laying out some of these unfortunate episodes on paper would prove cathartic, but it doesn't really help all that much. I can vividly recall every single one of them to this very day, and their memories still make me nauseous. I can't help it. One of my most basic fundamental beliefs is that I owe my worthy adversaries a quick, humane death when the trigger is pulled, and every time I fail to get that accomplished it feels as if I've dishonored the bird himself.

Yeah, I know what you're thinking; "for a guy who claims to be so concerned with making the initial shot count, screwing it up sure seems like a prominent theme in his stories." I certainly can't argue that point too much, other than to say this probably has more to do with the particular tales chosen for the book. Blown opportunities are the ones which have left the strongest impact on my psyche, so they naturally tend to bubble up in my writing.

I will freely admit that a lifetime "failure-to-kill" rate of 11% is higher than I like, but this figure pales in comparison to the 25% clip that the people I take hunting have under-achieved. I can't express just how exasperating it is to work hard at bringing in a tom to sure killing range for someone, and then watching helplessly as they screw it up. Every time this happens I tell myself that I'll never guide again, but I know that's just emotion talking. Before too long I'll have gotten past it, and once again be eager to experience the thrill of the hunt through the eyes of friends and compadres. My own misses and cripples, on the other hand, are much harder to take...

After the Indiana season sputtered to a close, I headed back to West Virginia for the third year in a row. Nothing in the world is tougher to chew on and harder to swallow than tag soup, and this state had long been feeding me a steady diet of my least favorite dish. It therefore didn't come as any great surprise when this unwelcome trend continued in 1998. Six days of torture later, I finally reached my fill of the bitter taste and headed for New York with two unused tags still in my pocket. On the positive side, I did leave there having learned some tough-love lessons which made me a better turkey hunter...

I had arrived at Elk River WMA very early on a Sunday morning, but because West Virginia is another of those backassward states that doesn't allow hunting on the Sabbath, all I could do was hike out onto a ridgeline and listen for several hours as a hot tom ripped the woods apart. He gobbled more than 200 times in all, which allowed me to study his movements and patterns until I was confident of busting his noggin' the next morning.

In hindsight, perhaps I was a bit *too* confident. Maybe I even jinxed myself, because I never heard a single gobble at dawn. The weather conditions certainly couldn't be blamed for that silence, as the temperature was crisp and cool, the skies were clear, and there was no wind. It also seemed highly unlikely that the tom heard the day before had moved to another zip code overnight, so maybe he'd simply tuckered himself out the previous day with all of that infernal gobbling. Because of that, I felt like my best option was to just hang tight in some of his favored spots and then blind-call/scratch in the leaves. Maybe he'd come sneaking in silently.

My first setup was atop a high knob where the tom had carried-on for quite a while on Sunday. When I began hearing footsteps in the leaves coming towards me an hour later, hopes of a quick WV kill started to take root in my brain. Then, an 80%-white piebald deer ambled up to within spitting distance of me. After another hour I once again heard footsteps, and while this time it was, indeed, a male turkey, he turned out to be merely a jake. Once he'd left I again heard something walking in the hollow to the west of me, and several times I thought that I might've even heard drumming, but I wrote those subtle sounds off as just the figment of an overeager imagination. I should've known better than to question either my ears, or that inner voice which guides so many of my moves. They seldom lie to me.

At 9:15a.m. the tom gobbled for the first time all day. He wasn't more than a hundred yards directly in line with where I had earlier thought the drumming to be coming from, but with only five days of the season remaining, and not knowing how much pressure this public land bird had already experienced before my arrival, I didn't want to be overly aggressive by running him off with too much calling. Instead, I merely clucked lightly a few times with my mouthcall.

The tom answered nothing I had to say, but he did gobble four more times unsolicited in the next half-hour. I continued to play things coy on my end, and he continued to show no apparent interest, whatsoever. Or, maybe he was just playing me all along - either way, I was content to hold the high ground and wait him out.

Eventually, he began gobbling on his own every fifteen minutes, but unfortunately, he was also gradually slipping further away with each one. With just over an hour of legal hunting time left I decided that a move on my part was necessary in order to make something good happen. Arising to my feet, I started incrementally slipping towards him whenever he'd gobble. Down through the hollow and up onto the next ridgeline I went, with the tom somewhere over the top and on the slopes below. Oh, if I could only gain another five yards to a wonderful-looking setup tree standing on the crest of the ridgeline...

The dreaded "putt...putt" of an alarmed turkey was my only reward for trying to force the issue too fast, instead of awaiting another gobble before making my next move. Then, I caught a glimpse of the tom flying off through the trees. I felt like a total dipstick.

Even though I was disgusted with my bumbling self, I looked around and quickly realized that I might very well have chanced upon the absolute perfect spot for killing this tom on another day. Not only was the ground under that old white oak where I'd been intending to set up absolutely scratched to pieces, but there was just enough brush surrounding it to supply cover without hindering vision; making for an easily constructed and exquisite natural blind. Furthermore, this spot just felt *right* to me. After a little rearranging of strategically places limbs and branches, I vowed to slip in there long before the sun even thought about coming up the next morning.

There have been many times in my turkey hunting career when I simply got my butt whooped by a superior opponent, and the following day proved to be a perfect example of that scenario. Perhaps things might've turned out differently if I'd been smart enough to plant myself at that oak tree and refused to budge until the gobbler showed up, but the siren songs of that old tom turkey kept beckoning me unto the rocks, and I willingly went along with whatever temptations he cast in my direction. During the course of the day's travels over hill and yon there were five different times when I just *knew* the gobbler was about to die a glorious death, but in every instance he somehow found a way to avoid my dastardly plans and escape with his life. Twice he even led me right back through the very spot where we'd started our battle at dawn, but again, I just wasn't smart enough to catch on that he was playing me for a fool, and I obliged him every step of the way.

So began a distressing pattern of coming oh-so-close to killing this tom on occasion after occasion. The crusty old curmudgeon led a charmed life though, and he always outmaneuvered, outfoxed, or simply out-lucked me time and again. The longer our private war raged, the more frustrated I became. That dad-blamed turkey, however, appeared no worse for wear, and in fact, he almost seemed to enjoy putting the screws to me as fate kept shining its golden glow upon his warty old head.

The fourth day of our ongoing duel was rainy and very dark, with lead-colored clouds hanging low overhead. The tom had shown a pronounced habit of roosting along a particular ridgeline, so I had snuck up onto it more than an hour before the first hint of dawn. Because he hadn't gobbled at all the evening before, I had no firm idea of his exact roost location when I owl hooted in the drizzle. However, there was no mistaking where he had slept the night away when a loud gobble blasted out *directly* above my head in answer to the owling. I was standing there leaning against a big red oak at the time, so all I could do was freeze and wish myself small - he was *much* too close, and it was *much* too risky, to even chance sliding slowly downward into a sitting position.

Well, the next gobble rattled my very soul a couple of minutes later, and left no doubt in my mind that this turkey was in the exact same tree against which I was leaning. For those of you who have been around turkeys much while they're still on the roost, you'll know what I'm talking about when I say that there's a particular thing which happens soon after they begin to awaken and stir around. In humans, this action is called "The Morning BM," and I swear that this next statement is totally true: when the gobbler subsequently released his bowels, a large load of the stuff came tumbling past my face in the dim light so close that I could actually smell the fragrance as it went by! A second helping was forthcoming a few moments later, and it too missed me by mere inches.

154

Ever-so-slowly and cautiously, I then cranked my head upwards (fearful at any moment of receiving a face full of turkey manure) to spot the tom in the very top of the tree we shared. However, despite the ongoing days of frustration and aggravation bestowed upon me by this evil bird, for all practical purposes he was safe from harm - I had not the slightest inclinations or intentions of shooting him out of that tree; whether legal, or not. I was, however, hopeful that he'd pitch nearly straight down and land within gun range when he left the roost. While I wasn't particularly anxious to shoot him in this way either, putting the hammer to him when his toes touched dirt would've been perfectly acceptable to my sense of propriety if circumstances dictated such a move.

I should've known that luck might provide an escape route for this rabbit's foot-carrying gobbler, because a few minutes later he left his roost limb and glided a good 200 yards downhill before landing clean out of sight. I hustled after him to reposition, and soon thereafter began yet another day of me being led around like a bull by his nose ring. When the season ended a couple days after that I was still no closer to killing this tom than I had been upon our initial introduction. But, in those six days of hard hunting there were at least 12 separate times when he was mine except for a hair's breadth of luck separating his life from eternity.

The grim reality of the situation was that I would've and should've killed this tom - *if* I had simply parked my stubborn butt on that ideal white oak which sat amidst all the scratchings and stayed there until he showed up. Invariably and inevitably, that rascal would pass within shooting range of it every single day, but instead of hunting smart, I followed him around like a puppy dog, convinced that I could call him in wherever I chose to do so. Time and again I ended up in places where he'd already been, rather than where he wanted to go. I'd also spent way too much time and effort trying to interpret his movements, anticipating his actions, and hustling to head him off; undoubtedly arriving late, missing out on the show, and being forced to begin the whole process over again.

Those were some of the keen observations rattling around in my brain as I made the drive north to New York, and another one came to me as more of a question: might it have been a far wiser move to leave behind a tom that seemed to have my number and go find another bird, rather than being bullheaded and staying the course like I had done all week? After all, I had paid good money for that WV hunting license, and now, here I was with two unused tags in my wallet. In hindsight, I could certainly see unfulfilled promise and perhaps lack of intelligence in my having failed to change course in midstream, but no matter how hard I tried to sell myself on that profundity, I couldn't say that I truly believed in the action.

My entire life, if for nothing more, had always been a study in lessons learned from negative events. While there was certainly something to be said for heading out to greener pastures when the going got tough, it was also undeniable that the emotional beatings and marathon hunts for particularly wicked birds were the ones which most stuck in my brain years later. I liked testing myself against the best that nature could throw at me, and struggling to find out who would persevere in a battle of wits and wills was the very essence of what I considered a good turkey hunt to be. However, whether I ended up as the winner or loser in any of these hard-fought duels didn't really matter in the grand scheme of things. There was knowledge and wisdom to be gained from the experience in either case.

Well, sticking with a particular tom until the fight was decided one way or the other might've been my preferred methodology, but that wasn't how I started the final hunt of the year in New York. I actually switched birds three different times that morning before eventually finding one willing to play the game, and after killing this tom I began walking back to my van parked beside a green hay field on the highest ridge of Tony Bay's dairy farm.

For several years I had been driving this same rig - a white extended-length Dodge with a high-rise roof. Its roomy interior configuration gave me plenty of headspace in which to stand straight up, so I considered it the perfect platform to serve me both as a carpenter's work vehicle for hauling materials and my entire tool set while back home, and as a 'home on wheels" filled with hunting and camping gear during turkey season. Because it looked so much like a big white whale out on the road, I nicknamed the Dodge, "Mobile Dick." This moniker may've had multiple layers of meaning...

As the top of my van came into sight over the hay field I did one of those "double takes" that you hear people talk about, because there, plainly framed against the white dome of my rooftop, I could see the fanned-out tail of a gobbler in full strut! Checking it out more thoroughly with a set of Swarovski mini binoculars that always hang around my neck when hunting, I confirmed that there was, indeed, a tom parading about for a hen 30 yards from where I'd parked before dawn. His position on a little elevated knoll aligned him perfectly with Mobile Dick, and although I was still a couple hundred yards away, I couldn't help but think of how the visual would've made a really cool photograph, if I'd only been carrying a camera with a good zoom lens.

While the bird over my shoulder strongly supported the previously discussed "run-n-gun" theory of not getting tied down until you find a gobbler willing to die, the next tom making his way into the camp cooler could best be defined by my more-preferred, "find one you want and stay with him" approach. I'd seen this tom strutting in a cornfield while driving into town to get an ice cream cone (remember my "good luck" theory on that favored treat?), and he looked like a "sho'nuf good'un." In fact, when I pulled off to the side of the road and glassed him with a set of full-size Swarovski's, I could plainly see his long, sharp spurs.

It took me two more days of hunting this bird before I could convince him to waltz up within killin' range, and because of our relative positions in that final duel, I could make out his leg hardware sky-lighted in silhouette before I took the shot. The tom had been walking along the edge of an elevated and just-planted cornfield, while I was down below him in the dark woods, 19 yards away. An in-hand examination afterwards confirmed that these spurs were not only long (1- 1/4 inches), but tri-colored like the old-time "candy corn" that we ate as kids. Very cool.

Then, as I drove back to camp I saw a pair of gobblers strutting by themselves in the field closest to Jake's house, so I went straight on up there to roust my buddy for a try at smacking one of their noggins. Twenty minutes later Jake was standing on a tom's neck, and while our two kills weren't exactly a classic "double" in turkey hunting parlance, they were close enough for the gals we dated. The very next morning we finished up Jake's two-bird limit with a tom shot from a group of at least seven strutters on our friend Charlie Leuberger's farm, thereby capping a very strange and unusual season filled with nearly as many lows points as high ones.

Overall, I had called in 74 toms to less than 40 yards and hunted on 64 days stretched between seven different states. These were definitely great numbers, and so were the 19 toms which had been brought to bag. However, any thrills derived from the good times had been somewhat counterbalanced by watching eight additional birds either missed, or crippled and lost. Un-fortuitous circumstances and bad breaks had seemed to be the rule all spring long, with recurrent difficulties continually serving to keep me feeling off-balance and out of synche. Even the weather had contributed to my general malaise, with lots of nasty, cold, thunderstorm-filled days.

Taken as a whole the good had still far outweighed the bad, but it wasn't an easy spring by any stretch of the imagination. The incongruities it had produced were taxing my brain as I drove home contemplating how everything had turned out and what I could do to improve upon it, and then, I was struck by a much-simpler thought which summed up the contradictions of 1998 in a little better way; I was both sad that the season had come to an end, and yet glad that I had been able to experience so much of the magic contained within those turkey woods that stir my soul. It just doesn't get any more basic than that.

Jake and I, along with young sons Trevor and Oria.

CHAPTER 10

Yardage and Ammo

I've often made reference in these volumes to the fact that I like my turkeys up close and personal because of the thrill that it brings to the hunt, and how that excitement grows exponentially stronger with each of his advancing footsteps. This is a time when your eyes automatically squint real narrow to keep the tom from homing in on your predator's gaze, and once he gets right there "in your lap" the adrenalin will be pumping so hard that it feels like the old ticker might burst open at any moment. I can't even count the number of times when passing out seemed inevitable from holding my breath for so long, out of fear that a gobbler would see my chest heaving if I snuck even one little lungful of air, but it's moments like that which make a hunter feel alive.

Once the echo of the gunshot has faded away I always check my watch to see exactly what time it happened, and then I pace off the distance to where the tom had been standing. These figures are both recorded in my hunting journal even before the picture taking begins, as anyone accompanying me into the turkey woods can attest. My companions might also vouch for the fact that I'm a stickler for letting a bird walk off if he's deemed too far away for a sure, killing shot, even though some of them will at times try to talk me into letting them "take a poke" at a gobbler standing out there at the edge of lethal range. My stubborn stance has undoubtedly resulted in fewer birds brought to bag over the years, but I have no regrets whatsoever because I'm also confident that it's resulted in less crippling losses. In a nutshell, it all comes down to this; I want to *know* that tom's a dead turkey walking before I'll sign off on the trigger-pull.

Unfortunately, there is no such thing as an "absolute" in turkey hunting, and that goes for the moment of truth when a shot charge exits the gun barrel or an arrow leaves its bow. I've freely admitted for all to see that my "shot well…nothing fell" percentage of 11% is too danged high to be happy about, but at least it's well short of the 25% miss rate for the people sitting beside me, and for many years their figure hovered around the dismal mark of 33% - meaning; *one out of every three toms shot at were not killed!* My companions' disturbing habit of blowing easy shots at wide-open toms absolutely drove me bonkers and made me want to pull my hair out in frustration, so I'm sure you can figure out where I place most of the blame for my now follicly-challenged head…

In total fairness, though; I certainly do acknowledge that a lot of strange things can happen in that last millisecond of a hunt, and the reasons/excuses for missing can be wide, varied, and sometimes even valid. Many of these low points in my own past have been totally inexplicable in hindsight, so I always try to be understanding and empathetic with friends and cohorts when such an occurrence befalls them. Sometimes that's a very hard thing to do, but I try. Fortunately, the folks in my company have tightened up their act in the last few years and killed far more toms than they've missed. I sure hope the trend continues, because I'd really like to keep what little hair that's still left clinging to my shiny dome.

Calmly and accurately estimating range to the target is yet another important part of becoming a consistently successful turkey hunter, and it's imperative to practice the skill in order to do it well. In my everyday life this entails regularly guessing the distance to something that I'm walking towards, before counting steps to see if I was right. I do this all the time. During the heat of a turkey hunting battle it's easy to miscalculate how far away a bird might be standing due to surrounding brush and ground cover, terrain, weather, amount of daylight, etc., but if you actually practice estimating yardages year 'round it almost becomes second nature when you're hunting. Then, if you insist on waiting until the tom's definitely "in tight" before taking the shot, even a big mistake at crunch time still assures enough pattern density to make the kill.

The yardage data gleaned from my hunting journals will confirm that the longest shot I've ever taken which resulted in a dead turkey was 51 yards. For nearly an hour I had been internally debating about the distance out across that wide open fescue field, and my mind eventually convinced itself that the range to that strutter was "about 40 yards." When I stepped it off afterwards and realized what a terrible mistake I'd made, I felt both ashamed and incredibly lucky to have killed that tom. Then, after calming down from the excitement and sitting back at my setup tree to take another gander at where my fallen foe had been standing, I could hardly believe how *far* it looked! The mind can play some funny tricks on you in this cerebral game called turkey hunting, and that day really drove this fact home for me. Since then I've tried to be more aware of the potential for errors in judging distance while being stared-down by a big old gobbler.

It takes a strong constitution to wait for the close shot. A lot of people these days are not only undisciplined to resist temptation, but also willing to do whatever it takes to bring that turkey to bag. I think this is, unfortunately, reflected in the current advertising campaigns among certain ammo companies which highlight just how far their products can kill a gobbler. In my opinion this is both way off the mark, and going in the wrong direction.

Focusing the public's attention on maximizing their effective range is bound to result in an increase of crippling losses by anyone trying to push the limit of what these shells can consistently do, and I think as hunters we would be better served if these companies would instead stress the intimate nature of the sport and its excitement, along with the responsibility we have for making sure our opponent is up close before the shot is even taken. Their products should then be used to demonstrate how a dense and uniform pattern at *reasonable* ranges will put turkeys down for keeps in a quick and humane manner. Wouldn't it be great if these companies also made an attempt to actually dissuade the practice of long-range gunning, instead of encouraging it? But hey, that just silly talk coming from me - an opinionated old codger. In today's world flash sells, bigger is better, consistency is boring, and doing the right thing is obsolete.

On the positive side of the ammo industry, there is a new material called Tungsten Super Shot (or, TSS for short) which is a blend of metals that's actually heavier than lead. The beauty of this product is that it allows for the use of smaller-sized shot to attain the same or improved killing energy per pellet. Smaller shot means more projectiles per ounce, so not only do these loads hit harder, but they also result in a far greater number of pellet strikes to the kill zone of a turkey's brain and spinal column. That's a win-win proposition all the way around, and I think if used judiciously and at proper ranges this new material shows great promise for reducing misses and crippling losses. In short, it kills the crap out of turkeys, so I certainly applaud that.

Being heavier than lead, TSS also retains more downrange energy, and along with that comes an accompanying potential for killing birds much further than we ever thought possible beforehand. As stated earlier, this has been embraced and highlighted as a major selling point, but I strongly disagree with that. Ours is *not* a sport built on long-range marksmanship. The whole concept of turkey hunting is to see just how close you can lure in your opponent, and I think it's dishonorable to treat our quarry in any other way. Have you really won the game if 60 or 70 yards is as close as you can get to that gobbler? If it was all about killing him at any cost, then rifles would be legal and we'd just shoot our birds at 200 yards. That's not turkey hunting in my mind; it's ballistics. My old buddy Ron Ronk and I have a saying that reflects our deep-rooted feelings on this subject. Whenever we split up in the woods to go hunt our respective spots, we always tell one another to, "Call 'em close, and pound 'em in the face."

While I don't support using TSS in order to stretch the effective killing range of the initial shot, the superior aspects of its physical properties does offer advantages over more conventional pellets whenever an occasional yardage miscalculation occurs. Knowing that your shot charge carries enough downrange energy and pattern density to make up for mistakes made in range estimation can be a great confidence boost for anyone using this product, but again, if you focus on getting your turkeys in tight this needn't be much of a factor, at all. Still, I can certainly see the value of using TSS, and many of its proponents absolutely love the stuff.

There have only been a small handful of drastically wrong yardage estimates for me and my buddies over the years, but it does occasionally happen and I can see comfort in knowing that the ammo in your gun might compensate for a lapse in judgment by your brain. For example; out of the six shots that I've recorded which were taken at greater than 55 yards, there have been exactly zero kills made. Part of me wonders how many of those incidents would've turned out better if we'd been using TSS, but my honest opinion is that these shots were taken at ranges too danged far to begin with, and we didn't really deserve to kill any of the toms.

Although it sounds like I'm a firm believer in this "newfangled" stuff and its advantages of increased pellet numbers and subsequent killing power, I still have some reservations. The greatest of these concerns is cost. The price of this material is a *substantial* hindrance to it general acceptance. In fact, it's so danged expensive that only the most serious of reloaders are using it very much. That's a terrible shame. I personally don't shoot it because of that, but also because of the fact that I insist on killing all of my birds at short range. Why pay ten dollars or more per shell for TSS, when the factory loads that I shoot will kill my turkeys just as dead for only about a dollar apiece?

Hopefully, the cost will come down in the years ahead and make this material more affordable for the average hunter. If so, I might start using it, but for now I'll just "stick with the date what brung me." Or, to put it in the equally colorful words of that Missouri biologist who once described why his state didn't change their rules to legalize afternoon hunting, "if it ain't broke, don't fix it."

Let's now take a look at the chart below which displays the yardages and results of shots taken by me and my comrades in the past 35 years. I've published this only because it demonstrates some things that I've been talking about, and one of them is how we try to wait for a close shot. The chart makes it graphically obvious that the vast majority of trigger-pulls have occurred in the 15-35 yard bracket; in fact, it happens this way 83.5% of the time.

Shot Yardages (includes Fall archery)
Combined

Yardage	Shots	Graphic	Yardage	Shotgun Kill	Shotgun Miss	Shotgun Cripple	Archery Kill	Archery Miss	Archery Cripple
1	0		1						
2	1	x	2		1				
3	0		3						
4	1	x	4	1					
5	1	x	5		1				
6	2	xx	6	1			1		
7	2	xx	7	2					
8	4	xxxx	8	4					
9	2	xx	9	1					1
10	3	xxx	10	2	1				
11	6	xxxxxx	11	5				1	
12	8	xxxxxxxx	12	7				1	
13	10	xxxxxxxxxx	13	8					2
14	10	xxxxxxxxxx	14	7	1		2		
15	16	xxxxxxxxxxxxxxxx	15	12	4				
16	31	xxxxxxxxxxxxxxxxxxxxxxxxxxxxxxx	16	29	1				1
17	22	xxxxxxxxxxxxxxxxxxxxxx	17	20	2				
18	18	xxxxxxxxxxxxxxxxxx	18	15	1			2	
19	30	xxxxxxxxxxxxxxxxxxxxxxxxxxxxxx	19	23	3	1		3	
20	38	xxxxxxxxxxxxxxxxxxxxxxxxxxxxxxxxxxxxxx	20	31	6			1	
21	33	xxxxxxxxxxxxxxxxxxxxxxxxxxxxxxxxx	21	32	1				
22	37	xxxxxxxxxxxxxxxxxxxxxxxxxxxxxxxxxxxxx	22	31	2	2	1	1	
23	36	xxxxxxxxxxxxxxxxxxxxxxxxxxxxxxxxxxxx	23	34		1			1
24	46	xxxxxxxxxxxxxxxxxxxxxxxxxxxxxxxxxxxxxxxxxxxxxx	24	42	2	1	1		
25	37	xxxxxxxxxxxxxxxxxxxxxxxxxxxxxxxxxxxxx	25	33	5				
26	29	xxxxxxxxxxxxxxxxxxxxxxxxxxxxx	26	19	6	4			
27	30	xxxxxxxxxxxxxxxxxxxxxxxxxxxxxx	27	28	1			1	
28	26	xxxxxxxxxxxxxxxxxxxxxxxxxx	28	22	3	1			
29	27	xxxxxxxxxxxxxxxxxxxxxxxxxxx	29	25	2				
30	19	xxxxxxxxxxxxxxxxxxx	30	15	3	1			
31	20	xxxxxxxxxxxxxxxxxxxx	31	17	3				
32	21	xxxxxxxxxxxxxxxxxxxxx	32	18	2	1			
33	15	xxxxxxxxxxxxxxx	33	13		2			
34	15	xxxxxxxxxxxxxxx	34	11	2	2			
35	14	xxxxxxxxxxxxxx	35	9	5				
36	7	xxxxxxx	36	3	2	2			
37	5	xxxxx	37	5					
38	9	xxxxxxxxx	38	7	1	1			
39	3	xxx	39	1	1	1			
40	8	xxxxxxxx	40	6	1	1			
41	3	xxx	41	1	2				
42	2	xx	42	1					1
43	4	xxxx	43	2	2				
44	2	xx	44	1	1				
45	3	xxx	45	1	1	1			
46	3	xxx	46	2		1			
47	1	x	47		1				
48	2	xx	48	1		1			
49	0		49						
50	1	x	50		1				
51	1	x	51	1					
52	0		52						
53	0		53						
54	0		54						
55	3	xxx	55		2	1			
56	0		56						
57	1	x	57		1				
58	0		58						
59	1	x	59		1				
60	1	x	60		1				
	670	Average Yards Per Shot = 24.95 (16,715 Yards)		548	72	30	4	11	5

This is a portion of what my "Yardage Results Table" looks like.

Like I said before, my preferred Winchester Double X factory loads containing 1-3/4 ounces of #5 copper-plated lead shot kills turkeys dead as dead can be at these ranges, so I'm perfectly happy with their performance and not looking to change a thing. However, full disclosure dictates that I acknowledge other companies in the market making various shell combinations just as lethal as these, and I make no claims that my choice is anything other than that - my own personal choice, derived from *ample testing* at the gun range. Please note the highlighted portion of that last sentence, because it's the most important part.

Just as I have experimented a lot to find out what works best in my own firearms before settling on a brand and shell combination that gives me great results at both paper targets and live ones, so too should all of my fellow turkey hunters. A shotgun will actually show a "preference" for one particular brand/load of shell over others (even between individual guns of the same make and model), so it's paramount that we take the time and make an effort to sort that out before heading into the woods. What we're looking for is a shell that produces dense, uniform patterns with no holes or gaps. Although it only takes a single pellet in the "right" spot to kill a gobbler, I want to see a minimum of five delivered to the brain and/or spinal column *every single time* before I am happy with the results from a particular load, fired from any chosen range.

By testing your gun's pattern on turkey-head targets which are readily available at sporting goods stores or printable from the internet, you can tally the pellet holes in the kill zone of each shot to determine whether a particular load/choke combination is throwing a sufficiently dense pattern to attain the goal of five minimum hits where it counts the most - in the brain and spinal column. Start at 10 yards, and work your way out at 10 yard increments until you no longer achieve the minimum hits every time. That will tell you your maximum effective range. Why start so close? Because you'll occasionally have turkeys in that tight and you need to know exactly what your pattern looks like at that range, too. Hint: it's pretty darned small, so you'd better *aim* small.

As you can imagine, thoroughly patterning a gun with all the possible combinations of brands and loads can get complicated and entails some serious time and money. You don't have to test every one, and you can go online to find out what others have had success with to help narrow the focus, but the more you can test, the better. Once you've settled onto the right combination of choke for your gun, coupled with the brand and size of shell firing the type and size of pellet that gives the most optimum results, it will give you the confidence and capability to handle any situation that comes up during a turkey hunt. Even more importantly, you'll no longer be able to blame the inevitable misses on the gun or shells used, and you'll be forced to come to terms with what's called, "driver-error" - something that we will all need to face at some point. That's a vital part of maturing as a turkey hunter.

Seriously though; patterning your gun is an important task that shouldn't be taken lightly or ignored, and at the risk of repeating myself yet again, we owe it to the birds that we hunt to hit them with all the force necessary to administer a quick, humane death. The best way to assure that happening is by intimately knowing your weapon, its capabilities, *and* its limitations. Time and effort on the shooting range is the surest way to figure all of that out.

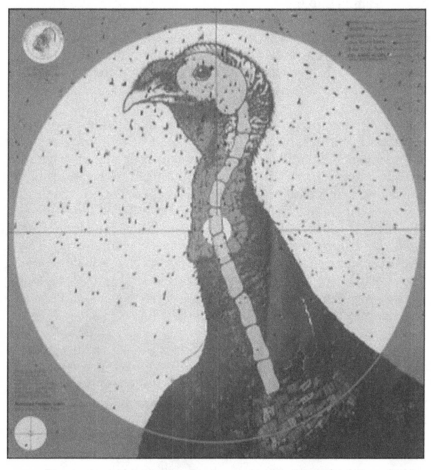

A good pattern on a turkey-head target demonstrates at least five pellet strikes to the brain and/or spinal column.

Referring back to my yardage chart, I think it's worth noting that the single range at which most shots have been taken is 24 yards. The total score from that distance is 42 kills, two misses, and a lost cripple – showing a pretty high percentage of kills at 93.3%. Another distance which has been particularly lethal is 23 yards; its 97% kill rate has been marked by only a single lost cripple to go along with 33 dead birds.

As for the worst results in the charts; 26 yards holds that distinction with a compilation of 19 kills and 10 lost birds (six misses and four cripples), for an effective kill rate of only 65.5%. I'm not at all able to explain how a couple of extra yards can logically account for the difference between the best and worst success rates, but I have a feeling that the yardage itself wasn't the issue. For example, at 20 yards there have also been six misses, coupled with 31 kills (83.7%). What that shows me is there was no obvious direct correlation between the range of the shot and lethality, so other factors must've been at play. Perhaps the sample just isn't large enough to provide any concrete answers for why certain yardages have higher miss/cripple counts. However, I do think you can look at what I might call the "extreme ranges" on this chart and draw one very solid conclusion: with only 10 dead birds out of 28 shots recorded beyond 40 yards, the meager success rate of 35.7% proves that ours is *not* a long-range sport.

Yet another way that I've used these charts is to calculate the average distance at which we shoot our turkeys, and after doing the math equations I've determined that it comes out to 24.95 yards. What this shows is a dedication to letting turkeys get "in tight," and I'm very happy about that. However, there is definitely such a thing as *too* close. I once shot at a turkey from a range of about five *feet*. He had been coming in to my calling down a sandy two-track in Oklahoma, but was then spooked by a road-hunter trying to drive up and kill him from his jeep. In running away from this bozo, the turkey headed straight towards me and passed my hide like he was Usane Bolt in the Olympics. I tried to take his head off as he sprinted on by kicking up sand into a roostertail, but I missed. Luckily, I killed him the next morning. Even better; he was banded!

Anyways; I digress. The most important thing that I want to stress in this chapter is that every one of us should strive to know exactly what our chosen weapon and load can do at any reasonable yardage. That can only come from shooting and practicing a lot on the range.

Familiarity breeds confidence in knowing that a trigger-pull will get the job done every single time, and it will definitely result in an overall reduction of misses and cripples. Attaining the highest lethality rate should be, after all, the ultimate goal.

Please trust me when I say here that the only feeling in turkey hunting which is worse than missing a tom completely is when you cripple one that's never recovered. It's imperative that we do everything within our power to avoid both of those scenarios, or at the very least, reduce their occurrence. The best way to accomplish that is with a combination of diligently practiced yardage estimation, thorough testing of our guns and ammo, and striving to make every shot count. We owe it to our noble adversary to do so, and we owe it to ourselves to be responsible and diligent in trying to live up to a higher standard.

Ok; I think it's time to go hunting again. Let's pick back up where we last ended in the field, and see how things went in 1999.

This New York tom was taken with a tight patterning shotgun. In duck hunting parlance, he's definitely a "beaker!"

CHAPTER 11

Partying Like It's 1999 –
Turkey Hunting Style

The previous spring had been an "El Nino" year, which means that it was very wet and full of powerful storms. Wet years also mean lots of bugs in the first state I hunt every year (Florida), and they had been absolutely horrible during that 1998 season. The swarms of gnats, mosquitos, and deer flies made for very difficult hunting; so bad, in fact, that I still consider the trip to be the toughest and most brutal of the 28 times Florida has found itself included on my annual itinerary.

The one good thing about this type of a weather pattern is that it's cyclical, with an El Nino event typically followed by a much dryer season call a "La Nina." Such was the case in 1999, and during the eight days that I hunted down there the soles of my boots never even got wet. That enabled me to much more easily traverse the swamps and cypress strands that make up the majority of Green Swamp WMA, and it also resulted in a *serious* reduction in the number of bugs encountered. In fact, not once in all those days and

169

nights of hunting and camping in some of Florida's most notorious swamps and thickets did I so much as get bitten by a single mosquito. Best of all, the buffalo gnats were non-existent! While the previous season could've easily been classified as a living hell, 1999 was pure, unadulterated heaven in comparison.

The turkey hunting was great that year also, and I quickly killed a pair of excellent toms which each sported spurs measuring 1- 3/8 inches. Other folks in our camp were having quite a bit of success too, and although both Frank Emert and Larry Sharp failed to make a return appearance, I was able to get in on some of that action, as well. For instance, I helped Rick Brown recover a tom that he'd shot with a bow from a thick stand of palmettos, and then I called in toms for a couple of his friends. The second of these was for a fellow named Steve Fincher.

Rick Brown's public land archery Osceola - a true trophy bird if ever there was one!

Steve stands about 6'10." He's an ex-baseball player who spent time with the St Louis Cardinals and the New York Yankees before blowing out his elbow in the days prior to "Tommy John Surgery," but in his prime, he'd been throwing fastballs at around the 100-mph range. Steve kept us entertained with colorful stories of life in the major leagues, and one that I found infinitely interesting was how he described throwing so hard and creating so much torque on the mound that he would blow out a size 18 shoe by the 5th inning of every game that he pitched. The enormous hiking boots needed to cover those gargantuan feet were quite a sight to behold in turkey camp too, and it didn't take long before we all started calling him, "Sasquatch."

Well, Sasquatch and I were hunting one day and easing along a firebreak lined with gallberry bushes when I froze in mid-stride - I had heard the distinct and unmistakable "pfffft...dmmmMMM" of a drumming turkey! I could tell that this bird was real close. In fact, it sounded like he might even be just on the other side of those gallberries beside us, which were quite a bit taller than my head. When I turned and whispered this information to Steve, he merely straightened up into an erect posture, looked over the top of the bushes, raised his gun, and killed the tom strutting 30 yards away. Being a rookie, he hadn't realized that this was impossible...

After leaving all of my Florida friends behind, I next traveled to Mississippi. I had never been there before, but having long heard tales of how good the turkey hunting was in all of the southern states, I was eager to add this one to my lifetime resume. Although I started out anxious and full of hope for quickly punching some tags, twelve days later I limped on out of there totally beaten down and tattered - both physically, and mentally.

During that eternity spent in Mississippi, I only heard four turkeys gobble in total, and while I did manage to call one of these in and kill him on Day 10, for the most part it had been a miserable experience of long days hunting in hot, humid, rainy weather. And snakes – let's not forget the snakes. I saw more cursed cottonmouth moccasins than I'd imagined in my worst nightmares! Overall, I was not impressed by my first visit to the Magnolia State.

Now, let's be clear; I can take just about any hardships encountered when turkey hunting, and tough out adverse conditions for as long as it takes for things to turn around. But, I've got to know there are actually birds in the neighborhood. Hunting for days on end without hearing any gobbling, or even finding much sign, is pure torture for me. After enough time has passed I will invariably catch myself grumbling to the turkey gods; urging them to just put me in the game. I don't mind riding the pine once in a while, but I sure can't change the outcome of the contest if I'm not in it!

This Mississippi tom finally fell after 10 days of tough hunting.

Sometimes, the difficulties encountered are simply due to a dearth of live turkeys in the area I'm hunting. This can be especially so on public land late in the season. If there isn't any gobbling going on whatsoever, you just don't know for sure if you're hunting gobblers, or ghosts of birds already killed by someone else. Working hard without positive results can be very frustrating, and the aggravation tends to build upon itself by the hour. I freely admit to becoming a little "toxic" and surly in those situations, but inevitably, at some point I'll realize that the worst day hunting beats the hell out of the best day working, and that helps calm me down.

Such was the case after leaving Mississippi, and it didn't hurt my improving attitude one bit that the next destination on my schedule was an awesome place where I'd hunted the previous year - Kentucky's Higginson-Henry WMA. This stop would also give me the chance to spend some more fun times with Larry Sharp and his family, which was reason enough for uplifted spirits. These fine folks are like kin to me, and there is never a dull moment when we're around each other. Larry is now retired, but at the time he was the manager of this WMA. His lovely and sweet bride Barbara is also one of the premier cooks with whom I've ever had the distinct pleasure of dining, and their sons Kenneth and Philip are both consummate woodsmen and cold-blooded killers of everything that walks, flies, or swims in the out of doors. It's always a good time when we get together, and I cherish their friendships greatly.

My old buddy Ron Ronk was also in attendance that year, but this time we would be hunting separate from one another. By now he already had a couple of archery toms under his belt and no longer needed my help. Plus, I was bound and determined to get my first turkey killed with the stick and string, and I thought my chances were better if I went at it solo. I've always preferred hunting turkeys one-on-one, anyway. It frees my mind up to do whatever it takes and whenever I choose to do it, without worrying about coming to a meeting of the minds with someone else. Besides that, as much as we love each other like brothers, Ron and I never seem to agree on anything when we're hunting together. He's one of my dearest friends in the whole world, but we get along better in camp than we do in the tight confines of a turkey blind.

I had purchased my own ground blind the previous year. It was much smaller and easier to assemble than the Leroy Braungarte model which Ron owned, and that fact alone allowed for a more mobile style of hunting. I tend towards being rather aggressive in how close I like to set up on gobbling toms, and I'm also prone to moving often as conditions and tactics dictate. This smaller version of a blind seemed to better suit my style, and on the second day of the hunt its advantages became abundantly clear.

Dawn broke with no turkeys gobbling near me, even though I could hear four or five just ripping it across the road. However, these were all in Ron's hunting area, so my only option was to sit tight and hope something wandered my way. When nothing came of that sedentary plan by lunchtime, I decided to move operations to a completely different part of the WMA.

Not a hundred yards after hiking out of the parking lot with my portable blind hanging from a shoulder strap, I rounded a corner in the road and came face-to-face with a pair of strutting toms. Neither of them seemed particularly alarmed by the sight of me, and merely eased off through the woods to the west, so after giving them time to clear out I continued on up the trail towards the sound of at least two other birds gobbling their brains out. They were hammering enthusiastically like it was the break of day, when in fact, it was 2:30 in the afternoon.

Before too long I'd snuck in tight, and in less than a minute I had my blind set up about 75 yards from the closest of these gobblers. I could tell from the very first call on my Cane Creek slate that this turkey was going to play the game right. It also became readily apparent that he wasn't alone, when at least two of his buddies stepped all over anything I had to say, as well.

For the next 15 minutes this trio of hot toms just about ripped the woods apart with intense gobbling. As they gradually drew nearer, their drumming began booming louder and louder, too - causing my knees to start shaking uncontrollably. The sound of sticks breaking just over the knoll between us kept me honed in on their exact path of approach, and even before that first bright red, white, and blue head popped into view at about 20 yards, I was already locked, loaded, and staring intently. A second tom soon followed the first one over the hilltop, and when they each then stepped behind big white oaks at the same time, it gave me the opportunity to reach full draw.

The range was 14 yards when the leader strutted out from behind his oak. My sight pin naturally settled directly amidships of his big black body, and as he turned around to face his buddy, my fingers instinctively knew the time was right to let the string slip from their tips. As the arrow met flesh it made a resounding "WHACK." The tom flew straight up into the air, but he immediately came right back down to earth on the other side of the knoll. The third, unseen tom gobbled at him when he landed, and this was followed immediately by the sound of heavy wings flogging each other as they began to fight. The tom still standing in front of me hustled back over the contour to join the unseen melee, and a double gobble blasted out when he reached the scene of the battle.

Further off to the east another bird answered this challenge, and he soon began rapid-fire gobbling all on his own. Over the next ten minutes the toms beside me gobbled back at him every time he said anything, while steadily moving away in his direction. I was just certain that the victim of my shot was lying dead where he'd landed out of sight, so I waited patiently for his living, gobbling companions to wander off. After all, I still had a second tag in my pocket, and this seemed like a pretty darned good area to hunt the next day. I didn't want to booger any of these other toms if I could help it.

Finally, I could stand the suspense no more. My knees had almost quit knocking by then, so I exited the blind to go recover my prize. Can you imagine how surprised I was when he wasn't lying there in the leaves? Shocked, perplexed, and heartbroken were how I felt when all I saw was a single cut feather. That just didn't seem possible; I had seen the arrow protruding from his side after the shot, and I knew that the razor-sharp 100-grain Rathaar Snuffer broadhead should've opened up a good-sized hole in his hide. Where were all the feathers such a wound would be expected to produce, and why no blood?

I quickly moved downhill to see if I could intercept the departing toms and determine if my crippled bird was in their company. Their frequent gobbles made that an easy thing to do, and I found them strutting in a wide-open mowed field. Sure enough, there were only two toms present, with neither of them showing any sign of being wounded. Obviously, the targeted bird must've peeled off to go die alone.

Hustling back to my blind, I commenced doing a more diligent search. It didn't take long to discover what I had at first overlooked, because a few yards beyond the point where I'd found that single cut feather, there were several more of them - along with quite a bit of blood. The splashes of crimson left an easy trail to follow, and there was so much of it that I couldn't see any way for a turkey to survive the loss of that much of his vital bodily fluids. But, where was he?

The woods ahead were clean and open, with no dead turkey anywhere to be seen. Tracking the bird all the way out of the woodlot, I came to a large field of Big Bluestem, and while the trail was harder to follow in there, occasional splashes of crimson were still fairly frequent. On I went, often down to hands and knees looking for specks of blood, until finally, I glanced ahead through the tall grass and spotted my gobbler sprawled out in full glory - dead as a wedge. He had gone an amazing 240 yards after the shot!

Immediately, I became elated, proud as a peacock, and thrilled beyond all reasonable measure. The initial shot had been a little low and a little far back from perfect, but the broadhead had still nicked the liver and caused massive bleeding. It didn't even seem possible that a bird could travel so far after suffering such a devastating wound, but he most certainly had done just that very thing. Yet again, for the umpteenth time of my life, I shook my head in amazement at the toughness and tenacity of the wild turkey.

For the next week I tried to fill a second tag, but the weather turned cold, rainy, and windy as could be. I also made a series of boo-boo's and blunders seemingly every day, and ran off a number of gobblers in a wide variety of ways. Oh, well; that's turkey hunting - especially so with a bow. Despite all the hardships, trials, and tribulations, it had been a good hunt. Furthermore, I left for home happy and content, because I'd racked up my first archery tom.

My first archery tom.

I arrived later that afternoon at Tea Mountain Lodge in Brown County, Indiana for our annual get together with Tom and Don Foley, DeWayne and Russ Feltner, Joe Harrod, Bill Udderback, Bruce Wilson, and an assortment of other "characters." DeWayne, Russ, and Bruce always liked to set up their own tent camp in one section of the property, and they would traditionally cook dinner for everyone there on the Tuesday before our season opened the next morning. One of the dishes we ate that night was "coot kabobs" made by Bruce. They didn't sit very well in my stomach, and by 1a.m. I was puking my guts out. I was still violently ill when morning broke.

Of course, immediate suspicion was cast towards Bruce for poisoning me in order to gain access to the section of the property that Donny and I always hunted. I wasn't having any of that – despite how close to death I felt, we headed out there, anyway. I really should've just stayed in bed, because the day ended up being a total wash. Time and again we worked turkeys, only to come away empty handed. Finally, I felt so weak and rotten inside that I couldn't take it anymore, so I limped on back to the cabin, where I was soon sweating under a thick pile of covers. I didn't stand upright again until 5 a.m. the next morning. This meant that I had missed out on a golden opportunity to exact some revenge on Bruce, since Wednesday was my night for cooking fried wild turkey strips and morel mushrooms.

I was still feeling pretty green around the gills, but for the second day in a row Don and I headed out to our preferred north-eastern quadrant of the property. Once again we failed miserably in dealing with the turkeys in that sector, even though we heard lots of birds gobbling. I blamed all of our failures on my partner, who had decided to take over the calling duties that spring and henceforth ran every turkey we encountered into the next county. Likewise, he blamed me for my highly-suspect, "expert" guiding abilities. Nobody else in camp killed anything either, so maybe all of us just sucked at the turkey hunting game. It didn't matter, though - every single one of us harvested a limit of good times, and we all took home lots of lasting memories. I also came away with some valuable Intel for future get-togethers; never again would I eat anything Bruce Wilson cooked!

With the Tea Mountain shenanigans now behind us for another year, I turned my attention to the Amish farms of Jefferson County where I would be guiding for the next couple of weeks. The first bird we killed down there was shot by ophthalmologist Frank Emert. Although we had hunted together quite a bit since he'd operated on my eyes in 1994, and several of his friends had killed birds on those trips, this was the first tom actually shot by Dr. Frank while in my company. Of course, full disclosure dictates reporting that he'd missed a couple of others prior to our 1999 success, but it did feel good to get him on the positive side of the scoreboard.

Several days later I took three of the Amish boys hunting at the same time, and all three of them ended up shooting jakes. None of these guys (Joe, Ervin, and Soloman Wickey, Jr.) did much hunting to begin with, so they were all perfectly thrilled to bring home young, fresh turkeys for their families to eat. That was fine by me, too, because any turkey is a trophy if the hunter believes it to be true. However, the next bird to fall was certainly worthy of special recognition; it was shot by Gary Shepherd, and went 25.5 lbs. on the Manville General Store scales. A gobbler that big is a pig of a turkey anywhere you go, and Gary was really proud of him. Bill Powers was Gary's partner on that trip, following the death of Louie Rusch. Bill is a doctor from Lyons, Indiana. He's really fun to hunt with because of his fascinating stories recounted from the pursuit of game all over the world, and while he didn't get his turkey with me on that particular trip, a return the following week took care of that.

Gary Shepherd and Bill Powers

With a day finally to myself, I took the opportunity to hunt on a new farm for the first time and killed a fine, long-spurred old tom that led me on a marathon hunt over hill and dale. It was a real chess match of a contest, and in the end I used a technique that I'd never tried before. I can't unequivocally say whether it was the turning point in the duel, or even if it worked at all, but when this bird hung up for the last time at about 60 yards I began spitting and drumming with my voice. Maybe this didn't affect the outcome either way, but the circumstantial evidence strongly points to it helping to turn the tide. What had been a five-hour battle of stubbornness up to that point culminated ten minutes later in a 21-yard chip-shot.

The next hunt will live on in my memory banks forever, and not just because it ended in another dead turkey. This was a remarkable day for a number of reasons, including the company with whom I was privileged to keep - not just one, nor two, but three women. All three of these bright, beautiful, sweet gals deserve a chapter of their own in this book, but we don't have the space for that. Suffice to say that I, as their guide and supposed guru, was the one who learned the most that day, and I consider myself to be a better person (and hunter) because of the experience. Hunting with women is so very unlike hunting with other guys; they are enlightening, refreshing, and lend a whole new outlook to things which I had heretofore taken for granted.

One of these gals (Christine Gerace) had previously hunted with me a couple of times, and in fact, had killed her first bird in 1997 while in the company of Frank Emert, Eric Coonrod, and myself. Christine is an absolute peach of a person, a joy to be around, and an extremely talented massage therapist living in Michigan. Another (De) is now the wife of Ron Ronk, but at that time she was a highly trained and fully capable wildlife biologist in her own right. Since then she's taken on a whole new career as a nurse, and excels at that, too. De is also a marvelous chef, smart as a whip, and I admire her on a whole plethora of levels. The third woman to accompany us that day was Joanne Stacy. Joanne is married to Mark, who only hunts with hawks that he catches himself. They are both fantastic people.

I was really hoping to help Joanne take her first turkey. In fact, she had sort of been my "project" for the year, because I just knew in my heart what a thrill she would gain from the experience. Joanne is also a massage therapist like Christine, and she's one of the sweetest, kindest, and most wonderful humans I've ever met. I was anxious to share the experience of her first turkey hunt, and looking forward to hearing/seeing things from her perspective.

Little did I realize at the time what an overload of "perspective" I would get from hunting with all three of these incredible women at the same time!

De had already taken a bird on her family's farm down in southern Indiana, so she was coming along as my co-guide. That meant Christine and Joanne both carried guns, but CG knew that our number one priority was to help Joanne pull the trigger. Our hunt was set to occur in Sullivan County, on the Minnehaha Fish and Wildlife Area, since this was close to where all three of these women lived and it had a good turkey population.

We chose to hunt the Busseron Bottoms area of this property, since nobody else had checked into this spot and it always held turkeys. However, not a peep greeted our ears at daylight, and while none of the gals were the least bit disappointed in that development, I certainly was. I wanted action, and I wanted Joanne to experience the thrill that gobbling produces in a hunter's heart at the crack of dawn. But, that's not what we got, so off we tramped in quest of a cooperative tom.

Finally, at about 6:30 a.m., I heard a bird gobbling good all on his own. We closed the distance just as quickly and quietly as four sets of feet could travel in a crunchy hardwoods bottom, and after wading across a shallow slough we snuck up onto dry ground much closer than I had thought possible - only about a hundred yards separated us from the loudmouthed tom, who was going absolutely ballistic. He sounded very lonely, and very workable.

While Joanne and I crawled on hands and knees to a big soft maple ten yards ahead of us, CG and De did likewise to another great setup tree twenty yards to our right. Things were looking good and I was actually starting to let myself believe that we could get this thing done as I slid into place and pointed to where I wanted Joanne to sit beside me. Then, I watched in abject horror as she stood upright and walked around the tree to get there. Big mistake! All gobbling immediately ceased, and a couple seconds later I caught a glimpse of the tom running off down through the bottoms like a ghost was chasing him. Bummer; boogering this tom wasn't really Joanne's fault, but rather my own, because I had failed to brief her beforehand that wild turkeys have absolutely zero curiosity when it comes to hominoids walking upright…

180

Ordinarily, one might think that a hunt was over-and-done after scaring off a turkey in such a manner, but this bird was hot as a firecracker and I thought the odds were decent that he wasn't entirely finished for the day. Joanne and I went over to quietly discuss our options with the other girls, and I told them all how I felt things might still play out if we just gave the tom some time to calm down.

Sure enough, 25 minutes later De said that she heard a gobble far away on the same compass bearing as his departure, so we hustled 150 yards in that direction and stopped to listen. When nothing else was heard we made another quick move of about the same distance, and that brought us within hearing range of the old boy, who was once again bellowing out rapid-fire gobbles in the same manner as when we'd originally found him.

This time I planned our setup more conservatively by stopping a couple hundred yards short, and from there I worked the tom gently by only answering him at the tail end of his gobbles. I probably needn't have been so timid with my calling, but after scaring the bejesus out of this tom once, I sure didn't want to risk running him into another zip code!

The strategy obviously worked, because after my second answering yelp the tom ripped off four gobbles in a row and immediately began coming our way. He then started veering off to the left, but one soft yelp turned him right around and on he came, seemingly gobbling with every five yards of advancement. When he again started drifting off course I brought him right back with a final yelp, and this time he stayed true and strutted into sight directly in line with Joanne's gun barrel. At 28 yards she shot him dead as a wedge - that's when the yelling, squealing, dancing, and rejoicing commenced. Joanne was giddy, De was thrilled, and CG was simply CG; euphoric as always. Me? I was the recipient of a lot of hugs from three beautiful women, so what do you think?

For the rest of the morning we wandered around admiring flowers and trees and insects and all of the beauty that surrounds us but which is too often overlooked or at least taken for granted, and then we went and showed off the fruits of our hunting prowess to everyone who didn't get out of the way quickly enough. I'm quite serious when I say that seeing this hunt unfold through those gals' eyes was an enlightening experience for me, and I enjoyed it *immensely*.

My Great Grandma Bertha used to own a restaurant in Franklin, Indiana. This place was a seedy little dive of a greasy-spoon diner that had a variety of cute/snide/abrasive signs hanging all over the interior walls. One of them is still vivid in my mind's eye to this very day, and its written message fits nicely with how this hunt felt to me, so I'll try to describe the sign thusly: two toddlers are standing side by side wearing only diapers - one is a boy, and the other a girl. They have each pulled the front of their own diaper out away from their bellies and are gazing straight down at what's between their legs. The caption reads simply, "There IS a Difference!" No truer words have ever been written, and they don't refer simply to the physical aspects of our respective sexes. It was an honor to share a different perspective with these three very special ladies.

De Ronk, Joanne Stacy, and Christine Gerace with Joanne's tom.

In the remaining days of our 1999 Indiana turkey season I success-fully called birds in for Dr. Bill Powers (his first Indiana wild turkey) and my cousin Bob Torrance. My general theory on calling in those days was to try and not say any more than enough, and no more than what was needed. I still think that's generally a pretty good creed to live by in the turkey woods, although there are certainly times when I'll let 'er rip in earnest. The most important element in my mind is to strive for making whatever sounds you utter "real" in terms of tone and cadence, and to actually *say* something instead of just making turkey noises. Attempting to share an actual dialog with the birds works much better than simply replicating the gibberish that you've learned by listening to TV shows and "experts" on cd's, and the more you can do that, the successful'er you'll be.

One more interesting hunt occurred on the final day of the Hoosier season, and it was shared with Ron "Pee-Wee" Day, who had been a friend of my cousin Bob for many years. Pee-Wee owned a small farm in Eagle Hollow, which lies just outside the town of Madison, Indiana. He was a retired iron worker by trade, and had raced winged sprint cars for many years. Riding around countless dirt tracks strapped to those loud engines had left him very hard-of-hearing, but he was always funny, mischievous, and quick with a joke. He was also country through and through and good people all around, so we struck up an immediate friendship the first time we met back in '96. Although he loved to hunt and had done some horseback big game excursions out west earlier in his life, the wild turkeys that were stacked up on his farm like cordwood hadn't ever interested him very much - that is, until Bob had told him how exciting the sport got when a strutting gobbler was whirling around in front of your gun barrel.

I had periodically taken Pee-Wee out hunting since our initial introduction, but every single turkey I called up for him (and there were several) had been subsequently run off by the old coot. We'd be sitting there side by side with a tom gobbling his fool head off 50 yards away, and Pee-Wee wouldn't have the slightest clue that a turkey was within a mile of us. I'd then lean over and practically shout in his ear for him to get ready, but about the time our tom was stepping into sight I'd see Pee-Wee's head swing around to face me while loudly asking, "WHAT DID YOU SAY?" He never heard the alarm putts that this always caused, but I sure did!

I think a variation of this same scenario had happened three or four times, but now I had a new secret weapon that I was sure would turn the tide in our favor - my archery blind. The potential that this item held for helping to hide Pee-Wee's inopportune movements at crucial moments was just the ticket we needed, and I couldn't wait to try it out. When we finally got a chance to hunt together again on the last Sunday of the 1999 season, I was stoked and chomping at the bit to see if we could finally break the spell of bad luck that had doomed all of our previous attempts.

The weather that day was perfect; crisp and cool at dawn, with no wind or clouds and a high of about 70 degrees by afternoon. Pee-Wee raised goats and a few horses on his narrow farm of mostly very steep terrain bracketing either side of a pasture running through a main hollow. The turkeys usually roosted high on either ridgeline, but they would wander downward as the day progressed. For several reasons, I thought it best to just set up our blind in the pasture and await their arrival.

First of all, turkeys were definitely going to show up in that field at some point, and although I suspected that a heavy dew might delay their arrival in the pasture grass, it was almost a foregone conclusion that they *would* be there eventually.

Secondly, Pee-Wee was no spring chicken, and while he was in great shape for his age and wired tight as a banjo string, those danged ridges were *steep*. As my cousin Bob would gladly attest, chasing turkeys up and down them was a major chore to best be avoided if at all possible. Why climb those cursed hillsides when we could sit around in easy chairs on flat ground, inside a comfortable blind, and await the toms' arrival?

Thirdly, Pee-Wee was just about the noisiest person whom I ever took hunting, and while he wasn't a big man, the guy could make more racket while walking a hundred yards through the woods than a small herd of elk might generate in a week. Why chance spooking every bird on the farm, if we could help it?

For all of these reasons and more (the most obvious being Pee-Wee's deafness, and the accompanying need for loud talking and movement in order to get him facing where the turkeys were coming from), I felt like our best bet was to hang loose in the pasture and see how the morning progressed.

Sure enough, when dawn broke there was a tom on either side of the farm. They were gobbling very well, and I really had to fight the urge to hot-foot it uphill to get in tight on the one east of us. This bird was going absolutely berserk, but we held our ground.

Eventually, both turkeys flew down and began traveling away from us to the north - gobbling as they went. I quickly realized that we'd soon find ourselves sitting all alone in a pasture that was soaking wet and thus probably not overly attractive to a couple of birds who were out looking for female companionship, so a move seemed necessary.

Quickly dismantling the blind, we headed up the hollow. Our route took us in-between and parallel to both toms' departure paths. After hiking out beyond them quite a ways, Pee-Wee and I began climbing east to get on the same level as the firecracker-hot tom up there. By now he'd found a spot which pleased him, and commenced gobbling practically non-stop.

Once we'd attained his contour level we crept back towards him a little bit, stopping at a safe distance to get situated in the blind undetected. I really thought we were in perfect position, and the first time I touched a call the tom triple-gobbled in response. At that point I hushed to give him a chance to come looking for us, and that is exactly what he did, too - drumming loudly the whole way. I knew Pee-Wee couldn't hear that beautiful music, but I sure could, and I kept him apprised of the tom's position with taps on the shoulder and a finger pointed in the appropriate direction.

Once the tom had closed to about 25 yards and was just out of sight below the lip of the ridgeline, he gobbled. Pee-Wee actually heard the sound this time, and his eyes grew wide with excitement. Less than a minute later I saw a bright white orb rising above the contour line with a whole lot of black feathers following it. When the tom's neck reached full extended height I made a trigger-pulling motion with my finger, and two seconds later Pee-Wee's gun roared - sending the turkey blasting into space like his feet were on fire and his ass was catching.

Well, we both just sat there for a few stunned moments. Then, we began recreating the hunt in not-so-quiet whispers. Pee-Wee admitted that he knew his gun shot high, but in the excitement of the moment he'd forgotten to account for it. Up to this point of the season my clients were a perfect 10-for-10, so this miss was disappointing. However, I didn't feel too awfully bad, because I knew it had been a total whiff at close range, and we needn't worry about a crippled bird. Pee-Wee was thrilled with the hunt, so that made it all worthwhile – kill, or miss.

Then, while we were sitting there jaw-jacking, a turkey gobbled on our ridgeline. Pee-Wee of course never heard it, but I most certainly did, and I told him of this new development while in the act of gathering up our stuff. I briefly considered going down to the farmhouse first to get my own gun and swap it out for Pee-Wee's high-shooting Remington 870, but man, haven't I already mentioned how steep and tall these ridges were? Instead, I just reminded him to aim lower the next time, before shuffling off to close the distance.

Stopping shorter than I ordinarily would due to the human noise-making machine breaking branches behind me, I quickly got the blind set up and we began working this new bird. He wasn't nearly as cooperative as the first one, but after about an hour of gentle persuasion mixed in with lots of scratching in the leaves on my part, the tom finally half-strutted up to 28 yards. He then stood there looking around like he was powerfully confused and ready to go back the way he'd come, so once again I gave Pee-Wee the universal hand signal for "pull that damned trigger."

The concussion of the shotgun blast sent Pee-Wee careening backwards against the wall of the blind. It didn't collapse around us, but it sure knocked everything asunder! Hence, it was a few seconds before I could get my face up to one of the windows in hopes of seeing a dead turkey flopping around in the leaves. Unfortunately, I saw nothing of the sort. I assumed at the time that the bird was just lying out of sight below the edge of the hillside, but after we got out of the blind and went to retrieve him, there wasn't anything there to fetch. Yes; Pee-Wee had just missed his second turkey of the day! Only my buddy Ron Ronk had attained that particular infamous distinction with me prior.

Pee-Wee and I then made an attempt at a tri-fecta when I called in another tom on the way back to the house. Fortunately, this one only came sneaking by at about 75 yards before quickly fading away. I say "fortunate," because I'm not sure if either of our hearts could've taken another exciting calamity.

Following Pee-Wee's display of exemplary marksmanship on the last day of Indiana's 1999 spring turkey season, I set off to further pursue my goal of killing turkeys in all the eastern states that interested me. Next up on that list was one where I had never hunted before: Ohio. This neighboring state had long intrigued me, but their spring season always overlapped with ours to a large degree, and I'd never been able to squeeze in a trip there during my annual state-hopping schedule.

I was really anxious see what the southern part of that state might have to offer, so I headed to their Wayne National Forest. I'm sure you can imagine my surprise when I spotted a big sign along the highway as I neared my destination which depicted a flying gobbler. Underneath this image was a written claim for how this particular county was the premier turkey hunting destination in the entire state. At that moment I felt like I might've made the right choice in regards to a starting spot, and those feelings were certainly strengthened the next day when I shot my first Ohio gobbler.

The hunt for this tom had been a very satisfying battle lasting several hours, but what really stands out years later is the bird's physical condition. Even though he appeared healthy and robust while gobbling and strutting all morning long, at some earlier point of time he'd had an accident while flying pretty darned fast. That was evidenced by a stick impaled all the way though his thigh! About an inch of this 5/8″ diameter stob protruded out the back side, while five inches of it were still sticking out the front. Stranger still was the fact that the wounds were totally healed up, with no sign of infection or gang green. It's hard telling how long the tom had carried this foreign object imbedded in his flesh, but he certainly didn't appear to be suffering in any appreciable way.

Three days later I filled my second Ohio tag only nine minutes before their noon quitting time, and when I looked at my journal afterwards I realized that he was also a milestone bird - my 100th springtime tom. It had been 17 years since I'd started into this maddening compulsion, and even though sheer numbers weren't then, and certainly aren't now important to me, in the grand scheme of things I felt pretty darned good about where I was at in my evolution as a turkey hunter.

I sat there for a little while thinking about my mentor Bill Madden - reflecting on his wry smile and imagining what words of wisdom he might offer if still alive today. Bill and my Dad were both incredible men with vast knowledge about the ways and habits of wild creatures, and all I'd ever wanted as a young lad was to be like them. I still don't believe that I'll ever attain their level of wisdom for the natural world, but sitting there beside my dead gobbler and contemplating it all made me feel like I was on the right path.

Those positive feelings were still running strong when I arrived in West Virginia later that afternoon. Brimming confidence and an ideal weather report for the coming week had me really looking forward to once again hunting in one of my favorite states. What could possibly go wrong?

A fine Ohio tom taken on public land.

The next morning dawned magnificent, even if I didn't hear a single gobble. Then, it got even better when I walked up on a brood of ruffed grouse poults and their angry mother, who tried to lure me away from them with the old "broken wing" trick. Her babies were itty-bitty tiny, and finding their nest just 15 feet away led me to believe that they had hatched from their eggs only hours earlier. I could've bent down and caught every single one of those 10 little bundles of fuzz, but of course, I knew that it was best for them if I quickly snuck away and let their mother lead them to safety.

That encounter with another of my favorite gamebirds left me grinning and feeling light-hearted as I traipsed on looking for turkeys, but after five seasons of hard luck in this state, I should've known better than to get too upbeat. West Virginia is a very cruel mistress – despite how deeply I love her beauty, she obviously hates me with a passion unbound.

Troubles started the very next day after I worked long and hard to finally bring a tom to within easy gun range. Inexplicably, I then pulled the shot to the right and crippled him. The question of why I hadn't putted loudly to stop his walking progress before taking the shot left me shaking my head in wonder. It seemed like I was always doing stupid stuff when hunting in this state, and I felt frustration building in my gut.

Many hours of unsuccessful searching later, I was still mentally kicking myself and questioning why things always went awry in this place. It felt like I was possessed by a self-perpetuating fear of failure which guaranteed disaster. In other words, I was so nervous of screwing up that this is exactly what happened every single time the opportunity presented itself. Confidence certainly breeds confidence in the turkey woods, but the opposite is equally true.

I had previously committed to driving seven hours home for an important pool tournament, so I left that evening. Then, I turned right around and came back to West Virginia. A couple days later I was on my way to town for supplies and a hot shower when I spotted a teenage boy and girl sitting on a guard-rail along the highway. I took notice because they had fishing poles leaned up beside them and a tackle box at their feet. The stream running along the highway looked like awesome trout water, and I wondered why they weren't down there fishing. When I returned along that same route three hours later, they were still in the same place, so I stopped to see if there was a problem.

These super-nice kids (boyfriend and girlfriend, aged 18 and 17), told me that their Grandpa was supposed to pick them up hours earlier, but he'd never shown. I offered to give them a ride, and they hopped in my van. The young man's name was Mark Cutlip, and when he spotted all of my turkey hunting gear, he excitedly began relating how his own hunts all season long had garnered zero success. He said there were at least three big gobblers living behind his Grandpa's house, but no matter what he tried, they wouldn't come close enough to give him a shot. It seemed only decent and fitting that I ask if he wanted some help.

Once we got to their home I found out that Mark and his Dad lived with an old man who wasn't really related to them, but whom they called, "Grandpa" nonetheless. His truck had broken down, so that was why he hadn't shown up to fetch "the kids." It didn't take long to realize that this family was barely getting by; in common parlance, they didn't have so much as a pot to piss in. However, they were incredibly friendly and sincerely nice people who made me feel welcome.

At dawn, Mark and I stood on a high ridge behind the barn, and my first owl hoot started a bird gobbling about 500 yards away.

"That's where he always gobbles from," said my hunting companion, "but he never comes any closer."

"Well, we've got to cut the distance," I told him.

"I always just call from here," he replied.

"And how's that been working for you," I asked?

Off we went, and before too long found ourselves set up about 125 yards away from the tom, who was still in the roost and ripping it up practically non-stop. Time ticked on by as he continued to belt out gobble after gobble. "Aren't you gonna call," Mark asked? "I call a lot."

"Tell me again how that strategy has been going," I whispered with a wink.

Turkeys had been flying down around 6:10 a.m., but by 6:22 the tom was still treebound and seemingly content to stay there all day. At that point I finally offered out my first sleepy, nasal-sounding, four-note tree yelp - promptly being cut off by a vicious response. I leaned over and said, "That's all he gets."

"Shouldn't we call more? I always call more..." Mark started.

"Do you want to hear him gobble from the tree all day, or do you want to kill him," I asked?

After another twelve minutes of furious gobbling we heard the tom pitch out of his tree. Immediately, I spotted his dark form flying through the woods towards us on a path no more direct than if he were riding a zip line. On he came, closer and closer; bigger and bigger he loomed. I swear; that bird looked like a Boeing 747 on final approach as he homed in on our position.

I really thought that he was going to set down at about the 35-yard mark, but then he caught a little more wind under his wings and kept right on coming. Finally, he touched ground exactly six steps away from the muzzle of Marks 20-gauge.

"Kill him," I whispered.

Nothing happened, except for the tom's head periscoping upward.

Still nothing, as it went even higher.

For what seemed an eternity there was total silence, as that red, warty head stretched higher and higher, until it reached absolute full extension. The rapidly building anxiety level in my guts was about to make my heart explode into a million bits…

"BOOM!"

It would've been real easy to miss at that range, but Mark didn't. After the flopping around had subsided, only a small strip of skin approximately a half-inch wide kept the head of that turkey attached to its body. As for Mark, he was absolutely beside himself in pure, unadulterated joy. I'm quite certain that he must've pumped my hand and thanked me fifty times before we got back to the farmhouse.

I couldn't have been any happier for him, either. Helping anyone kill their first wild turkey is always an honor and a thrill for me, but this was particularly special because of how much that bird meant to this fine young man. Over the next few hours we carried that turkey around to show him off to everyone Mark knew, and the perpetual grin on the kid's face couldn't have been wiped off with a bulldozer. In all my days I have never seen a person so thrilled with their first gobbler, and rightly so, for he had killed an absolute giant. The right spur of this behemoth measured 1- 7/16 inches, while the left one was just 1/8" shorter.

That day of helping Mark to attain the designation of "turkey hunter" was a spirit-uplifting experience for me, but two days later I would once again take a precipitous fall from the lofty perch of those emotions. Once again I would stumble into the bottom-dwelling depths of yet another personal low point. Once again I would cripple and lose another West Virginia tom…

The infamous event left me with so many horridly intense emotions running through my mind (anger, anguish, frustration, humiliation, dejection, disappointment, shock, and sympathy for the bird) that I couldn't decide whether to cry, puke, or both.

I mulled this latest tragedy over in my mind for hours. Finally, I came to the realization that all of my troubles occurring in this state were because of mental attitude alone; I had become very timid and tentative in mindset, and reluctant to act in a decisive manner at the crucial time of each turkey encounter. My "killer instinct" had been damaged by so many negative results that I was scared to do anything out of fear of screwing up everything. Instead of being intent and focused on making moves that would improve my odds of success, I was sitting back and waiting for things to happen - too afraid to be bold, and scared of making a mistake.

The smile says it all for Mark Cutlip in West Virginia,
but those hooks speak volumes, too!

I vowed right then and there to become more assertive and once again start listening to the little voice inside my head that often told me how and when to act. The potential cost of such a change was that I would probably spook some birds by being *too* aggressive, but that was a risk worth taking in order stop missing and crippling turkeys. My mental wellbeing *demanded* that I stop missing and crippling turkeys!

The very next day was my last opportunity to put West Virginia's jinx on me asunder, and that is exactly what I did with a bold move on a nice tom shot full in the face from 11 yards. It sure felt good to put everything together and get back on track, and I immediately began feeling like the real me once again.

Headed for my traditional season-ending hunt with the Bays clan in New York, I first picked up Frank Emert at the Binghamton airport. He was anxious to experience some of the fun that this place always produced, and had planned a three-day trip. Unfortunately, the weather turned terrible and it dumped rain on us the whole time of his stay. We never even came close to killing any turkeys.

While the weather didn't improve a whole lot after he left, at least I was able to get in a few good hunts with Jake and his brother-in-law Kent Blanchard before season's end. Jake shot one gobbler and I added two more, but the main focus that year was on Kent. His beautiful daughter Julie had been killed in a snowmobile accident the previous Christmas.

Kent was understandably having a very hard time dealing with Julie's death, and our hunts ended up feeling more like therapy sessions, of sorts. Being out there in the woods had a calming, soothing effect on Kent, and we were able to spend a good amount of time talking through all of his emotions. I think the two jakes he shot were therapeutic, as well, because Kent felt like Julie's spirit was right there beside us at each instance.

This was a very sad time for the Bays clan, and although it would not be the last heartbreak we would share, at the time I was just happy to think that I might've had a small part in helping some of my "family" move through the grieving process.

When I looked back on the 1999 season in my journal, I realized that it had been a rather tough year overall. Statistically, it looked decent on paper with 60 toms called "in camp," but that was only because I had managed to lure in enough multiple toms to override the many days of striking out completely. A large part of the difficulties were due to the effects of that La Nina weather pattern mentioned at the beginning of the chapter. It had thrown the whole spring season for a loop, with warmer temps and an earlier leaf-out everywhere I went. Spring was so far advanced that the turkeys hadn't been particularly cooperative, and gobbling numbers were way down from my seasonal averages.

Still, I had persevered through all of the difficulties and managed to squeeze out 67 days of hunting in seven different states. Between clients, friends and myself, we had managed to kill 24 gobblers in that timeframe. I had also added a pair of new destinations to my lifetime resume, boosting that figure to 21 states hunted. I hadn't as yet even considered the prospect of a U.S. Slam; my main goal was simply to hunt in all of the eastern states that tickled my fancy, while continuing to hit Florida every single year.

As always happens, I began planning for the next spring's itinerary even as I was driving home. With the new Millennium dawning, I was really anxious to get it stated with a big bang!

A dandy tom from New York to end the season.

CHAPTER 12

Cleaning and Eating your Turkey

Conservationist; since the days of Aldo Leopold, that term has been used to define someone who believes in and practices the wise use of our natural resources. This group includes hunters, and one basic creed of most hunters is that we eat what we kill. This was a point driven home to me and millions of my fellow lovers of the outdoors very early-on in life by the person (often our fathers) who gave us that first BB gun, taught us about safety and how to shoot it responsibly, and then set down certain ironclad rules. Included in this list was a basic covenant of "if you kill it, you eat it."

I can still vividly recall the first animal I ever shot (it was a small bird miraculously plinked out of mid-air), and everything that subsequently happened after rushing home to show Dad my prize. Although I will forevermore feel fully-qualified in claiming that sparrow ain't too bad on the dinner table, suffice to say the lessons taught that day were well received on my end - to the point that I no longer had much of an interest in shooting songbirds! I did, however, become certifiably hell on wheels for legal game like rabbits that were foolish enough to let me track them up in the snow and then sit still long enough that I could zero-in for a head-shot. That little multi-pump BB gun had plenty of power to get the job done, too.

As my hunting interests grew to eventually include the wild turkey, another memory etched into my brain is of the laborious effort I took in carefully hand plucking that very first tom and then preparing him for my family's dinner table. I even went so far as to drive into town and search the library (no internet in those days) to find a scrumptious-sounding recipe for what was described as "Roasted Wild Turkey with a Traditional Peanut Stuffing." Whether or not you've ever had the slightest insanity-based inclination to smear peanut butter on a turkey sandwich is irrelevant; I can assure you that this dish came out tasting just exactly as it sounds. Now, I love peanuts, and I love turkey, but together the combination is nothing short of hideous! However, I sure wasn't going to let any of that precious bounty go to waste if I could help it, so I ate every single morsel in the days to follow. Leftovers from Thanksgiving dinner are a favorite of mine, but that was a hard week's worth of dining…

Since that time I've shot a few more wild turkeys, and I've prepared them for the table in a wide variety of ways. Turkey flesh is so incredibly tasty and nutritious that it's truly one of my favorite foods. I enjoy cooking them, I enjoy eating them, and I enjoy serving them to my guests. I've also become quite adept at caring for my birds in the field before they ever reach the kitchen stove, and I take great pride in that skill set, as well. Just as in other types of hunting, the care with how your wild game is treated after being shot is paramount to achieving rave reviews at the dinner table.

Generally speaking, gone are my days of plucking turkeys. I'll do it if someone really wants to try roasting or deep frying their bird, but it's both too much work, and impractical for most cooking methods that I use. Wild turkeys aren't built like their store-bought cousins, and in my opinion they don't cook up particularly well (i.e.; evenly) in either the roasting pan or the deep fryer without special attention and considerable effort. Instead, I generally skin and separate the turkey into pieces (breasts, legs, thighs, wings, internal organs, neck, and carcass) as I go, and then use different cooking methods for each type of body part.

Many people dread the task of cleaning game, but I actually enjoy butchering turkeys. It's not hard to do, doesn't take very long, and if done correctly the mess created can be quite minimal. Around the hunting camp it seems like everyone is always turning to me for help and/or advice in this process, but that's ok; I guess it just makes sense because I've cleaned about a bazillion of 'em. I'm always willing to show other folks my cleaning methods and the various shortcuts that I've developed through time and repetition, and here in this chapter I'll try to describe a few of these tips and tricks on how to get the most meat out of your dead turkey.

Unfortunately, I don't feel like the written word can adequately describe the process very well. Well, at least, not *my* written word. A hands-on demonstration is much better at conveying the intricacies involved, so a couple years ago Bill George, Doug Pickle, and myself produced the first rough draft of an instructional video showing the butchering process. I think it came out pretty good, so after some additional tweaking, refining, and reshooting to make the whole thing look a bit more polished and presentable, we plan to post it on Youtube in the near future. I sincerely believe that most turkey hunters could benefit from watching our video, so please try to find it and let your friends and fellow hunters know about it, as well.

For the rest of this chapter I'm going to try and peck out some inadequate words to help cover the basics in cleaning turkeys, and then I'll offer up a few ideas and recipes for how to get the greatest culinary enjoyment from your hard-earned trophy. However, the very first thing I want to talk about is that in discussing this subject with literally hundreds of turkey hunters over the years, I have found that just about half of them simply breast out their bird and throw the rest away. Every single time I hear someone admit to that act it makes my skin crawl, because I find this practice to be no less than reprehensible for a number of reasons. First, they are throwing away approximately HALF of the available meat, and I am one of those people who would argue that it might even be the very best tasting half of the bird. Don't get me wrong here - I love fried turkey breast just as much as the next guy, but that dark meat is so delicious that it boggles my mind to try and understand why anyone would do such a dastardly thing.

Discarding all of that high-quality turkey meat also seems to at least border on being a criminal offense covered by the "wanton waste" laws of most states, and in my mind it actually steps well beyond that line. This would be like pulling the back straps from your deer and then leaving the rest to be nibbled on by scavengers and maggots. I think as hunters we can universally agree that such a practice would be wrong on a number of levels including both moral and criminal, so don't even try to tell me how tossing over half of your bird into the trash is any different.

Of course, there's also the old adage covered in the first paragraph of this chapter: if you kill it, then you eat it. I've heard some people claim that any turkey meat other than the breast is dry, tasteless, too tough, gamey, etc., but if that's really the delusion under which you're living, then all you've got to do is give those unwanted portions to someone who can adequately appreciate the gift. It only takes another ten minutes of labor to glean every usable part and parcel of meat off that bird which you've worked so hard to bring home, and believe me; your kindness when you give it away will be most graciously received. I have gifted quite a bit of turkey flesh while on the road and far from home, and I have yet to find a single soul who wasn't absolutely thrilled to get it.

Ok; let's get started. One of the most important things that I do when cleaning a bird is to let it sit for a while. I know there are some people who insist on butchering their turkey when it's fresh, but that's seldom desirable in my mind. Field dressing to remove the guts is also an unnecessary task so long as you can get started on the butchering process within a reasonable timeframe, but even in the hottest of environs I don't want to begin that job for a minimum of two hours. A delay of six to ten hours or more will likewise produce no ill effects to the meat if the weather allows, although I think the optimal waiting time is usually from three to five hours after the bird's been shot. Of course, this greatly depends upon the ambient temperature where he's being stored, and how the turkey was killed is also paramount. For instance; penetrating wounds to the body cavity from either pellets or a broadhead would warrant a more expedient approach. I sure don't want intestinal juices tainting any of the meat that I'm so anxiously planning to eat, so this would be an example of a time when field dressing might be a good idea.

One reason why I let my birds sit for a while is because if you clean them too soon you'll find the cooked product to be a bit tougher than if it had been slightly "aged" for a few hours. I've experimented with this concept for years, and the positive results garnered from waiting are analogous to why we hang deer for as long as possible; it allows the cell membranes to begin their initial decomposition and leads to a general tenderization of the meat. The only difference between deer and turkeys would be the length of the aging process necessary to attain our desired goal, and again, that's more a factor of the ambient temperature where the aging is being done.

While I might let a deer hang for two or three weeks if it's kept at a constant 35 degrees in a walk-in cooler, springtime turkey hunting weather dictates a much more condensed timetable. We've probably all heard stories of how royalty in olden times would hang their dead fowl from the neck and not cook the bird until the body had fallen away from its head, but that's a little too extreme for my taste. Instead, I try to stick with that 3-5 hour timeline, which seems to give the best results for both the tenderness of the finished product, and in helping to make the cleaning process easier.

The very best indicator of when your bird is ready to be butchered becomes obvious after you begin filleting the breast meat off the carcass. Lying underneath those two big hunks of deliciousness are the tenderloins, and on a bird that is aged "just right," these will easily peel right off the carcass without using your knife for anything other than to cut the tendon at its forward end. On a fresh kill you would actually need to slice the meat away from bone. This is also true for where the breast meets the skeleton below the breastbone; on an ideally aged bird this meat can gently be pushed off the carcass with your fingertips, and your knife is only needed for the final detachment, up near the wings.

I now want to focus a bit on something that I've never heard anyone else discuss in regards to the cleaning of wild turkeys, and that is the bloody mess which tends to accompany the removal of the breast meat. All this blood comes from two arteries which feed the breast muscle, and if you so much as nick either of them with a knife they bleed out. This can create quite a puddle of blood underneath the bird as you're cleaning him. However, I have found a way to greatly reduce or eliminate this altogether, and when I demonstrate the method to other hunters, I quite often hear comments like, "Oh, that is amazing" or, "I've never seen that" or, "Doc, you're brilliant." Well, this isn't exactly rocket science, but it is a rather slick trick.

When cleaning a turkey I first remove the lower legs, tail, and beard for memento purposes, and then I lay the bird flat on his back on the cleaning table. My next move is to remove the secondary flight feathers from the middle section of the wing by slicing down between their attachment points and the wing bone. After that, I get rid of the outermost section of the wing and its accompanying primary flight feathers by sniping or cutting the cartilage and tendons between the first and second sections.

With the wings taken care of, I next begin the skinning process by making a small incision in the flap of skin between each leg and the body. When you then push the legs/thighs down towards the table, the rest of this skin will rip open as the hip joints pop out of their sockets. This leaves the legs lying flat on the table. There will still be a section of skin remaining intact between the lower tip of the breast-bone and the anus, so I'll work my fingers underneath it to separate the skin from the body, and then cut it through. Holding the flap of this skin that's attached to the breast in one hand, and with my other hand holding the bird down flat to the table with his head towards me and hanging over the edge, I then pull all the skin covering the breast towards me. It strips off the breasts easily, and by pulling it all the way past the craw, the bulbous "limb knot" of the breastbone will also be exposed. Brace the heel of your off-hand against this knob, and push the skin straight down towards the ground. This peels all the skin off the entire breast and leaves them totally exposed.

Like I said, this is a far easier task to demonstrate than write about, so you might want to give the video a look as we go through this chapter. On camera you'll see that I next cut through the fatty tissue around the craw (or, crop), before pulling that food storage "sack" out of its pocket lying between the two breasts. Then, I run my knife down along the wishbone which has just been exposed. Another filleting cut along the breastbone allows the breast meat to fall to the side and reveal the tenderloin underneath. With a little snip of its tendon, it's free to be gently pulled off the body. Again, if the tenderloin doesn't just slip right off of the carcass, then the bird is too fresh and you'll have to use a knife.

Now, look closely at a spot about halfway between the thigh and wing, where the breast meat attaches to the body. You'll see there a sort of hollow "cavity" on the inside of the thigh meat, which is covered by a clear membrane. By pushing your finger into this hollow spot and running it down towards the rear portion of the breast, you will strip this layer of "fascia" tissue away from the meat. This also exposes the most important point of discovery for controlling the amount of blood generated in the cleaning process - that pair of arteries which feed the breast muscles.

By gently pushing the breast meat away from the carcass with your fingers, these two "bleeders" can plainly be seen lying just underneath the surface of the meat. If you then slip a sharp knife blade underneath them and follow their path out into the breast for a couple of inches, you can remove about a half-teaspoon-sized portion of meat at their terminal ends to virtually isolate the blood that they contain. However, be forewarned that the slightest nick in these arteries will cause them to bleed a *lot*. Utmost care must be taken when performing this little task.

Once the "bleeders" have been bypassed, the rest of the breast can be removed from the carcass via a combination of pushing with your fingers and cutting with a knife. Next, do the same thing on the opposite side of the carcass, and place both breasts, along with their accompanying tenderloins, in a one-gallon zip-lock bag. This is approximately half of the turkey's edibles (the "white meat" portion), but we most certainly aren't done at this point; there's still quite a bit of delicious flesh to salvage.

My next move is to remove the legs and thighs, and I start that process by first pulling all the skin from the leg. Peel it off the thigh as well, going clear up to the center of the backbone, because I'm about to reveal another little trick. By rolling your turkey onto its side, you can see the attachment points which hold the thigh to the carcass. They're defined by the shape of the underlying boney skeleton. Slip your knife blade down along these attachment points and score the flesh shallowly in three strokes; a simple one inch cut at the rear, another 4 inch cut above the thigh bone, and a semi-circular cut tracing around the forward attachment point of the thigh. All of these cuts are guided by the natural curvature of the skeleton, and none of them need to be made very deeply.

Next, roll the turkey onto his back again, and using the curvature of the skeleton beside the hip joint as a guide, make a deeper cut from the hip socket to the rear portion of the thigh. You don't need to go all the way through, but it doesn't hurt to do so. Then, grasp the leg bone in one hand like you were getting ready to eat a drumstick, and place the other hand firmly on the carcass for support. Give a quick, forceful pull away from the body and slightly towards the front, and the whole leg/thigh portion of the turkey will pop off slick as a whistle. I then separate the thigh from the leg by severing the cartilage between them at the "knee," before placing both portions in the second zip-lock bag. Repeat for the other side of the bird and you'll now have most of the "dark meat" of your bird packaged. But, again, we aren't done just yet.

The wings also contain a good amount of prime meat, so skin these out before severing the connective cartilage of the wings from the carcass at the shoulder. Don't forget to fillet down along the shoulder blade as you take off the wing, because there is a little nugget of deliciousness approximately two or three ounces in size which covers it.

The breast, legs, thighs, and wings are the main parts to be retrieved off of your bird, but even after this has been accomplished there's more. The neck can now be used as you would any other turkey neck - boiled and pulled for use in gravy, etc. However, since the neck is usually where we aim our shotgun, it's generally full of pellets and I seldom utilize it in my kitchen. If you like the liver, heart, and gizzard then by all means slice the belly flesh below the tip of the breastbone and crack the carcass backwards to fully expose them for retrieval. Likewise, you can remove the guts and remaining internal organs, finish skinning out the skeleton, and then boil the whole thing down to make soup stock and/or pick the few remaining morsels of meat from the bones. I don't usually go to this much trouble when I'm camping in the field, but some of my friends are quite religious in their devotion to the practice.

Now that I've covered the basic tips and tricks for cleaning your bird, let's get down to some actual cooking methods. I don't have the space here to make this into a real cookbook, but I do want to share some of my favorite ways to prepare wild turkey with you. One of these is to simply fillet the meat off the bones of the wings and thighs before running it all together through a grinder. This makes the most fantastic burger imaginable, and you can use it in any recipe that calls for such. Or, you can form it into patties and just cook them as is. Turkey burger really has a *fantastic* flavor, and anyone who would knowingly throw those portions of a bird away after trying it is a lost soul, in my opinion.

Legs are another part of the turkey which I often hear terrible things about, but if you take a little time to prepare them, they can be a fantastic source of scrumptiousness. What I like to do is wait until I have six, ten, or more legs in the freezer before putting them all in a big pot of boiling water. Add a medley of spices (black pepper, salt, garlic, and whatever else sounds good), and then cook them for a couple hours. At that point turn off the stove, let them stand until cool enough to handle, then commence pulling the meat from the bones like you would do when making hog or beef BBQ. Wild turkey legs have a number of annoying "sheath" bones in them, so this type of preparation allows you to easily find and remove all of these by hand. Once the meat is separated from bone you can use it in soups, stews, turkey salad, the aforementioned BBQ, manhattans covered in mashed potatoes and gravy, or any number of different ways. It has an absolutely DELICIOUS flavor, and is undoubtedly one of my favorite portions of a turkey to eat.

I'm now going to conclude this chapter by sharing a couple of specific recipes that I use quite often, but like I said earlier, by no means is this going to be a comprehensive listing for all the ways you can serve wild turkey. First of all, I am not an overly talented chef; I'm more utilitarian in the kitchen than fancy, and while I can get something edible and tasty onto the plate, it isn't going to be anything too complicated. Elegant cuisine is beyond my pay grade. However, if that's what floats your boat, then by all means feel free to explore other ways to prepare your hard-earned prize. You might even want to start by perusing any of the many good wild game cookbooks on the market. There is no finer eating than wild turkey, no matter which way you choose to prepare it, and my only suggestion would be to stay away from any recipe that calls for peanuts!

OK; I'm no different than anyone else when it comes time to sit down at the dinner table, so my favorite go-to recipe for wild turkeys is to simply fry up their breast meat in a hot skillet. This is always a staple at my camp. The main reasons for that are because it's quick, easy to prepare with a minimum of basic ingredients, and extremely delicious. I've probably cooked this dish for thousands of people over the years to rave reviews, and here's how you can do it, too:

First, slice the turkey breast across the grain in about 5/8" thick strips. Lay them flat on the counter top, and sprinkle each piece with as much Lowry's Seasoned Salt as you like, along with a little garlic powder and quite a bit of black pepper. Rub these spices into the meat, then flip them over and repeat for the other side. Put about a half-inch of peanut oil in a skillet and get it real hot. Dredge the turkey pieces in flour before placing them in the oil. Fry for about two minutes, or until white foam begins forming around the edges of each piece, and then flip them over and fry for about another minute. Do NOT overcook, unless you like your turkey meat dry and tough as leather! Remove from the oil and drain on a paper towel, and while they're still hot, sprinkle with a magic ingredient that further enhances the culinary experience - parmesan cheese. That's all there is to it. Step back, stand clear, and watch the hooligans you're feeding go berserk in scrambling to get ahold of these hot, golden delicacies.

Another recipe that I like a lot is what I call Buffalo Turkey Strips. Again, I start by slicing the turkey meat (breast, thigh, or anything else) into strips and chunks, although I'm not as concerned with cutting across the grain as when I'm frying it. I just want the flesh reduced to bite-size pieces. That's not crucial though, as the bigger portions eat just as well as the small ones.

Next, make a solution using the following ingredients, in these proportions, based on how much meat you're cooking. In other words, this recipe is good for about a breast-worth of turkey flesh, so if you are preparing more, then multiply these ingredients accordingly. The important thing here is to have enough liquid so that when you pour it onto the turkey meat in a big bowl and thoroughly mix it all together, every piece is coated with oil and spices.

> 1 t salt
> 1 t black pepper
> 2 t hot sauce of your choice
> 2 t oil

The original recipe for this dish said to next grease up a couple of baking trays, but I've found a better way – I now use parchment paper. I still smear the paper with a little shortening to keep the meat from sticking to it, but cleanup is *so* much easier when the turkey isn't in direct contact with the metal. Once your oven is heated to 400 degrees, simply dredge/shake all of the turkey pieces in flour before spacing them on the paper and baking for approximately 25 minutes. Flip each piece over after the first 15 minutes. Sample occasionally to make sure they're done, but as is the case for all of the turkey meat I cook, I don't want them to be TOO done. Overcooked turkey is tough and dry.

While the strips are cooking you can mix up the main sauce on a warm stove, and again, if you are preparing more than one breast-worth of meat, then multiply this recipe so you end up with enough liquid to thoroughly coat all the pieces after they come out of the oven. This is the original recipe for "Buffalo" sauce, and it's way-good:

> 1- 1/2 T white vinegar
> 1/4 t cayenne pepper
> 1/8 t garlic powder
> 1/4 t Worchester
> 1 t Tabasco

204

1/4 t salt
6 T Frank's Hot Sauce
6 T Butter

After the strips are done I place them all in a big Tupper Ware bowl, then pour on the Buffalo sauce, seal the bowl with a tight-fitting lid, and shake thoroughly until every piece of meat is evenly coated. Serve.

I really enjoy this recipe, and I know that you and your guests will, too. It's a staple that I bring to Tailgating Parties and other gatherings regularly, and if you make enough ahead of time (be forewarned that your guests will absolutely devour this dish), I like to dine on warmed-up leftovers until they're gone. Many of my friends have commented that this is their favorite way to eat wild turkey, and that's a hard statement to argue against.

While these are some of my own personal favorite recipes for the bounty of my harvests, the ways that you might choose to prepare your own wild turkey are limited only by imagination and cooking skills. This gamebird that we all spend so much time hunting is a great source of delicious and nutritious meat, so please try to utilize every bit of it. We owe that much to our noble adversary, and our family and friends will appreciate the effort when they're sitting down to a meal featuring its scrumptious flesh.

With that, I wish you all, "Bon Appetite!"

A plateful of deliciousness: fried wild turkey, gravy, and
fried potatoes with onions and morels.

CHAPTER 13

The Year 2000 – A New Millennium

Beginning the New Millennium, my main goals in turkey hunting continued to be fueled by a simple desire to visit various Eastern states and Florida every year, with an occasional foray out west if friends and trusted hunting companions expressed the interest in going for Merriam's or Rio's. Yes; there was plenty of turkey hunting magic to be found closer to home in the beloved deciduous forests of my youth, but an unquenchable wanderlust to explore new territory compelled me to travel from state to state at every opportunity in order to extend my season and get the maximum number of hunting days out of each spring. Turkey hunting in such an all-out manner had brought me so much excitement over the years that it was unthinkable in my mind to do it in any other way, and the annual travels had become a huge part of not only who I was, but who I wanted to be. I thought of myself as a turkey hunter above anything else in life.

My seasonal journeys always begin in Florida, where I have long observed that their turkeys are strongly influenced by climatic conditions. Indeed, I might even venture to say that weather is the single most important factor in determining how those crazy swamp birds are going to act from day to day. The degree to which it plays an influence has always been rather surprising to me, because common sense might seemingly dictate that turkeys living in a place which is warm and drenched in sunshine year-round would be relatively stable in their behavior, as well. Not so. Osceolas are downright fickle!

The West is something altogether different. Major daily temperature fluctuations of 50 degrees or more can happen fairly regularly, and snowfall can blanket the ground all the way into early summer. Those are conditions which I would expect to cause wild mood swings in turkeys, but Merriam's and Rio Grande toms hold no such sway over their thin-skinned Osceola cousins in this department. A swamp-loving Florida bird might clam up for days with the slightest variation of temperature, humidity, cloud cover, wind, or myriad other climatic conditions. Hunting them always holds a higher degree of challenge due mainly to the quantity (or rather, the *lack*) of gobbling heard.

Of particular effect on these birds might be a couple of season-long weather patterns which I have discussed in previous chapters. In review: El Nino years produce extremely wet conditions, and the La Nina's are just the opposite. These usually follow one another cyclically, but they don't necessarily rotate through like clockwork every two years. In fact, there might be several seasons of relative "normalcy" in between an occurrence of either one.

Such was the case in the year 2000, when even before my arrival I'd been receiving reports of relatively calm conditions and good gobbling. Winter had been fairly dry as well, so that was welcomed news. Dry years mean that the bugs aren't going to be as bad, and it's no secret that I don't care much for mosquitoes, ticks, deer flies, or biting gnats. Never have; never will!

I planned to take my time in 2000 and enjoy what I had so come to love about Florida; the fun and games of messing around with one of the most difficult subspecies of turkey to be found anywhere, coupled with good times and camaraderie shared by a whole cast of interesting characters. Included in that group are a number of local Floridian friends, as well as "beetleneckers" like me from up north who had initially come down to pursue an Osceola in hopes of conquering the Grand Slam, only to then fall in love with the land and its many unique aspects to such a degree that it became a part of their very soul. I most-certainly qualify as one of those!

I've been hanging around with this motley crew of excellent turkey hunters and eccentric personalities for so long now that I could write a book based solely on our camp life. Each and every one of these people are folks whom I count as not only my friends, but beloved family members, and I cannot imagine a turkey season beginning without a prolonged stay in their presence. You will undoubtedly meet many of them in stories and/or pictures from this book or other volumes, but I want to take a brief moment here to publicly offer a heartfelt salute to every single person (named-or-not) who has graced my life with their presence in our Florida camp. This has been an exquisitely wild ride for many years, and I can only hope that it continues for a very long time to come.

Florida itself was at one time a place that I absolutely abhorred and couldn't wait to leave behind, but over time it became like a second home to me - so much so that I am always and forever missing the place and anxious to come back, even before I finish up my annual pilgrimage.

The hunting down there can oftentimes be tough, but in 2000 things started off with a bang. In fact, a pair of very loud bangs during the first three days of the season quickly filled my Florida bag limit, leaving me with only two options: I could either leave the state much sooner than I wanted to, or else I could stick around for a while and guide other people. Hmmm....

Larry Sharp had again come back to seek vengeance on an Osceola devil-bird that had evaded him in 1998, and this time he'd brought along his son Philip, who like his Dad, is a wildlife biologist working for the Kentucky Department of Fish and Wildlife Resources. Both of Larry's offspring are exceptional woodsmen and hunters in their own right, but work commitments had kept the eldest son Kenneth from attending our Florida shenanigans.

Kenneth loves to hunt as much as anyone I've ever met, so I knew how badly he wanted to be there. I also knew how much Larry wanted to get a Florida bird killed, following the painful missed shot on his previous trip to the land of gators and gobblers. Osceolas have a way of getting under a fella's skin like that. Unfortunately, for the first two days of his trip we basically struck out swinging. In fact, there was only one single gobble heard during that timeframe. Then, on the third morning, we hiked deep into one of my favorite spots along the Withlacoochie River via an old tram grade, and we were rewarded at dawn with a tom gobbling hard from only about 250 yards away

A 100-yard gap in the raised-sand railroad grade at this spot had at one time supported a wooden bridge spanning a creek feeding into the river, but it had long ago been torn out and/or rotted away into oblivion. The gobbling was coming from off towards the river channel at this cut-through, so Larry and I quickly snuck 75 yards closer to the tom and set up on a huge Live Oak. A tree-bound hen behind us then began lightly yelping in the soft light of half-dawn.

Just as we got settled-in good and proper, this hen glided earthward. When she then yelped from the ground, I answered in a like manner. She answered me, I answered her, and the tom gobbled loudly from out front. To be perfectly honest, I couldn't even imagine a better setup, with Larry and I directly in-line between an eager tom and his equally anxious girlfriend. Unfortunately, these two turkeys hadn't read the script of how this deal was supposed to go down, and they circled our position just out of sight to join up amidst the Cypress knees of the river swamp hard to the left of us. The woods were much too open to risk any move that would get Larry's gun pointed in a more favorable direction, so all we could do was hold our positions and wait.

At that point I began issuing sharp one and two-note cuts on a glass call, hoping to fire up the hen. She immediately responded in kind. I was sitting to Larry's right, and in short order I heard the tom drumming loudly from somewhere *close* on the other side of him. I dared not move a muscle. Then, Larry nudged my arm and hissed that turkeys were coming from the left, but again, he was facing almost 90 degrees to their right and in no position whatsoever for taking the shot.

I was hoping that the two lovebirds would circle around in front of us, and as the hen's sharp cutting calls got closer and closer, that is exactly what I thought was happening. I could almost feel the tom's drumming as it boomed louder and louder. Then, I heard the telltale sound of wingtips dragging on the ground as the tom strutted up to what sounded like mere spitting distance from us.

All of a sudden everything grew quiet. I could almost feel the tension in the air as my brain visualized both birds abruptly popping up into erect mode and staring hard. Seconds ticked by like hours on the clock, but it couldn't have been more than mere moments before all Hell broke loose in the cypress swamp. There was no mistaking the meaning, urgency, or panic in the sound of staccato putting echoing off the trees, or in the desperate churning of leaves as turkey feet ran away. There was also no mistaking the lack of effect from two quick and explosive shotgun blasts.

The previous fall I had hunted turkeys at Larry's WMA in Kentucky, and after arrowing a fine old gobbler by myself, he and I had doubled up and tried to duplicate that feat in the next few days. During that time-frame I watched my buddy miss seven turkeys in a row with his bow. *Seven.* If you add in the one he'd missed with me in Florida during the 1998 season, that made eight, and now the total had suddenly grown to nine (or, ten if you count each individual shot), because he'd just whiffed on yet another! To say that Larry was frustrated and aggravated would be a grave understatement, so I was very reluctant to say anything too hurtful or insensitive. That would have to wait for later, back at camp, after we had a few beers to dull the painful memory.

Instead, we sat there reconstructing the calamitous event in whispers, and Larry told me how the tom had been strutting off of his left shoulder at a range of only five yards. For some reason the hen had suddenly become alerted and sprinted for safety, forcing a rushed attempt at a running head shot on her boyfriend. The shot pattern had hit nothing except cypress bark down through the swamp, and a second trigger pull of the 20-gauge Benelli was no more successful in drawing feathers than the first. Just like that, another promising situation full of hopeful expectations had spiraled straight down the tubes into the abyss.

With no other turkeys gobbling in earshot, and our collective negative attitudes threatening to pull both of our souls deep down into the river muck, we backtracked to the cut in the tram line and sat down to contemplate the value of life. Right then things didn't look very sunny in the Sunshine State, and an hour and a half later it hadn't gotten much better.

Larry then snuck off to colloquially feed the bears, so during his absence I pulled out my Cane Creek glass call and began practicing some kee-kee's. Then, I threw out a few loud yelps with a powerful cutt sequence on the end, and a far-away turkey gobbled from the direction that Larry's missed bird had flown. I quickly gathered our gear together as Larry came out of the bushes pulling up his pants, and after a hasty move of 50 yards to a better setup tree, I got another response to some urgent-sounding yelps. The tom was still a long ways off though, so we immediately arose and moved another 100 yards to cut the distance. Following yet a third answering gobble, we repeated the move sequence a final time.

Each of these strategic shifts in position had taken us right down along the swamp edge like a real hen might normally do. The tom's next unprovoked gobble was obviously closer, and since he'd already jumped on each of my previous calls, I couldn't think of a good reason to say anything else for a while. It was time to let *him* search for *us* . Over the next ten minutes the pressure grew intense as silence reigned, and while part of me wondered if the tom had decided to slip on by, I also had a powerful feeling that something good was about to happen.

Suddenly, the tom walked out from behind a big cypress tree 60 yards away, but at the 9 o'clock position to Larry's gun barrel. Just as quickly, he turned and vanished back behind the tree from where he'd first appeared. I whispered for Larry to swing his gun to cover that spot before I offered up a sweet sounding 5-note yelp, which the tom enthusiastically answered. Less than a minute later he popped right back out from behind that very same cypress, and this time he stood there tall as an ostrich, gazing hard to try and find the hen that had made those calls.

Softly purring on my glass made the gobbler puff up into a half-strut and start working closer, and although it took seemingly forever for him to get there, he eventually reached good killing range. His bright red head was framed against a big Cypress tree when the shot folded him up like a deflated balloon. I was on him like lightening, and Larry soon joined the party. A huge grin stretched from ear to ear on his face as he said, "Will wonders never cease; we finally kilt one!"

That was a happy time for the both of us, and we glad-handed around like a couple of village idiots. Then, I caught sight of

Larry's entire shotgun pattern centered on the tree bark of that big cypress behind the gobbler. Splatters of blood and brain matter highlighted its lethality.

Larry Sharp - Killer of Turkeys.

Unfortunately, this would be the last success found in Florida during the 2000 season. The only other positive hunting-related event was when Steve Fincher gave me a gift for guiding him to his first bird the previous year; it was a set of Ping Red Eye golf clubs. For the past several springs a few members of our camp had been gathering annually to play in a golf tournament that we'd started and named, "The Greater Green Swamp Cracker/Beetlenecker Invitational Golf Tournament." It was always a ton of fun to play in, and I had even built a very special trophy that stayed with the winner from one year to the next - despite a few objections from some of the winner's spouses! Kenny Dorman's dog chewed on the legs one year after he won it, but this prestigious trophy still today manages to find its way into a place of honor (such as on a fireplace mantel) at the winner's home. Everyone who plays in this tournament wants nothing more than to have their name engraved upon it, but win or lose, we always have a blast.

The trophy for our Greater Green Swamp Cracker/Beetlenecker Invitational Golf Tournament. Who wouldn't be proud to display this masterpiece in their home?

Next up on my schedule were a couple of new states for me: Louisiana and Arkansas. Tree planting had taken me to LA three times back in the early '90's, so I was somewhat familiar with the town of Natchitoches and the nearby Kisatchie National Forest. I had really enjoyed that area and its fun loving people, and in doing some research I figured out that this large swath of public land was regarded as a fairly decent place to find turkeys.

Once in camo it didn't take long to confirm that, as I heard a tom gobbling on my very first morning's hunt. Unfortunately, the old boy hooked up with some yackity hens soon after flydown and never said another word. At least I was encouraged about the possibility for success, and when I called in three jakes numerous times the next morning, I felt like it was only a matter of time before I might fill one of the two tags burning a hole in my pocket.

Such are the hopes and dreams of an eternally optimistic turkey hunter, but during the course of the next week those promising feelings got battered around quite a bit by henned-up gobblers, too many competing hunters, and a series of intense thunderstorms with lots of lightening and sporadic tornadoes.

At least I was hearing an occasional bird gobble when the weather allowed, and finally, on Day 9 I called in three big toms. The first one that gave me a good shot fell victim to my Ruger. It felt great to put this bird in the cooler, and I really thought at the time that my success was just a pre-cursor of good things to come, but I was badly mistaken; four more days of rapidly diminishing returns and minimal gobbling put my nerves on edge and made leaving for Arkansas an easy decision.

I'd heard 11 different gobbling toms gobbling during that 13-day Louisiana trip, but due to the tight grid of drivable roads on the National Forest, the only "successes" I realized were in hearing gunshots and wings flogging the earth, after four of them were killed by someone else. I like to hunt on ground so big that if I hear a bird gobbling, there's a good chance I'm the only person within walking distance. Crowds are something I usually avoid like the plague. I just couldn't seem to get away from people on this hunt.

The Kisatchie National Forest was also some of the most garbage-strewn ground I'd ever hunted, and that was a severe disappointment. I will *never* understand how anyone can despoil the very wilderness that we all so claim to cherish! Way too much of my time was spent picking up other people's trash and carrying it out in my game pouch, because in the grand scheme of things, whom is the greater sinner - the one who throws their garbage down in the woods, or those who walk right past without picking it up?

Despite these negatives mentioned, there were certainly some highlights. For instance; I had managed to call in nine separate jakes, besides those final three adult toms. I'd also personally witnessed a smokey-gray phase hen as she'd fed right on past me at really close range. She glowed like a neon light in the pre-thunderstorm dark timber surrounding us. Beautiful!

I'd also met a fellow whom I consider to be one of the few true Turkey Men that I've ever encountered in my lifetime - a Wildlife Tech for the LA Department of Wildlife and Fisheries by the name of Charles Boles. Charles is a consummate woodsman, a great guy, and quite a character known locally as, "The King of Kisatchie" for his intimate knowledge of that National Forest and its wildlife; particularly, the wild turkey.

Another thing that I always enjoy whenever I'm in Louisiana is the food. If you haven't figured it out by now, I really like to eat – and so do those Cajuns and Coonasses living in the Bayou State. Any time I'm in that part of the country I make a habit of sneaking off to little diners, meat markets, and grocery stores for favored delicacies such as Boudin, cracklins, gumbo, pickled quail eggs, etc., etc., etc. So much good food; never enough time! After buying a final five pounds of boiled crawfish to snack on along the way (that was a *big* mistake - they're just far too messy to be considered "road-food"), I headed out to meet Ron Ronk in Arkansas.

Neither one of us had ever hunted this state before, but during the winter we had purchased some topographic maps of the Ozark National Forest and spent considerable time looking them over for spots which figuratively cried out to be hunted. That was Standard Operating Procedure back in the "old days" when preparing to hunt new places. The internet hadn't even been invented at that time, and satellite imagery most certainly wasn't available for everyone at the click of a mouse, so topos were the next best thing to being there. They were an extremely valuable resource that we utilized to a huge extent then, and for some of us old fogies, they still are.

The first thing I always look for when perusing these maps is ridgelines of timbered forest that terminate in a number of fingers and points that stick out above hollows and isolated creek bottoms. Turkeys in hill country seem to show a marked proclivity for roosting just down off the end of these points, where their gobbling can project out over a broad area to attract members of the opposite sex. Oftentimes, the birds will then pitch out to the ridgeline above and work their way towards saddles between two high points, or drop down onto shelves below the ridgeline that provide relatively flat ground for strutting. Any high knob along the ridgetop is a natural vantage from which to listen for gobbling at daylight, and of course, I'm always checking out other natural ground features like fields, open areas, and edges that tend to pull turkeys towards them like magnets.

All of this valuable information, and so much more, can easily be found on topographic maps. It's there for anyone who takes the time to study them. Personally, I can sit "reading" maps like this for hours on end like some people might peruse a book. I consider my huge collection of topo's to be an extremely vital part of my turkey hunting arsenal, and I never leave home without some in my vehicle, *and* my hunting vest.

The Arkansas trip started off on solid footing when the area I picked for an initial hike put me within hearing distance of three gobbling toms at dawn. However, once I moved in and set up on the closest pair, I could hear someone else calling to them. I backed off and started making my way towards the more distant bird, but this plan didn't work out very well, either. A gunshot soon quieted that tom's ardor forever. Such are the trials and travails of hunting public land...

With nothing else within earshot, I began hiking out a long trail which meandered away from the fellow working those initial two birds, and after a couple of miles I finally heard another tom gobble at a flock of noisy crows. The woods were popcorn dry following a long spell without any rain, so I stopped well-short of where I might ordinarily set up before yelping on a Mad MVP diaphragm. Immediately, I got cut off by the tom bellowing out an answer, and he rapidly advanced towards me. Then, he hung up at a shallow ravine between us. While I could hear drumming and occasionally catch glimpses of him strutting back and forth behind some heavy brush on the other side, for over an hour he refused to budge from that spot.

This whole time I had been trying to sound coy with gentle perts, purrs, and light yelping on a Cane Creek Glass, and finally, my tactic appeared to work when I spotted the tom easing down the slope between us. Then, he inexplicably took a hard right at the bottom of the hill and kept on walking down along a small, meandering creek. After he was out of sight I picked up my stuff and circled wide to intersect a tributary stream that ran down into the main bottom ahead of his path. I was just preparing to sit down and call from there when a loud gobble rattled the woods. Would you like to know where it came from? Why; yes - right back where I'd previously been sitting for so long.

The creek bottom was much too open to allow for a direct approach. I also wasn't eager to retrace the briar-choked path that I'd just fought through in order to get back where I'd already been, so I decided instead to stand pat. Another hearty gobble rewarded the first soft yelp on my MVP, and then the tom really ripped into a louder, "kawking" call on the glass. Not four minutes later I heard something walking deliberately in the dry leaves above my position, and this advance notice gave me plenty of time to swing ahead of the tom's travel path with my gun barrel. His big white-topped head soon stuck up above the contour line, and after he peered down over the ridgeline at 20 yards, he never knew what hit him. Just like that, I had my first Arkansas gobbler flopping in the leaves. One day hunted; one tom down; one tag left to fill.

My first Arkansas gobbler.

Four different birds could be heard gobbling the following morning. It began to drizzle as I set up on the closest one, and after a series of moves and countermoves, I finally had him drumming loudly from about 40 yards away. But, he was being very reluctant to advance the last few steps to where I could actually see him. That's when the *real* rain started, and it effectively put a screeching halt to all gobbling and drumming. I held my ground; sure that the tom would eventually come sneaking in to find the hen who had been whispering sweet nothings in his ear for the past 20 minutes.

An hour later I was still sitting there getting drenched to my very core. I was also cold and starting to shiver. Finally, I convinced myself that the battle had indeed been won by my opponent, so I resigned myself to defeat and dropped off the ridgeline, seeking shelter under a spacious limestone overhang. Once safely underneath its protective cover, I gathered up a stack of brittle branches and broken sticks, and started a nice, roaring fire.

Stripping completely naked, I hung my clothes on some tree limbs to help them dry faster, and then I took a seat on a comfortable log. The crackling flames quickly warmed my bones and dried my clothes, even while the rain continued to fall hard. I sat gazing into the embers, locked in a fireside reverie that wandered all over the place. I even contemplated whether I might be the first person to find safety underneath this overhang, but I thought the odds of that were pretty slim. This area had been heavily populated by Native Americans for eons, and surely, such a place as this had been both well-known and utilized many, many times before...

I'd absentmindedly been yelping lightly on a mouth call to pass the time, and after my clothes were toasty-dry I was reaching for my pants when, quite suddenly, a hen's head popped into view above a mound of earth fifteen yards from the cave's entrance. I froze in mid-reach as she began clucking and purring. When she dropped back down out of sight, I grabbed my shotgun and aimed it where she'd been - just in case there might be a boyfriend in tow behind her.

My previous calling in this natural amphitheater must have lured her in. Once again clucking on my diaphragm to see if she'd come back, I immediately, saw her head pop into view in the very same spot. For an eternity we each stared at one another without moving an inch or batting an eye. Then, she dropped out of sight.

Thirty seconds later she was back. After another long stare-down, she disappeared yet again, and this time I thought she was gone for good. However, two minutes later she was right back in the same old spot. Over the next twenty minutes she repeated this odd behavior three more times, all the while keeping up a nearly continuous dialog of gentle clucks and soft purring.

Finally, she wandered off about 40 yards and began scratching around in the wet leaves. She was all alone. By now my arms were shaking uncontrollably from holding the gun up for so long, and I welcomed the opportunity to lower it for some relief. I should've just let her go at that point, but now, curiosity had really got ahold of me, so I clucked once more to see what she'd do.

Rushing back to her previously held position behind the knob, she stood there for about 30 seconds before launching into flight and landing in a tree about 50 yards away. She only stayed there for a couple minutes though, and then flew right back towards me – alighting on a closer limb that gave her an unobstructed view of me and my cave. At that point she began craning her neck downward and staring at me so intently, for such long periods of time, that I began to feel real uneasy and uncomfortable in my nakedness.

By then I had the very distinct impression that this hen couldn't be run off if I wanted to, so I slowly stood up. No reaction. I began walking around. Again, nothing; all she did was continue to stare. I then put my pants back on, followed by my t-shirt and long-sleeved hunting shirt. Getting progressively bolder with my movements, I checked the gear in my turkey vest and prepared to go back to hunting. It was by far the strangest behavior I had ever seen in a wild turkey, and I was both amazed and flummoxed. Was she a tame bird? There wasn't a house for miles in any direction, so that seemed unlikely. Maybe she was just confused, having never seen a naked human being before…

When the rain finally came to a halt I calmly walked out of my shelter without causing the least bit of noticeable concern from that goofy hen. Her melodic cluck/purring was still audible as I worked my way back up to the ridgetop and moved steadily away.

Then (it was already past noon), a tom blasted out three unprovoked gobbles in quick succession from about 300 yards away. After this brief flurry of excitement he hushed up as suddenly as he'd begun, so I decided to just set up right where I was at and send out a long series of lost yelps. I made sure they were loud enough for him to hear. No gobbles came in response, but I continued to hold my ground, hoping that the tom might come sneaking in silently. Or, maybe he'd at least start gobbling again so I could safely make a move in his direction. Either way, I kept an alert vigil in scanning my surroundings carefully.

I was *not* prepared for the sight that appeared a few minutes later - that same silly hen which I'd left a quarter-mile back behind me was now sauntering up like she didn't have a care in the world, cluck/purring for all she was worth. For the next hour she scratched and fed contentedly within a 30-yard semi-circle of my setup tree, and never showed the slightest concern.

When a far-distant gobble finally echoed out, I jumped up and hurriedly began cutting the distance between me and this new tom. My "girlfriend" stood right where she was at and merely stared forlornly as I hustled out of sight. I was tempted to call to her "Pied Piper-style" and see if she wanted to come along and help lure in the gobbler, but then I decided to abandon that silly plan. Using her like a live hen decoy would've felt like cheating.

Once set up near the tom's position, I cutt hard into the tail end of his next gobble using a mouthcall. While he didn't vocally respond, I did heard the sound of drumming ten minutes later as he eased closer. Soon after that, I laid eyes on the tom strutting into view at about 40 yards; too far to risk taking the shot. Then, for some reason only the tom could decipher, he suddenly straightened up and began putting while walking away. I had absolutely no idea what alerted this bird, but as so often happens in this sport, our hunt was over in the blink of an eye.

Well, maybe I should change that statement a little bit to say this particular *battle* with the tom had ended, because ten minutes later he was right back gobbling again. Once more moving quickly to intercept his path, I set up, called, and was robustly answered yet again. Then, I noticed that the surrounding woods had inexplicably erupted with turkeys gobbling in every direction! I could easily count at least five or six of them within earshot, and despite the clock now reading 4:30 in the afternoon, every single one of them was gobbling *good*.

Suddenly, a volley of seven gunshots erupted from where two or three of these gobblers had been carrying-on in earnest - causing the tom who had just stepped into sight over my gun barrel to turn on his heels and run away. I surely hadn't expected that kind of a panic-stricken reaction to the sound of distant gunfire. This bird had a bad case of nerves!

Despite this latest setback, I still felt confident. After all, these woods were obviously chocked-full of turkeys, and it seemed like only a matter of time before I might catch a break in my favor. I also felt certain that the closest tom wasn't done gobbling just yet, and sure enough, he started back up gobbling ten minutes later.

For what seemed like the umpteenth time of the day I closed the distance on this tom and got set up, and for what seemed like the umpteenth time he blasted out a gobble to my first call. Unfortunately, that know-it-all little voice inside my head then pointed out a better-lookng position 60 yards closer, but I didn't make the move quickly enough; a few minutes later the tom materialize exactly where I "should've been." I thought he still might come on in, but then a brazen little hussy of a hen ran in and led him away, thus saving his life.

Soon thereafter the sun began setting in the west. Although I hadn't pulled the trigger all day, I couldn't help but reflect on how this had been one of the singular most spectacular hunts of my life. It seemed only fitting when I heard several turkeys fly to roost at dusk, and one of them even uttered a "good-night" gobble to give me a starting position for the morning.

I headed back to camp happy and content with my lot in life, having been "into" turkeys all day long. Promises for the 'morrow were strong, and Ron was also feeling good, because he'd shot a fine tom at 11a.m. Spirits were high around our fire pit, and after a great meal, we tucked in for an anxious night of sleep; eager for what the morning might bring. I was totally unaware of the disappointments soon to come.

The troubles started with the first vocalizations of a "supposed" turkey hunter trying his best to imitate an owl 300 yards east of me at 5:50a.m. This was at least 30 minutes earlier than any gobbling I'd heard all week, and furthermore, the guy doing it was amongst the two or three worst owl hooters of all time! He continued to compound the fiasco by repeating his efforts at least once every minute, without fail.

At 6:10a.m. another worthy contestant for the "World's Worst" award began his own horrid renditions of owl talk 300 yards west of me. While his efforts were even more dismal, at least he wasn't quite as persistent. Unfortunately, this bozo then began moving towards me in the dark, and I seriously contemplated leaving the birds I'd roosted to go elsewhere – looking to hunt *anywhere* else besides near these two guys!

Then, a gobble ripped out from exactly where I'd anticipated a bird to be roosted. Time on the clock showed 6:21a.m. It amazed me that the racket around me hadn't silenced this bird, but I should've known better than to expect anything less than disaster. That happened a few minutes later when "Imposter #2" took out a Penn's Woods Gobble Shaker. I shudder to recall how bad his efforts sounded.

The tom's first gobble that day may've been the final one of his life. Surely, he was so embarrassed that anyone could think his own splendid gobbling sounded even remotely like what this interloper into his domain had uttered with the gobble tube, that he swore a vow of silence from that day forward! Of course, this is merely anthropomorphic speculation on my part, but what's undeniably true is that the tom never uttered another peep from his roost, and then flew off into the pinkening eastern skyline a few minutes later like he was tardy for a very important meeting.

Well, that was the final straw, so I wasted no more time in backing out of there and getting gone. The rest of the day was as frustrating and maddening as the previous one had been exhilarating and exciting. I covered more than 12 miles of rugged trails, set up on several obstinate toms without even an inkling of success, and returned to camp feeling beaten up and battered to a pulp. Ron had also experienced his own difficulties - crippling and losing a gobbler. We searched for the bird again after lunch, but found no further traces of him.

By 3 p.m. I was back in the vicinity of where all the gobbling had been heard the previous afternoon. I was sure hoping for some semblance of the action which that day had supplied, and at 4:30 a pair of toms separated by about 400 yards let loose with a volley of unsolicited gobbles. That raised my excitement level up a notch, but despite moving in between them and setting up amidst a large scratched-over area that just screamed "kill zone," I couldn't get a response to anything said. I sat there for the next two hours expecting at any moment to see turkeys at least moving through such a prime spot, but all I witnessed were squirrels aplenty and a lone fox that sent them scrambling for cover.

At 6:30p.m. a bird gobbled hard at a loud cut from my diaphragm call. He was only about 200 yards away, and over the next ten minutes he slowly closed that distance while gobbling twice more. I said nothing during his approach, and only offered up some gentle purring after I heard him drumming from just beyond eyesight.

A few moments later I spied a white-topped periscope at 50 yards. For what seemed an eternity he merely stood there, alternately standing tall and then puffing out into a half-strut. After 20 more minutes of building pressure I risked using my off-hand to scratch in the leaves like a feeding hen. That's all it took - he began slowly and cautiously working his way closer. A grey squirrel on the opposite side of me was rummaging around in the leaf litter, and I could tell by the tom's body language and posture that he was listening hard to the sounds it made; obviously contemplating whether or not this noise was the unseen hen (me).

Finally, he walked out into an opening at 25 yards and stood tall so I could kill him. However, after the shotgun went off he got up running. One of his wings looked like it was dragging behind. My follow-up shot centered a 10-inch tree a dozen yards from my muzzle, so I jumped up and gave chase while simultaneously breaking open the Ruger and fumbling in my pockets for extra shells. Trying to leap over a fallen log, I caught my shin on an unseen vine and did a face-plant in the dirt. I didn't realize it at the time, but that fall not only split the skin of my shin; it also cracked my gun's stock at the pistol grip. All I could think about at the time, however, was to get back up and catch that wounded tom!

Ignoring my bleeding, aching shin, I scrambled to my feet. No turkey was in sight; he'd run over the lip of the ridgeline and was gone from view. A sprint to where he'd vanished brought me to a *very* steep slope, which was empty so far as I could see. I tried to listen for the sound of feet running in the leaves, but all I could hear, instead, was my wheezing breath from the harried and frantic exertions to get there. Damn! Double Damn!! What had happened? How in the world had I blown such a perfect opportunity?

Returning to my setup spot and sitting back down to replay what had just transpired, the answer soon became crystal-clear. Twelve yards from where I sat, there was a four-inch dogwood limb angling up from the right. I shoot left-handed, so in tracking the tom over my gun barrel this limb had been completely hidden from my view. However, it had obviously not been invisible to my shot pattern, which was now graphically and raggedly displayed as the lower half of a circle of chewed-up bark and splintered wood on the top half of that cursed limb. While most of the pellets had hit this damnable obstruction, enough of them had gotten past it on the high side to strike the tom. The repercussions of this blunder were enough to make me sick.

I knew the tom was hurt, and hurt badly, so once again I walked over to the top of the slope and began working my way downhill, searching every brush pile and logjam along the bird's suspected path of departure. Try as I might, I never found the least bit of sign in the hour left before sundown, and I eventually had to call it off due to darkness. Camp was a miserable place to be that night, since both Ron and I had crippled turkeys on the same day. Neither one of us takes that kind of mishap lightly, or well. There was a lot of grumbling and bemoaning involved, centered around long periods of silence and blank stares into the campfire flames. Unlike our usual turkey camps, there was absolutely *no* jocularity.

After a terribly restless night with very little sleep, I headed back out to the "crippling zone" at daylight to begin a thorough and complete search. I just knew in my heart that this gobbler was dead, and I was bound and determined to find him. My plan was to work a ten-yard grid pattern over that whole valley and its encompassing hillsides. It was rugged ground and I knew that I was staring at a difficult task, but I owed that tom my best effort.

Ignoring two or three gobbling birds on surrounding ridgetops, I commenced walking/stumbling/crawling along the contour lines of the steep hillside, searching every nook and cranny for a half-mile in all directions. Then, I dropped down and covered the valley and its trickling creek before starting up the opposite slope. Hour after hour wore on, with my feet and ankles taking a terrible beating because of the rocky and rugged ground. It was really rough going, and as the noon hour approached I was exhausted and physically hurting. There must have been about 2.5 million likely hiding spots in that area, with lots of brush piles, fallen trees, limestone outcroppings, briar tangles, folds in the terrain, etc. Wounded turkeys are masters at tucking themselves up into the tiniest hidey-hole imaginable, and finding one is often as much luck as it is diligence. Still, I wasn't calling it quits until I felt like I had exhausted every last hope, and searched every last possibility.

Finally, at about 2:30 in the afternoon I admitted to myself that I'd done everything within my powers and far more than nearly anyone else would've done to find a bird that I felt certain was terribly crippled and probably already dead. I was physically and mentally torn, tattered, beaten, and battered. Early on in the search I'd been quite positive, with high hopes of finding the tom, but now I was just one miserable, wretched, and worthless turkey crippler - thoroughly disgusted with myself, and at a loss as to why in the world I hadn't just let him take one or two more steps into the wide open before pulling the trigger.

I still felt like I had to make one last pass up the valley before heading out to my van, and not 50 yards after crossing over the creek I spotted a suspicious-looking pile of leaves that appeared to be about the size of a bushel basket. Walking closer to investigate, I saw a single turkey feather sticking up from the top of this mound. Curiosity and anxiety welled up in my chest at the sight of that feather, and when I brushed back the leaves with my hand I found more feathers, then a very dead gobbler laying underneath them - MY TOM!

The gobbler's craw had been torn open a little bit, and there was about a golf-ball-sized chunk of meat missing from the breast where it joined the throat, but other than that he was in perfect condition.

Obviously, some critter had either killed him or found him there already dead, but whatever it was hadn't ripped him to shreds or eaten him. Instead, the perpetrator had merely covered up its find with leaves. Bobcat? Weasel? Feral cat? I can't positively say which one, but I sure was grateful in how well the tom had been cared for, and thrilled beyond measure to put my tag on his leg.

Ron was also successful that morning, killing a "fine young bird of the year." By late afternoon we were back on the road and headed for our favorite turkey hunting spot in western Kentucky; Larry Sharp's bow-hunting-only, Higginson-Henry WMA.

On the second morning at H-H I killed a tom while using a new broadhead called a Tri-Triska. Its 2 3/4" diameter mechanically operated cutting edges had administered devastating damage on the gobbler, and in fact, had nearly cut the bird in half! I was thoroughly impressed, and didn't think there was any way to fail in the future with this highly lethal addition to my gear. The following day, however, would once again prove that nothing is ever a sure thing in the world of turkey hunting.

Another bow kill at Kentucky's Higginson-Henry WMA.

My shot that day felt right and looked good, but the tom simply limped off looking really hurt. Several of his buddies then ganged up on their crippled flock-mate and battered him around for a few minutes before he could separate from them and hobble off alone. A half-hour later I slipped out of my blind to begin following his blood trail, which was so good that I expected to find the tom dead at any moment. Instead, after about 250 yards the blood began petering out, and eventually it stopped altogether. At that point I opted to go get Ron, Larry, and a pair of his dogs named, "Two" and "Tracker." I felt like the tom was surely dead already, but probably tucked up underneath the green honeysuckle which predominated this part of the WMA.

As we returned and closed in on the spot where I'd last found blood, I heard a turkey flush out ahead of us. I hoped that it was a nesting hen instead of the tom, but in hindsight, I think it was my gobbler. However, the dogs never showed much interest, and our diligent searching failed to turn up a dead turkey.

The disappointment and shame of losing that tom weighed heavily on my mind as the next week of hunting passed with nothing more to show for my efforts than a series of oh-so-close encounters and a growing level of frustration. Hunting with a bow had proven to be much more difficult than I'd ever imagined. Then, on the final morning I whiffed on not one, nor two, but THREE different toms; all complete misses. That was a real slap in the face to my sense of reality, and it stung. Of course, Larry and the gang barely made fun of me at all...

Getting a gun back in my hands for Indiana's season opener couldn't have come at a better time. I was mentally drained from the last week of bow hunting, and I was anxious to once again smell gunpowder and see turkeys flopping in the leaves after a trigger-pull.

During the last few years I had been focusing most of my hunting and guiding efforts on those aforementioned Amish farms of Jefferson County. I've also brought up the fact that each year it became a little more obvious that I was being edged out of the picture as the Wickey boys' love of turkey hunting grew stronger. In the year 2000 I found myself limited to only two of the original seven farms where we had enjoyed so much prior success, and I was thus forced to seek out other landowners who were friends with my cousin Bob Torrance. Luckily for me, my beloved cousin knew practically every farmer in the area, and many of his friends welcomed me on their ground.

However, access to good land doesn't guarantee success; it only offers the opportunity. It took me six days to get a bird killed. He was a beast of a bird and well worth the effort, but things got really tough after that. In fact, for anyone accompanying me into the woods during the year 2000, the actual killing of turkeys proved to be problematic, at best.

That season I took a total of ten different people hunting on twelve separate days. I called in 18 toms to within killing range for those guys, and twelve of them got shot at. Would you believe every single one of the first seven were missed? And, let's also not forget another infamous day when I called in a tom and three hens for a fellow whom I will refrain from naming for soon to be obvious reasons. When I whispered to kill the tom trailing up behind his girlfriends in a wide open soy bean stubble field at 25 yards, my buddy pulled down and murdered the very first hen in line. Totally shocked by this unexpected development, I looked at him and asked, "Why the hell did you kill her?"

This man is a good friend, and a very experienced hunter, but like everyone else in my company that year, he was seemingly living out an episode of *The Twilight Zone*. His attention had been so focused on the first bird that he never even noticed any others. As the gunner behind three of those misses to start the season, I'm sure that he was feeling a great deal of anxiety and pressure to make a kill, and there were definitely some vicious demons living rent-free in his head by the time of our last hunt. However, in my wildest nightmares I never would've expected things to turn out as they did!

Trust me on this one; there is *nothing* sadder and more hopeless in turkey hunting than having to butcher a hen and seeing all of those underdeveloped eggs in her body cavity. By the letter of the law it was illegal, but what else could we do? I sure wasn't going to leave her in the field for coyote food. We did the only decent, moral thing possible, and used the tragedy as a painful learning experiece.

I know how bad I felt about it, and I most certainly know how terribly my friend regretted his mistake.

Another epic failure occurred when Marvin Wickey and I took Ron "Pee Wee" Day out for another attempt at getting his first-ever bird killed. Marvin is the only true turkey hunter in that Amish clan, and I really thought the two of us might get it done by working in tandem. However, this was Pee Wee we're talking about, and nothing ever came easy with him. Instead of hitting the big tom walking past our blind at 16 yards, Pee Wee missed everything; everything, that is, except for the edge of the blind's shooting window. This, he hit *very* well!

The concussion of the shot blew the whole blind up over the top of us, creating quite a bit of momentary confusion as we struggled to extricate ourselves from the mess. When we subsequently got free and searched in the vicinity of where the turkey had been, we found no dead bird lying in the leaves. Yes; it was another blown opportunity for our old buddy, Pee Wee. This last one now deflated his failure rate while hunting with me to a lowly 0-for-3, and while he felt rotten and apologized profusely about the torn and tattered blind, I was much more concerned with how in the world I was ever going to make something positive happen for my nearly-deaf friend. Certainly the blind was the best option I'd tried so far in actually getting a bird in close enough for the shot, but how could I account for his inability to hit what he was aiming at?

Well, the next morning we gave it another go, and I am absolutely thrilled to report that Pee Wee Day finally got the job done! I had to call that particular tom in three different times before my gunner finally saw its flaming red head and touched off some gunpowder, but everything worked out swimmingly after that. In fact, this gobbler ended up being a true arsekicker of almost 23 pounds, with an 11 inch beard and long, sharp spurs measuring 1- 3/8 inches. Pee Wee was thrilled with the hunt, and proud as could be. His wife Carolyn was, too. Before that day, all we'd ever brought home to her were tales of woe.

Following the completion of that goofy Indiana season, I ventured back out to my old nemesis - West Virginia. I absolutely love this state's spectacular scenery, and was anxious to hunt there again.

I had previously struggled quite a bit to find birds in that rugged hill country, and my meager successes in actually killing some of them had been counterbalanced by several missed and/or wounded turkeys. Not so in 2000; I quickly made up for my string of bad luck by hearing multiple gobbling birds and killing two of them in only three days of hunting.

Ron "Pee Wee" Day and wife Carolyn admire his first tom.

Filling my tags so quickly allowed me to then race back to Michigan, where I had first hunted unsuccessfully in 1997. Now, Christine Gerace's invitation to hunt on her father Frank's 450-acre property near Midland sounded like a great way to correct that aberration; especially since she reported that the local toms were gobbling like crazy.

The weather took a severe nosedive before I reached Michigan, and during my five-day stay it was *very* cold and *very* windy, with a little snow thrown in for good measure. Despite these hardships, Christine and I averaged hearing four gobbling birds per day. They didn't gobble much, though, and we struggled to work any of them into shooting range. This all changed on the fourth day, when I was able to call in a stutter that circled wide through the open hardwoods and came in from a direction choked with tall ferns. When he periscoped his head up above the greenery at 24 yards, I added another state's kill to my "life list."

The next morning I tried one last time to help Christine fill her own tag. We failed miserably. That was no big deal for her, though; the unflappable "CG's" upbeat, energized, and ever-buoyant spirit kept her positively looking forward. Christine had killed a couple of toms with me in Indiana during previous years, and with her obvious passion for the sport, I now thought that it was time for her to step out and do things on her own. After all, a person can never quite become a full-blown turkey hunter if they are always just the one pulling the trigger. At some point the only way to fully learn this sport is to do it alone.

Subsequent years have proven that this was the right time for my friend to spread her wings and fly solo. Christine has done very well with the turkeys, and is now a highly successful hunting guide in Michigan.

My first Michigan tom.

Ah, yes; New York. Once again it felt almost like a homecoming as I stopped by the farmhouse at dawn and had my annual cup of coffee with Evelyn Bays, before heading down to find Tony out doing chores at the barn. Jake and his two young sons joined us shortly thereafter over at the deer camp, where I unpacked my belongings and got settled-in.

It was 9 o'clock before I even thought about donning camo and taking a tour around the farm. The first place I checked was an old favorite of mine – a big disked field beside Jake's "Christmas Trees." Sure enough, there was a tom right out in the middle of the field strutting for three hens. After sneaking in and hunkering down against the remnants of an old stone fence, I got a couple of the hens fired up with some harsh cutting calls. In no time they were hot-footing it towards me, passing by my outstretched legs within mere yards on their way into the woods.

The third hen, however, was content to stay right where she was at, with a boyfriend that never left her side. She busily scratched up freshly planted corn kernels like they were candy until the noon whistle in Smyrna signaled the end of hunting hours. Then, I stood up and shoo'ed them away. Tony hated turkeys - and geese - because of their fondness for wrecking his corn fields.

The next morning this same tom first gobbled at a rapidly advancing thunderstorm's deep rumbles. He was roosted in the thick hemlocks down below the "Beef Pasture," where the cover was so good that I could slip in tight and set up only 75 yards from where his toes were curled around a limb for the last time. I don't ordinarily say much to a roosted turkey, but that morning I tree-yelped several times. I did so because there were several vocal hens surrounding him, and I wanted to impress upon the tom that I was the first of the girls to fly down.

The hens talked back to me a little bit, before one of them pitched out and touched down 35 yards from my gun barrel. At that point I was pretty sure her boyfriend was in deep trouble, and a few minutes later this was confirmed when he flew down and landed 29 steps away from me. Tag Number #1 was promptly filled just before the sky opened up in a deluge.

I didn't care one bit whether I got drenched by that downpour, because there was a warming fire in the cook stove back at camp, and it wouldn't take long to have bacon, eggs, and pancakes sizzling on the griddle. Later that afternoon we had our annual feast, and that was always a special time for all of us. This year's menu included fried turkey breast and morels, along with steamed wild asparagus and my semi-famous pan-fried Parmesan potatoes. For desert we had vanilla ice cream atop one of Evelyn's still-warm-from-the-oven chocolate cakes. Then, we all sat around camp telling stories and cutting up. What a blast!

During the next week Jake and I didn't really get after the turkeys too hard because of perpetually rainy weather, but I still managed to call up one tom to fill my second tag, and a strutting, bearded hen that kept me entertained for a good half-an-hour as she paraded all around me. Jake's brother-in-law Kent Blanchard also accompanied me into the woods and shot a jake, and then "The Jakester" himself missed a big tom on May 31.

This last miss ended the year on a rather disappointing note, which seemed only fitting. It had been a trying season at times, with more misses than I'd ever thought possible. True; my friends and I had accounted for 19 dead gobblers, but the 13 misses set an all-time high unmatched either before, or since.

Four of the errant shots had been made by yours truly, but three of those had been with a bow, and the other was the Arkansas tom that I'd found the next morning. I didn't feel nearly as bad about my own accuracy issues as I did about all the other hunters in my company. They had consistently missed or crippled toms toms that were standing statue-still in perfectly killable range!

In that regard alone it had been a terrible season, and to say that I was frustrated would be a grave understatement. In fact, the missing part weighed so heavily on my mind that I seriously contemplated whether or not it was even worthwhile to continue working so hard for other people, only to then watch helplessly while they blew the whole deal in the final nanosecond. Still, I knew in my heart that I could never quit guiding completely, any more than I could stop hunting by myself. I definitely enjoyed my "solo time" more than I liked taking someone else hunting, but there was friendship and camaraderie to be found in sharing the experience with others, and I would undoubtedly miss that if I quit altogether. I just had to find a way to help my companions hit what they were aiming at, before the stress gave me ulcers or a stroke!

Despite more than just a few hiccups along the way, the New Millennial truly had started off on a good note, with 67 days spent in pursuit of elusive gobbles coming from both unknown and familiar lands of eight different states. I had also called in no less than 64 toms during the season, which wasn't too shabby.

My Michigan bird had also tidied up a particular source of annoyance for me, and I could now claim dead turkeys in every one of the 23 states where I had hunted. With plans to add a couple more new ones in 2001, I was looking forward to a day in the not-so-distant future when I might boast of success in over half of the 49 states that held a spring turkey season. I still harbored no aspirations, intentions, or even thoughts of trying to hunt in every single state in the country; my goals were simply to hit it hard in those places that most interested me. I craved the exciting new adventures that each trip brought to my life, and the only negative, as happens to me every June, was in having to wait nine more months before I could do it all again.

Kenny Dorman listening to a few notes on a Cane Creek glass pot.

Epilogue

This volume takes us up through the spring season of 2000. With my turkey hunting skills finely honed by that point, I thought that I had everything pretty-well figured out - turkey hunting around the country for nearly three months straight, then working the next nine to help pay down any debts incurred to a manageable level before starting the routine all over again. I had a boss that, while not exactly encouraging my beliefs, nonetheless supported them by allowing me the freedom to leave my job for the entire turkey season. I also had a birth family that endured my shenanigans without too much complaining. Life was good, and I was generally happy with where I stood in it.

However, there were some huge sacrifices necessary on my part to keep this lifestyle going. For instance, maintaining any type of a quality romantic liaison was problematic, at best. I mean, really; what gal in her right mind was going to put up with a partner being gone from home for so long every spring? Certainly not the kind of intelligent women to whom I was attracted! But, my love of the woods and its feathered denizens held such a sway in my heart that I was willing to forego the type of ordinary relationships which most of my friends enjoyed, and remain an avowed bachelor. Just keeping a girlfriend for more than a month or two at a time was so hard that as I entered my fortieth year of life I'd already resigned myself to the fact that marriage and raising a family of my own didn't seem to be in the cards for me. In one regard, this felt like an awfully steep price to pay for the hand that I'd been dealt. However, I had quite willingly jumped into this ultimate game of Solitaire, so I had no one to blame but myself.

Another rough spot in my life was finances, but again, most of that was self-imposed agony of my own design. Turkey hunting was so very important to me that I wasn't willing to compromise on my time afield, and I felt not only compelled, but totally powerless, to resist hunting from the first opening day in the south (early March) until the season finally ground to a halt at the end of May (even on into June, in Maine). This time period when I wasn't earning a paycheck stretched to approximately 12 weeks or more, and when you couple that with a general lack of interest in pursuing the almighty dollar during the rest of the year, I knew that I was destined to be working class and relatively poor for as long as I held onto a yearly schedule which kept me carefree and wandering around in the woods for months on end.

I had always consciously tried to separate the things that I loved to do from how I made a living, in order to keep my favorite activities fresh and vibrant, and my mind free from burnout. While that still felt right to me philosophically, I watched with at least a small degree of envy as other people around my age made their own passions pay in the burgeoning outdoor industry. The growing successes of companies like Mossy Oak, Primos, and others made me, at the very least, contemplate whether I might have made a dire mistake by not centering a working career around the important things in my life. It looked to me like those guys were doing well and hunting just as much as I did, but without beating up their bodies in the process (as I was doing in the construction trades). Hard manual labor might help to build character in a person's soul, but man, as I reached my 40's I wondered if that career path wasn't in reality breaking me down prematurely without sufficient compensation as just reward. My pockets always seemed to be empty, and my joints were beginning to ache.

Despite these and other negatives, people whom I encountered along the turkey trails were consistently listening to my exciting stories and then telling me that it was *they* who were envious of me and my life-style. I must admit that such praise helped to grease my ego quite a bit, and when I actually sat and thought about it, there really wasn't any other way that I wanted to lead my life. I was having a ball traveling to all of these unknown places, and it was exciting to match wits with turkeys in the different types of habitat found scattered across this country. Besides that, I was getting pretty darned good at not only the turkey hunting game itself, but in all the little intricacies involved in making these trips a reality - what might be called the dreaming, scheming, planning, and implementation phases that went into finding turkeys where I'd never set foot before, and then convincing them to go for a ride in my van once I entered their domain with gun in hand and ill intentions in my heart.

As with any endeavor passionately pursued; the more you do something, the better you'll likely become at it. Hence, the whole process of gathering the information needed to make my hunting trips go smoothly was getting easier by the year. No sooner would I return from the annual "turkey wars," before I'd be busy writing letters to game departments of the various states which I was considering for the next spring's itinerary, and then arranging all the incoming information in a way that was both logical and easy to access. My stack of manila files for all of the individual states were thusly growing larger and more complete by the season, and it was becoming a much simplified task to pick out areas in each one that offered what I was looking for; mainly, large tracts of public land with decent turkey populations and the option to set up camp while I was there. In short, these were the three most important criteria that I used when researching new ground back in those days, and they are still at the top of the list today.

I've mentioned this several times previously, but the first thing that I do when investigating a new state is to check to see whether it has any National Forest property within its borders. If it does, then the next step is to buy a copy of the "Land Use Map" for that particular forest. After narrowing my search down to a few areas that interest me, I might also buy some of the United States Geological Society 7.5-Minute Quad Topographic Maps which cover those places, but with their high cost these days, I don't do that nearly as much as in years past.

What I do unfailingly buy is an *Atlas and Gazetteer*, published by DeLorme. These are basically a booklet of smaller scale topo's covering the entire state, and while they don't have quite the same detail as the larger USGS maps, they still contain a plethora of vital information. Most public land is even highlighted on their pages, although the boundaries aren't always 100% correct, and some holdings might be completely missing. Still, I wouldn't even think of venturing into a new state without one of these things close at hand beside the driver's seat, and while they run about $20 each at most Wal-Marts, I find their value to be absolutely priceless as a resource.

It's important to correlate these mapping tools mentioned above with the technical data supplied from Game Departments and/or the Internet, so after I have everything in hand it's time to begin cross-referencing. County-wide kill sheets and turkey population density maps are especially helpful, as are personal recommendations from wildlife biologists and other professionals.

The goal here is to narrow my focus down even further, and really hone in on a particular area. I want to have a pretty good idea of where to find turkeys before I ever arrive for the hunt. By doing my "long-distance scouting" months in advance, I can hopefully minimize wasted time afield traipsing around in areas that are devoid of gobblers. Vacation days are too precious to waste, and time is of the essence once the hunt begins. I'm not out there to take pictures of beautiful scenery - unless it serves as a backdrop for feathers and meat!

Thoroughly investigating new areas from the comfort of your home or office gives you at least a rudimentary introduction to the land and its potential. As far as I'm concerned, the more information you can gather in this way, the better. Knowledge is power, power builds confidence, and confidence keeps you going when the going gets tough. This is especially true late in the season, when you might not be hearing any gobbling or finding much sign of the birds. Attitude is everything when that happens – and adversity *will* happen to all of us.

Difficult times without much positive feedback can cause our brains to begin questioning whether we're hunting gobblers or ghosts, but if you've done enough research beforehand to know that there are definitely turkeys in the vicinity, it is much easier to stay alert and hunt smart until fortune turns in your favor. Just as bad times are inevitable, so too will things change for the better – sooner, or later. That is something I've had to tell myself many, many times during the course of a long and grueling season. Believe me, here; I cannot count the number of these self-administered "pep talks" that I've both given, and endured, throughout the years.

As for how to glean the greatest amount of useful information from the World Wide Web; I'll have to admit right here that I'm a dinosaur. Oh, I can most certainly putz around on a PC well enough to eventually find what I'm seeking from state game department websites and such, but when it comes to all the newfangled stuff like apps for a smartphone, I am way behind the times. Heck, I still carry a flip-phone - and love it!

I am also much more comfortable with a paper map and a compass to get me where I want to go, so I don't really need or want electronic gadgetry for that purpose. Admittedly, I do carry a GPS these days, but not so much for finding my way in or out of the hunting area. Rather, I use it to mark important points of interest like roost sites, brush blinds, or other hot spots that I might want to unfailingly reach long before the sun comes up.

I think too much technology detracts from the magic and enjoyment that I find in the turkey woods. I conscientiously try to minimize its use for that reason alone, and can easily think back on several hunting companions in the last few years who couldn't seem to take a step in any direction without first checking out their location on an ever-present smartphone. Trust me; it takes everything within my power to keep from grabbing the damned things and stomping them into the mud!

However, in all fairness, I can certainly see a degree of merit in having some technology at your fingertips while far out in the boonies. There are even a few apps that I think would make carrying a modern phone worthwhile. For instance, I've seen some identification programs for birdlife, trees, wildflowers, mushrooms, etc. that really interest me. It would also be nice to check the weather once in a while to see if a tornado or serious thunderstorm is bearing down on me.

A lot of the places I hunt are very remote, so it would occasionally behoove a man to know his exact location (or, more importantly, how to get *out* of there). Namely, I'm thinking of those cursed Florida blackwater swamps. Once you're deep within one of those things, each cypress tree looks exactly like every other one surrounding it. Getting turned around is *very* easy to do, and getting lost is a strong possibility. Daniel Boone is rumored to have once said, "I've never been lost, but I have been powerfully confused for months at a time." Well, he most certainly wasn't roaming around in some God-forsaken, mosquito-laden, Cottonmouth-infested Florida Hellhole and wishing with all of his might that a helicopter would show up to lift him out of there. I sure have, and on more occasions than I care to count!

The world of turkey hunting is certainly different than when I first began the sport back in 1983, and there is both good and bad that's come along with those changes. For instance; wild turkey populations are infinitely higher and more widespread now, but so are the numbers of turkey hunters. Most suitable land has already been stocked and harbors huntable flocks, but since the quantity of public property hasn't grown at all, those places get more crowded every year. License fees continue to rise, but available cash in my wallet is dwindling - oh wait, that's always been the case. Anyhoo, you get my point about bad news nearly always accompanying good, and vice-versa.

However, the one area where everything seems to be headed on a positive upslope is the ease with which today's hunter can plan a trip into unknown lands. Technology has made it a simple thing to gather all of the information necessary for finding and scouting new hunting ground, and it's no longer such a tedious and time consuming task. A few clicks of a button can bring forth gobs and scads of valuable Intel. In mere moments you can even be staring at a current satellite image of the very ground where you're planning to hunt, and focus down with Hi-Def resolution onto individual trees and other pertinent details. One time my computer guru Bill George and I were even able to read a sign on a fencepost to verify that parking in an area where we wanted to hunt was prohibited. That absolutely blew my mind!

Technology has made the world a much easier place to navigate, and this is certainly true of our sport, as well. It just gets easier and easier every year for the traveling turkey hunter to get out there and explore new ground where they've never been before. All of these tools at our fingertips make it a breeze to find the kind of hunting opportunties that fit our personalities and pocketbooks, whether that be staying in plush accommodations and hunting exclusive private property, or scrimping and saving to rub elbows with the masses on crowded public land holdings. There really is no good reason (baring other factors keeping them home) why anyone would limit themselves to the few days and low bag limits which most states impose on the spring turkey hunter.

I *strongly* encourage everyone who loves this sport to venture across state boundaries at any given opportunity. Hunting in a place where you've never been before is like opening your eyes to a brand new world. The wonders beheld in wandering across this great country in quest of the Grandest of Gamebirds have contributed incalculable value to my own life, and I know that it can do (and has done) the same for countless others who share my passion. Always remember this; the worst day hunting beats the heck out of the best day working.

Well, that's about all the space I've got for this volume. I really do appreciate you tagging along on some of my turkey hunts, and I hope that you've enjoyed the ride as we ventured out across the country together. My next book will begin with the 2001 season, when I decided to go ahead and pursue the quest of completing a U.S. Slam. It's already in the works, and promises to recount even more exciting tales from the turkey woods. Undoubtedly, Volume 3 will also include tips and hints on how my fellow hunters can get the most out of their own planned excursions to new ground.

If you'd like to purchase any of the books in this series, I would encourage you to order them directly from me. That way, I can sign them. Maybe when I'm dead and gone that might mean something, but probably not. Paperbacks will continue to be $25, with Hardcovers $35. I'll take care of all postage.

Again, my mailing address is:

Tom Weddle
PO Box 7281
Bloomington, IN 47407

If not too much trouble, I'd also like to ask any of my readers to leave feedback on Amazon. That's the best place I've found for buying turkey hunting books myself, and a little positive feedback goes a long way in helping someone else decide whether an unknown book is worth purchasing. Hopefully, the positive feedback outweighs the negative, but rest assured that I read them all either way, and pay attention to what people have to say about my writing.

With that said, I'm going to sign off. I sincerely hope every one of you enjoy many safe and wondrous travels across this fascinating country in quest of unheard gobbles coming from as-yet unseen lands. Just remember to enjoy the ride along the way. Good luck!

Printed in the USA
CPSIA information can be obtained
at www.ICGtesting.com
LVHW091453101123
763181LV00110B/218/J